HC
110
.E5
P68
1991

Preserving the global
environment.

$22.95

Preserving the Global Environment

THE AMERICAN ASSEMBLY was established by Dwight D. Eisenhower at Columbia University in 1950. Each year it holds at least two nonpartisan meetings that give rise to authoritative books that illuminate issues of United States policy.

An affiliate of Columbia, with offices at Barnard College, the Assembly is a national, educational institution incorporated in the state of New York.

The Assembly seeks to provide information, stimulate discussion, and evoke independent conclusions on matters of vital public interest.

THE WORLD RESOURCES INSTITUTE (WRI) is a policy research center created in late 1982 to help governments, international organizations, and private business address a fundamental question: how can societies meet basic human needs and nurture economic growth without undermining the natural resources and environmental integrity on which life, economic vitality, and international security depend?

The Institute's current areas of policy research include tropical forests, biological diversity, sustainable agriculture, energy, climate change, atmospheric pollution, economic incentives for sustainable development, and resource and environmental information.

WRI's research is aimed at providing accurate information about global resources and population, identifying emerging issues, and developing politically and economically workable proposals.

CONTRIBUTORS

CHARLES V. BARBER, World Resources Institute

RICHARD ELLIOT BENEDICK, The Conservation Foundation / World Wildlife Fund

ABRAM CHAYES, Harvard University

ANTONIA H. CHAYES, Georgetown University

RICHARD N. COOPER, Harvard University

NATHAN KEYFITZ, International Institute for Applied Systems Analysis

JESSICA TUCHMAN MATHEWS, World Resources Institute

KENTON R. MILLER, World Resources Institute

GEORGE W. RATHJENS, Massachusetts Institute of Technology

WALTER V. REID, World Resources Institute

PETER H. SAND, United Nations Economic Commission for Europe

TOM H. TIETENBERG, Colby College

THE AMERICAN ASSEMBLY
Columbia University

WORLD RESOURCES INSTITUTE
Washington, D.C.

Preserving the Global Environment

The Challenge of Shared Leadership

JESSICA TUCHMAN MATHEWS
Editor

W · W · NORTON & COMPANY
New York   London

The text of this book is composed in Baskerville. Composition and manufacturing by the Haddon Craftsmen, Inc.

First Edition.

Library of Congress Cataloging-in-Publication Data

Preserving the global environment : the challenge of shared leadership /
Jessica Tuchman Mathews, editor.
      p.   cm.
   At head of title: The American Assembly, Columbia University. World
Resources Institute, Washington, D.C.
   Includes index.
   1. Environmental policy—United States.   2. Environmental policy—
International cooperation.   I. Mathews, Jessica Tuchman.
HC110.E5P68   1991
363.7'0526—dc20
                                                          90-46672

ISBN 0-393-02911-5
ISBN 0-393-96093-5 (PBK.)

W.W. Norton & Company, Inc., 500 Fifth Avenue, New York, N.Y. 10110
W.W. Norton & Company, Ltd., 10 Coptic Street, London WC1A 1PU

1 2 3 4 5 6 7 8 9 0

Contents

Preserving the Global Environment

Preface

When the leaders of the G-7 countries held their regular meeting August 1989 in Paris, foremost on the agenda was the increasing deterioration of the global environment, and the need for international action to deal with environmental problems. For the first time, the environment had been given a place among the world's top political and economic concerns.

Earlier in the year, apparently for domestic political reasons, Prime Minister Margaret Thatcher of the United Kingdom had delivered a widely reported speech on global warming, and had declared herself a "Green." Throughout Europe, "Green" parties were having greater success at the polls; in Britain, they had been particularly successful in the elections for the European Parliament in the spring of 1989.

With the bursting forth of democracy in Eastern Europe at the end of 1989, the extent of environmental crisis there, caused by the centralized economies' emphasis on heavy industry without environmental controls, became public knowledge. Among developing countries, the accumulating effects of rapid "mining" of the resource base and the threat of global trends beyond their control have led many governments to the conclusion that environmental management was essential to long-term economic growth. Clearly, the 1990s are to become the "environmental decade."

This volume is the third in The American Assembly series addressing the changing global role of the United States. The series was designed to enable a significant number of leaders from around the world to make thoughtful and considered recommendations to the United States government concerning the appropriate role for the United States, as it moves from hegemonic power to a new role as one of several major powers. The first volume examined America's global interest for the 1990's. The second volume, *The Global Economy: America's Role in the Decade Ahead* edited by William Brock and Robert Hormats, considered America's role in the global economy. This book treats the question of preserving the global environment for the survival of the planet and the challenge to the United States of shared leadership for this purpose.

The American Assembly believes that it can contribute to the development of national policy on these issues by bringing together a number of citizens who would examine the central questions and come to a consensus among themselves on a vision to inspire U.S. policy. With the advice of a steering committee whose names are listed in the appendix, The Assembly joined with the World Resources Institute, and the two institutions together agreed to retain Dr. Jessica Tuchman Mathews, vice president of WRI, as the project director and editor of this volume.

Under Dr. Mathews's editorial guidance, a team of authors prepared the chapters in this volume to serve as background reading for an American Assembly held April 19–22, 1990, culminating on the twentieth anniversary of Earth Day. The group of seventy-six participants from eighteen countries met at Arden House to discuss the papers in this volume, and to issue a report that has been widely circulated and is included as an appendix to this volume.

The goal of this volume is to lay the groundwork for scholarship in the new area of policy analysis that lies at the intersection of four fields: foreign policy, environmental science, international law, and economics. Although environmental issues have made their way into the realm of international politics and diplomacy, only limited scholarly and human resources are available to support the new and difficult policy choices that must be made. Few political scientists, international lawyers, or individuals with broad experience in multilateral diplomacy are well versed in the major environmental issues, while few environmental experts have experience in international relations.

This volume is intended to provide a critically needed addition to the sparse literature on the international aspects of this vital issue. The American Assembly and the World Resources Institute hope that it will stimulate further thinking and discussion among informed and concerned citizens, and encourage the development of a broad consensus about the nature of our global predicament and the actions that should be taken to address it.

We are grateful to the following organizations for the support of this project:

Principal funder	Rockefeller Brothers Fund
Major funders	The George Gund Foundation
	John D. and Catherine T. MacArthur
	The Pew Charitable Trusts
	The Tinker Foundation
Funders	CITIBANK
	Compton Foundation
	The Ford Foundation
	John Merck Foundation
	The Overbrook Foundation
	Rockefeller Family Fund, Inc.
	Texaco, Inc.
	Volvo North America
	Xerox Foundation

Opinions expressed in this volume are those of the individual authors, and not necessarily those of the funders, the World Resources Institute, or The American Assembly.

James Gustave Speth   Daniel A. Sharp
President   President
World Resources Institute   The American Assembly

1

Introduction and Overview

JESSICA TUCHMAN MATHEWS

T he latter half of the 1980s saw more change in international relations than the several previous decades combined. The litany of transforming events needs no repeating.
What is notable here is that among these sweeping changes
was a fundamentally new appreciation of the importance of the
environment to the human condition. Before this watershed,
environmental issues were seen as local or regional concerns,
extraneous to economic growth, matters of health, aesthetics,

JESSICA TUCHMAN MATHEWS has been vice president of the
World Resources Institute since its founding in 1982, as well as director of research at WRI from 1982–88. Previously, she was director of
the Office of Global Issues on the staff of the National Security Council in the White House and was a member of the editorial board of *The
Washington Post* covering science and technology, energy and environment, and other issues. From 1973–76 she was a Congressional Science Fellow of the American Association for the Advancement of
Science (AAAS) in the U.S. Congress and served as a professional
staff member of the Energy and Environment Subcommittee of the
House Committee on Interior and Insular Affairs.

and perhaps ethics. After it, they assumed a global dimension, beginning to be seen as intrinsic to economic growth or decline, and to be recognized as significant determinants of nations' prosperity, governability, and security. As rapidly as communism crumbled, the environment catapulted from the quiet netherworld of "other" concerns to a place among international priorities.

To the extent that any such large trend can be pegged to a particular moment, the emergence of the environment into the realm of high politics might be said to have begun in the spring of 1987 with—as unlikely as it seems—the publication of a United Nations report. The report of the Commission on Environment and Development, *Our Common Future,* quickly became an international bestseller, although not in the United States. After nine reprintings in little more than one year, the Brundtland Report, as it is also known, had changed the terms of international debate by convincingly demonstrating to a broad audience that environmental degradation is a "survival issue," especially for the developing nations. Although individuals and other commissions had been making the same case for years, *Our Common Future* succeeded where others had failed in making poverty, hunger, debt, economic growth, and more into environmental issues.

The report concerned itself with economic growth in the developed, as much as in the developing, countries, adding the still elusive term "sustainable development" to the international lexicon. This it defined as economic activity that "meets the needs of the present without compromising the ability of future generations to meet their own needs." The report unashamedly embraced limits to economic growth, but with the essential difference that it did not mean the absolute limits whose existence was so hotly debated in the 1970s. The limits humans face, it argued, are the highly elastic constraints "imposed by the present state of technology and social organization on environmental resources." Whatever absolute limits there may be do not derive from limited supplies of resources, but from "the ability of the biosphere to absorb the effects of human activities."

Even the selection of the commission's chair, Gro Harlem Brundtland, former prime minister of Norway, seems in hindsight to have pointed the way toward a new political context, for Brundtland is the first head of government to have reached that post after prominent service as minister of environment.

In the fall of 1988, one year after the Brundtland Report's release, British Prime Minister Margaret Thatcher and Soviet Foreign Minister Eduard Schevardnadze, in back-to-back speeches, captured international attention by linking environmental concerns to global security. In a stunning reversal of a lifelong antagonism to environmental protection, Thatcher proclaimed that because of population growth, powerful agricultural technologies, and the use of fossil fuels, "we have unwittingly begun a massive experiment with the system of this planet itself. . . . Protecting the balance of nature is therefore one of the great challenges of the late Twentieth Century." So unlikely was the source of these otherwise modest remarks, that the speech garnered nationwide headlines in Great Britain and wide attention elsewhere.

A day later, before the UN General Assembly, Schevardnadze likened environmental threats to a "second front" that is quickly "gaining an urgency equal to that of the nuclear-and-space threat." Everyday human activities, he warned, are "turning into a global aggression against the very foundations of life on Earth."

After that, events began to accelerate. In March 1989 Prime Minister Thatcher called an international meeting to discuss stratospheric ozone depletion. One hundred and twenty-three nations attended, more than had attended any environmental meeting in nearly two decades and vastly more than had actively participated in negotiating the Montreal Protocol on ozone-depleting substances. Thatcher's plan to steal the spotlight with a dramatic announcement of British support for a 75 percent cutback in chlorofluorocarbon (CFC) emissions, rather than the 50 percent cut called for in the just-completed treaty, was very nearly scuttled by an outbreak of international one-upsmanship. In the days before the meeting, various governments and the European Commission scrambled to outdo each other in calling for even more severe cuts. By May, at the very first meeting of parties to the Montreal Protocol, over eighty countries were ready to join in a formal call to revise the infant treaty's terms from a 50 percent cut to a complete phase-out of CFCs by the year 2000.

Ozone depletion was not the only, or even the most prominent, focus of attention. One week after Thatcher's ozone meeting, the prime ministers of the Netherlands, France, and Norway convened a conference to consider global atmospheric change generally, but especially greenhouse warming. The resulting Declaration of The Hague was signed by twenty-four heads of state. It called for "the development of new principles of international law including new and more effective decision-making and enforcement mechanisms." Lest anyone should miss the point, it explicitly proposed that a "new institutional authority" be established within the UN framework, empowered with "such decision-making procedures as may be effective even if, on occasion, unanimous agreement has not been reached." This extraordinary document may be remembered best as further evidence of what can happen when heads of state meet without sufficient advance staff work, but it also accurately reflected a prevailing sense that changes in the atmosphere demand action that is, in the declaration's words, "vital, urgent and global."

Deliberations at The Hague, as well as Thatcher's change of heart, were surely influenced by a dramatic shift in public opinion. The previous autumn, *The Green Consumer Guide* had become an immediate bestseller in Britain. Sensing the public mood, the prime minister hammered home her new message in a speech to the Conservative party with the admonition, "No generation has a freehold on this earth. All we have is a life-tenancy with a full repairing lease [a lease that requires the return of the property in its original condition]." In the U.S., *Time* magazine chose a troubled planet earth for its Man of the Year cover. In March the French Greens captured 2,500 seats in local elections, up from 300. In May the Dutch governing coalition collapsed over issues relating to a national environmental plan, and the Greens more than doubled their share of the popular vote in British local elections.

The full import of what was happening, however, was not widely registered until the European Parliament elections in June, when the Greens more than tripled their share of the French vote and won 15 percent of the British vote, a fivefold increase over their best previous showing. Overall, Green parties won thirty-nine parliamentary seats in the six countries (out of twelve) in which they ran for office, although the large British vote counted for nothing in its winner-take-all system. The total remained a small fraction of the 512 seats in the Parliament, but the trend was unmistakable.

The developing nations joined the swelling rhetorical chorus in May 1989 at the nonaligned summit meeting in Belgrade. In a keynote speech, Indian Prime Minister Rajiv Gandhi noted that "the costs of development must integrally include the costs of conservation, which, if not paid for now will be extracted . . . later." With that, he proposed the creation of a Planet Protection Fund. All developed and developing countries, except the thirty-odd least developed, would be expected to contribute a fixed and equal percentage of gross domestic product (GDP). Contributions of as little as 0.1 percent from so many countries, he noted, would produce $18 billion annually.

Finally, in July, at the Paris economic summit, the leaders of the G-7 devoted almost as much space in their declaration to environmental matters as they did to economic ones. The Paris declaration emphatically linked economic and environmental well-being, saying that "good economic policies and good environmental policies are mutually reinforcing"; endorsed a phase-out of ozone-depleting chlorofluorocarbons no later than 2000; "strongly advocate[d] common efforts to limit emissions of carbon dioxide and other greenhouse gases"; and found that a framework or umbrella convention on climate change is "urgently required."

The same trend was evident in the Soviet Union and Eastern Europe. Spurred by the nuclear explosion at Chernobyl, the pollution of Lake Baikal and the dramatic shrinking of the Aral Sea, and by Mikhail Gorbachev's strong rhetoric on the subject, environmentalism became a hot political topic in campaigns for and the first session of the new Soviet legislature. In Eastern Europe, much higher population densities and forty years of aggressive industrialization without even the most primitive environmental controls combined to produce environmental conditions widely believed to be the worst in the world, particularly in Poland, East Germany, and Czechoslovakia. As in the Soviet Union, even highly repressive governments hesitated to take action against environmental groups organizing against obviously horrible local conditions. The Polish Ecological Club, for example, survived the 1981 crackdown against Solidarity. But the attitudes and political skills learned in one cause could not be contained, and in country after country (including the Soviet Union), environmental groups with local interests evolved inexorably into political groups with national interests. By the late 1980s, for example, the Ecoglasnost Association in Bulgaria had become one of that country's largest and strongest opposition groups. As revolution swept across Eastern Europe, such groups were transformed overnight into official Green parties and their concerns into political priorities.

Why did the latter half of the 1980s see such an apparent explosion of interest in issues that had been around since the early 1970s? The lessening nuclear threat undoubtedly played a role. Although our perspective today is too short to allow an accurate historical assessment, it seems clear that this was not the only, or even the major, force at work.

Public attitudes were clearly influenced by a steady drumbeat of internationally reported events: the oil price rise and widespread shortages that opened the decade; the chemical accident at Bhopal; the decimation of European and high-altitude U.S. forests from acid rain and other air pollutants; Chernobyl; ozone depletion and the discovery of a "hole" in the ozone layer over Antarctica; drought and famine in Africa; the Rhine River chemical spill; the homeless freighter that sailed the world for two years without finding a place to unload its cargo of toxic ash; steadily rising rates of tropical deforestation and of species extinction; closed beaches from Western

Europe to the Baltic to New Jersey; the Exxon Valdez oil spill; and as the decade closed, an outbreak of freakish weather—drought and record-breaking heat in the U.S., devastating floods in Bangladesh, the most powerful hurricane ever measured, and the warmest winter in Moscow in more than a century—bringing intense new concern to the possibilities of global greenhouse warming.

Governments were influenced also by insights flowing from a new field of research known as earth systems science, or more simply, global change. Composed of studies that crisscross the traditional boundaries of geology, ecology, oceanography, chemistry, paleobiology, and meteorology, earth systems science emerged for several reasons. Research over the previous thirty years had erased the old notion of a stable and fully formed planet, replacing it with a picture of a planet that is naturally in constant flux. The signs of this activity—earthquakes, volcanoes, mountain building, and continental drift—could now be consistently explained. The increased attention to change was buttressed by advancing understanding of the high degree of interaction among the planet's nonliving realms—water, the atmosphere, rocks, and soils—and its living realm, the always evolving biosphere, which overlaps each of these. Together these two trends virtually demanded a new approach to research.

Technological advance was also crucial, because for the first time it became physically possible to measure global phenomena on a vast scale and to handle and analyze the resulting mass of data. Remote sensing devices on satellites and airplanes and improvements in computer capabilities are the best known of these, but highly sophisticated new sensing devices on land and at sea also began to provide extraordinary insights into huge swaths of the planet that were largely unexplored. A new British long-range sonar, for example, discovered twenty-eight new volcanoes on the ocean floor on its first voyage.

Earth systems scientists studied the four chemical elements essential to life—carbon, nitrogen, phosphorous, and sulfur—and quickly found that their natural cycles through earth, air, water, and living things were being affected on a global scale by human activities. Humankind is altering the natural carbon cycle largely through the combustion of fossil fuels, having increased the natural carbon dioxide (CO_2) concentration in the atmosphere by 25 percent in the past 130 years, mostly in the last three decades. We are also *doubling* the amount of nitrogen that nature makes available to living things through the production of commercial fertilizer. One minor class of chemical compounds, the chlorofluorocarbons, is depleting the life-giving stratospheric ozone layer.

Nonchemical changes are equally massive. On land, soil erosion and deforestation are accelerating the flow of sediments and nutrients to the ocean in some places, while dams built for irrigation and electricity interrupt the natural flow in others. Deforestation in the Amazon, for example, could multiply the river's discharge manyfold in the near future, while the Colorado and the Nile, which each once discharged more than a million tons of suspended matter annually, now discharge essentially none. The loss of species—now estimated to stand at four per hour—utterly disrupts the natural balance between speciation and extinction.

The more closely scientists looked at the planet's structure and metabolism, from the top of the stratosphere to the ocean canyons, the more the evidence of rapid change accumulated. A sense of urgency gradually filtered through to governments that humans are now the principal agent of environmental change on the planet, and that if humanity is to live successfully with its ability to alter natural systems, it must first understand those systems and the ways in which human society depends on their normal functioning. Unless policies change, some scientists warned, human impacts on the planet are so profound and so rapid that irreversible damage could occur before—to put it bluntly—we have any idea of what we are doing.

Beyond the headline-grabbing events and the scientific discoveries, public and official views were also influenced by social and economic trends clearly linked to environmental conditions that seemed to augur ill for the future. The 1980s opened with a famine in Africa. By mid-decade, per capita

gross national product (GNP) in sub-Saharan Africa was falling at the appalling rate of 4.2 percent per year. The region
was also the only place in the world where per capita food
production and consumption were declining. It had—and
has—the world's highest rate of population growth, by far the
highest fertility rate; the highest infant, child, and maternal
mortality rates; and the lowest life expectancy. It has the heavi-
est reliance on imported food, the greatest proportion of land
area losing its fertility, and the largest percentage of the population suffering from severe malnourishment. It has the
world's greatest dependence on fuelwood for energy, and accounts for a bare 1 percent of commercial energy consumption. Looking ahead, the Economic Commission for Africa
predicted in 1983 that if these current trends continued, the
prospects for the region in 2008 were "almost a nightmare
. . . characterized by a degradation of the very essence of
human dignity."

As the 1980s progressed, a surprising international consensus grew that "the first answer" to Africa's crisis, in the words
of Food and Agriculture Organization (FAO) Director-Gen-
eral Edouard Saouma, lies in the management and protection
of its natural resources. The stress on Africa's cropland,
rangeland, and forests will, if not soon relieved, "impose sav-
age limits" on future production. This widely shared, though
by no means universal, view that Africa's uniquely fragile and
unforgiving environment lies at the heart of its development
challenge represented a striking break with the past.

Global trends also promised future stress. Throughout the
decade, academic and official studies used UN population projections, prepared in 1980, that saw global population ultimately stabilizing at about 10 billion people. In the spring of
1989 the UN Fund for Population Activities revealed that
growth had been considerably more rapid than projected, and,
if the current trend continued, the earth's population would
stabilize not at 10 billion but at a hard-to-imagine crowd of 14
billion—almost triple the present figure. And while concern
mounted over greenhouse warming and how it might be controlled, global energy use marched rapidly upward, rising by

almost 3 percent in 1987 and 3.5 percent in 1988.

Probably the most influential trend of the decade was the gradually spreading realization that environmental mismanagement—not just environmental cleanup—imposes large economic costs. As countries in Central America and Southeast Asia, endowed a few decades ago with vast hardwood forests, faced the prospect of soon becoming timber importers, precepts of forest management that preserve the forests while producing a steady annual income acquired new salience. As agricultural projects failed on land converted from tropical forests, governments began to count the fiscal costs of subsidizing the conversion. As a species of perennial corn—potentially worth billions—was saved on the point of extinction, scientists could point with new credibility to the costs of an extinction rate conservatively estimated at one hundred species per day. A widely publicized 1985 study, *Natural Disasters: Acts of God or Acts of Man?*, pointed out the degree to which droughts, floods, and famines, once assumed to be wholly uncontrollable, were in fact caused or exacerbated by human-caused environmental degradation. Around the world, for example, soil erosion on newly populated upland watersheds was contributing to flooding hundreds of miles downstream.

The costs of environmental decline were also being measured in human suffering as "environmental refugees" proliferated. In 1985 two-thirds of all refugees in the world were African. A large proportion of these were fleeing not war, but the consequences of devegetation and soil loss that made it impossible to grow food where they lived. In Haiti, where one-sixth of the population left, deforestation that stripped much of the country of topsoil was as powerful an impetus to leave as were the brutal Duvalier regimes. Even now, as borders open in Eastern Europe, the newspapers are full of accounts of families moving in search of breathable air.

All of these environmental troubles and warning signs must be set against the remarkable achievements of the postwar era. In the forty years since 1950, global economic output has grown fourfold, outstripping population, which doubled, by a healthy margin. Life expectancy has grown by one-third—the average person can now expect to live to be sixty years old (seventy-four in the developed countries). Infant mortality dropped by half in the developing countries, from 180 deaths per thousand births, to eighty-two, and by three-quarters in the industrialized countries, from fifty-six to fifteen. Most of these improvements, it should be noted, slowed dramatically or came to a complete halt for most of the developing world in the 1980s. Per capita income actually declined in Latin America and Africa, and rates of improvement in infant mortality decelerated sharply.

Global agricultural performance presents a similarly mixed picture. From 1965–85, food production grew by 59 percent—a 10 percent per capita improvement. Yet in 1988 the World Bank estimated that outside China almost a billion people—one-fifth of the world's population—suffered from hunger. Thus in spite of decades of rapid growth in agricultural productivity, including the Green Revolution and steady expansion of agricultural land at the expense of forest and wilderness, there were more hungry people on the planet as the postwar era drew to a close than there had ever been before.

Institutionally, the record of environmental achievement is also hard to assess. International attention to the environment began on a large scale in 1972 with the Stockholm Conference on the Human Environment and the founding of the United Nations Environment Programme (UNEP). At that time only twenty-five countries possessed national environmental ministries, eleven of them in the developing world. Environmental action was understood to be principally a matter of preventing or cleaning up pollution, and in the developing countries was seen as a luxury to be afforded only after industrialization. At worst, the developed countries' environmental concerns were attacked as "environmental imperialism" or even seen as a conspiracy designed to squelch economic growth in the developing countries and preserve the global division between rich and poor.

By the mid-1980s, more than 140 countries—110 of them in the developing world—had national environmental agencies, though many of them remain chronically underfunded, poorly

staffed, and near the bottom of the ministerial power hierar-
chy. The emphasis had shifted from pollution to the management of such resources as forests, fisheries, rangeland, soils,
genetic diversity, and wetlands. Environmental degradation
was now seen to be as much a consequence of poverty, the
result of billions of individuals striving for a living, as of successful industrialization. More and more leaders of developing
countries viewed environmental and resource conservation as
integral elements of economic development. In words that
could not have been uttered a decade earlier, World Bank
President Barber Connable concluded that "economic growth
based on any other premise is a costly illusion." The focus of
activity shifted steadily from local to regional to global.

The realization that environmental issues will be a major
concern of international relations in the 1990s has caught both
diplomats and environmentalists unprepared. There is little in
the way of scholarly or human resources to support the policy
choices that must be made. Only a few political scientists, international lawyers, or individuals with broad experience in
multilateral diplomacy are well versed in the environmental
issues. On the other side, only a few environmental experts
have experience in international relations. Economists are still
employing tools that distort or ignore the contributions of natural resource consumption and send badly misleading signals
to policy makers. All sides recognize the absence of a common
language and body of knowledge. Moreover, time is short:
many key negotiations are in their formative stages.

This volume explores part of this newly important territory
that lies at the intersection of political science, economics, international law, and environmental science. Its emphasis is
less on specific policies than on the processes of international
governance as they relate to the management of global environmental problems. Its focus is on the new directions required for U.S. foreign policy, but two features of today's international landscape, especially as regards the environment,
inevitably broaden its scope. First, there is no longer a sharp
dividing line between foreign and domestic policies. The
highly interdependent global economy has made that clear (in

theory, if not always in practice) with respect to economic policy. It is equally true for energy and environmental policies. As we shall see in the following chapters, environmental policies encompass fiscal, trade, and monetary policy, as well as choices in agriculture, the allocation of research dollars, technology development, and development assistance.

Second, the U.S. can no longer make its foreign policy first and consult with others later. The post-postwar era may still be unnamed, but its defining characteristics are already clear: multipolarity, replacing the bipolar U.S.-USSR axis around which nations used to array themselves; economic interdependence; and diverse invasions of national sovereignty. In this new global era, more and more issues demand broad transnational cooperation. No simple alignment of relations, East-West or North-South, will prove sufficient. Legislators, who expect to serve with the same colleagues year after year, know that their opponent on one issue may be a vital ally on the next. A detailed understanding of all parties' positions, careful consultation before initiatives are launched, and sometimes heroic patience are required. So too, in the new era, for nations. No longer can any country get what it wants by doing what it wants—even the richest country in the world. So in this volume, as in reality, the roles and positions of other key players are an important feature.

The chapters that follow fall into three groups. In the first, the major global environmental concerns are introduced. Nathan Keyfitz, trained as a mathematician and sociologist and a world-renowned demographer, explores global population growth. Kenton Miller, former director general of the International Union for Conservation of Nature and Natural Resources (IUCN) and his colleagues address tropical deforestation and the parallel loss of biological diversity. Ambassador Richard Benedick, who led the United States delegation during the negotiations, traces the issues and answers that led to the precedent-setting Montreal Protocol, examining the record for lessons that can be applied elsewhere. Chemist and political scientist George Rathjens draws on his years of experience in arms control and nuclear proliferation to delineate the challenge posed by greenhouse warming and the complexities of global energy policy that lie at the heart of its solution.

Each author first addresses the physical trends involved; their biological, chemical, or physical nature; and the timing of the threats posed to human welfare and to the natural environment. They then consider the present and foreseeable implications of these trends for international relations, including, for example: impacts on national economic growth and the governability of highly stressed areas; creation of regional tensions or of a growing impetus for regional or global cooperation; infringements on territorial integrity and national sovereignty; and effects on North-South relations. Finally, these experts look beyond the usual sectoral perspective (how should tropical forests be managed, how should family planning be supported) to suggest some of the changes in governance—at the national, international, and nongovernmental levels—that are needed. Priorities range from reform of land tenure to technology transformation; from changes in economic accounting to new forms of international financing and mechanisms for joint regulation and resource management; from greater roles for players outside of governments to the formation of new international blocs and coalitions. Within this spectrum, each author considers the priorities for the United States.

In the next section we turn our attention to the "dismal" science, with results that are surprisingly hopeful. Professor Tom Tietenberg, recent president of the American Association of Environmental and Resource Economists, describes a wide array of economic tools that can be used to arrive at workable solutions to environmental problems. Some of these are well known but applied in new ways; others are quite unconventional. All can be used in an international regime, and are designed to make the marketplace function more efficiently or to incorporate values and goals that are today treated as externalities. In a commentary on the pitfalls and opportunities that lie ahead, Professor Richard Cooper, former under secretary of state for economic affairs, outlines what he sees as the key macroeconomic trends.

In the last section, three experienced practitioners consider the crucial questions of how to achieve the necessary international cooperation. Lifelong international civil servant Peter Sand reviews a large menu of mechanisms that have worked well (and less well) at the regional and global scale on environmental issues, broadly defined. He examines both formal and de facto means of achieving agreement, hard and soft law, treaties, regimes, and international standards. Lawyer/negotiator and defense expert Antonia Chayes and international lawyer and former legal adviser to the State Department Abram Chayes take up the question of how international regulatory regimes of the types analyzed by Sand might be maintained in the face of the certain need for rapid self-adjustment to changing circumstances and powerful incentives for noncompliance.

From this diversity of experience, disciplines, and perspectives, a striking number of common themes emerge.

Rapid change is the keynote. Keyfitz explains how a "window now open could close within a generation or two" because of the scale and characteristics of human population growth, and the strongly nonlinear relationship between human activities and their environmental impact. Threshold effects occur when consumption of a resource even slightly exceeds its sustainable yield. Suddenly, the past relations between population growth and production are changed, and can produce a crisis even without further additions to the population or technological development. An interaction is set up between "the social and biological system that, if allowed to persist, ends with the destruction of both." The rapidity of current tropical forest loss, and even more, of the biological extinction rate, underscores how quickly such change can occur, even on a global scale. So, in a different way, does the sudden appearance of the Antarctic ozone hole after decades of chlorofluorocarbon use.

A corollary of rapid change is a high degree of uncertainty and the frequent need to make policy choices long before major scientific questions can be resolved. For Rathjens, as for most other observers, this is the central conundrum of dealing with the greenhouse effect. The history of the chlorofluorocarbon negotiations demonstrates, however, that even a very high degree of scientific and economic uncertainty need not block joint international action. Ambassador Benedick speculates that the ozone treaty "may signal a fundamental shift in attitude" because consensus was reached and action taken, based solely "on a balancing of probabilities."

Rapid change puts a very high premium on flexible regimes capable of fast adaptation to new facts or scientific insight. For Tietenberg this means an added advantage for market mechanisms over rigid command-and-control regulation. For Peter Sand and the Chayeses, it creates a powerful reason to look for ways to institute an ongoing process, rather than one or many treaties, especially if each of these must be separately signed and ratified. In times of rapid economic, technological, and scientific change, the Chayeses argue, "perhaps *the* major function" of a regulatory treaty is not to define specific standards of performance, but to "establish a binding decision process for resolving regulatory issues as they arise."

The second corollary of rapidly changing circumstances that emerges from these pages is the need for experimentation and bold policy innovation. The usual sluggish pace of policy development and of international regime formation is inadequate. Elsewhere, Harlan Cleveland and Lincoln Bloomfield have aptly captured this sense of urgency in their call for "postwar planning without the war." As one example, several chapters in this volume examine the pros and cons of unilateral action by one or a group of nations to address a global issue. Benedick and Tietenberg both point out that while this may entail a temporary economic disadvantage, it may also mean a long-term advantage by giving (more accurately, forcing on) industry a head start in developing new technologies and practices.

Environmental conditions are integral to the human condition. Solutions lie in mainstream political and economic policies. Human population growth is a central tie that binds human welfare and the environment. While this may seem a truism, it has not been widely recognized in scholarship, or acted upon in policy circles. The exact nature of the relationship remains a matter of some contention and a high priority for research, but that an important connection exists is now little doubted. The authors of this volume, whether biologist, economist, or political scientist, see population growth as of overwhelming importance to environmental outcomes.

There are also intimate connections between environmental degradation and poverty, explored here by Keyfitz and by Kenton Miller and his colleagues. These connections run in both directions. That is, impoverished people generally have no other option but to overstress the environment, even when they are fully aware of the fearsome long-term costs. By the same token, environmental decline *creates* poverty. The two problems are so deeply intertwined that successfully addressing one demands a simultaneous attack on the other. In many cases there are genuine trade-offs to be made between the alleviation of human suffering and environmental protection. In a surprising number of others, however, the trade-offs are apparent, not real. In all cases, the past tendency to treat environment and basic human needs as wholly separate, if not conflicting, concerns is obsolete.

Just as Keyfitz shows that population policy and environmental policy can not be disentangled, Tietenberg traces some of the ways in which fiscal, monetary, and trade policies, not ordinarily thought of as having anything to do with the environment, in fact have huge impacts on it. The policy lesson is that as governments and international institutions build their capacity for dealing with environmental issues, the preferred course is not to separate, but to integrate; not to hire environmental specialists to operate out of their own small departments, but to educate everyone else.

The nature of national sovereignty is changing. The global environmental trends—loss of species, ozone depletion, deforestation on a scale that affects world climate, and the greenhouse effect itself—all pose potentially serious losses to national economies, are immune to solution by one or a few countries, and render geographic borders irrelevant. By definition, then, they pose a major challenge to national sovereignty.

In this they are not alone. The pages of this volume abound with examples of policies and practices once held to be purely domestic and now recognized to be unarguably international. To cite two very different examples, Richard Cooper cites the integration of the global economy, with its internationalization of markets, sources of supply, capital, and, most recently, of location of production, as a determining feature of the world economy. As industry becomes more and more mobile, he predicts, governments' sovereign rights of regulation and taxation will be ever more constrained. The Chayeses point out that whereas a state's treatment of its own citizens was traditionally viewed as strictly its own concern, now it is widely accepted that states have human rights obligations under international law for which they can be held accountable in international forums.

The boundary-erasing effects of remote sensing technologies and of developments in telecommunications are also evident. One consequence is the rising influence of international public opinion, which crops up over and over again in this volume. This may or may not lead to better environmental policies. For example, Professor Cooper stresses that now there is an "all-but-universal aspiration for higher standards of living in all but the richest parts of the world. In this respect the world has been westernized; it has absorbed the notion and the expectation of material progress." Willy-nilly, governments must recognize those desires, making the task of environmental protection all the more difficult. On the other hand, Peter Sand notes in numerous instances public opinion has been a more powerful tool for enforcing international agreements than anything states themselves could bring to bear. Ambassador Benedick amply corroborates the powerful impact of public opinion in the case of the Montreal agreement. However, public opinion depends on the availability of information: while governments may be less able to purposefully withhold information they possess, all too often in the case of global environmental issues, the data necessary for policy making simply do not exist.

Despite the pressures from so many directions toward a pooling of sovereignty to serve mutual interests, greater international cooperation is not a foregone conclusion. Govern-

ments may respond paradoxically to the erosion of their influence by clinging even more tightly to their powers.

*National security depends increasingly on global security. Within that
context, North-South relations will be profoundly different.* In its original military sense, national security was a zero-sum concept:
the greater one nation's security, the less another's. (The distinction between offensive and defensive actions has never
been convincing: one country's defensive buildup is preparation for war in the eyes of its enemy.) As the concept broad-
ened to include economic strength, the element of common
security gained ground, as indicated, for example, by efforts to
cooperatively manage monetary policy and to achieve free
trade. Global environmental trends shift the balance still further. The trends described in this volume threaten nations'
economic potential, and therefore their internal political security, their citizens' health (because of increased ultraviolet radiation), and, in the case of global warming, possibly their very
existence. No more basic threat to national security exists.
Notwithstanding some of the real or perceived differences in
national interest that Rathjens describes in relation to changing climate, the developed countries on both sides of the East-
West axis are likely ultimately to see a broad area of common
interest in developing the mechanisms necessary for shared
stewardship of the planet. The prospect of bridging the North-
South gap is far more problematic.

With more than 90 percent of future population growth in
the developing countries, North-South relations will change
for that reason alone. In the coming century the developed
countries will account for less than 15 percent of global population, down from 40 percent at the beginning of the postwar
era. Moreover, population growth is intimately connected not
only to poverty and environmental stress, but also to the debt
crisis. Keyfitz highlights the importance of the latter, since "as
long as the flow of funds is from the LDCs to us, it is they who
will influence our policies, not we theirs."

As with population growth, environmental trends all tend to
widen the North-South gap. Again, climate change is the
prime example. While the Dutch may be able to build dikes to

protect themselves from rising sea levels and more frequent storms, for Bangladeshis, says Rathjens, the eventual choice is "likely to be between attempting migration . . . or death by drowning or starvation." Miller and his colleagues point out that while there are substantial impacts of deforestation and biological diversity loss on the developed world, the developing countries bear far greater costs.

On the other hand, past and present contributions to ozone depletion and greenhouse warming have come largely from the developed world, and it is they who have profited from the emissions-causing activities. Now, the issue on the table is abandoning or drastically altering those activities and many others. With pessimistic assumptions of the potential for technological and social change, this raises the question of how much economic growth the planet can handle. As Professor Keyfitz puts it, "If only so much development is possible in the world, then the question of who will have it is going to dominate international politics in the short term." Since the developed countries must have the active cooperation of the developing world in order to solve global environmental problems, the potential for conflict is clear. The developing countries can be expected to exercise the leverage this situation confers to the fullest extent they can.

Institutional reform and innovation are high priorities. The UN system and other international institutions set up early in the postwar period were designed to preserve the status quo and to manage conflict. The task of actively fostering cooperation has evolved slowly. So far the system has scored some clear successes in areas where nations had much to gain and little to lose by participating, such as the distribution of the radio frequency spectrum, controlling infectious disease, the World Weather Watch, and the management of civil aviation. Divisive issues have proved to be a very different matter.

Our authors do not directly address the various proposals that have been made to strengthen the UN system for dealing with the environment, but do describe the principles and goals that should guide reform and innovation. Peter Sand stresses the wealth of experience that already exists and the need to "activate and accelerate the presently available machinery." Ambassador Benedick and the Chayeses share his view that more can be achieved through a step-by-step process than through another "epic codification" like the Law of the Sea. There seems to be a preference for keeping these issues away from UN headquarters, and indeed Benedick notes that one reason the ozone negotiations succeeded was that the United Nations Environment Programme has remained relatively free from the extraneous political debates that hamper work in other UN agencies.

The Chayeses argue that "the world appears to be on the verge of a major period of international lawmaking in the environmental field," but that so far its proponents have shown "impoverished institutional imagination." They suggest that both the General Agreement on Tariffs and Trade (GATT) and the International Monetary Fund (IMF) are models that have much to offer. "Like a global environmental treaty, the GATT is a multiparty agreement dealing with activities in which long-run benefits are in constant tension with inconsistent short-run domestic economic interests backed by powerful political constituencies." There is much to be learned from its history, they say, including the steady shift away from a judicial approach to dispute settlement toward a process of negotiation and conciliation, and from the generous use of "escape clauses and safety valves" that allow the regime to bend under pressure rather than break. In the case of the IMF, the Chayeses emphasize the setting of specific targets separately with each state by a respected third party, in this case the fund's expert staff. The analogy would be most apt if the hypothetical environmental agency had substantial financial resources at its disposal.

Nonstate actors are increasingly important. This follows directly from the changing nature of national sovereignty. If nation-states have less within their control, others will play a greater role. When private banks move vastly greater sums of money around the world than do state-run banks, the private sector plays a larger role in determining fiscal and monetary policy, whether the shift is explicitly acknowledged or not.

Governments are already knowingly and unwittingly delegating power, both upward to international institutions and downward to nongovernmental organizations (NGOs) and the corporate sector. Our authors are united in seeing this trend continuing, and in urging that it grow. They see international centripetal forces that bring together, each in its own sphere, scientists, specialists in multinational bureaucracies, business interests, labor, citizens groups, and so on. These transnational communities offset the centrifugal forces that generally govern relations among states. Ambassador Benedick cites the very different key roles played by scientists and by the corporate sector in the chlorofluorocarbon negotiations. The Chayeses note the tripartite make-up of delegations to the International Labour Organization. Peter Sand relates the role of NGOs in the European Community. Miller and his co-authors point to another advantage of NGOs, exemplified by debt-for-nature swaps: their capacity for policy innovation and the small-scale experimentation needed to test new ideas.

Economics provides an inadequate toolkit. Some tools are broken; others are missing. The misleading signals sent to policy makers because of economic analysis that ignores crucial physical realities are a principal cause of environmental decline. Two analytic shortcomings are most important. One is the failure of national income accounts, as currently formulated, to value and depreciate a country's physical resources—its forests, soils, and so on. The result is policies that treat capital assets as though they were income, a mistake so basic that it would be unforgivable in the rawest neophyte in the business or financial world.

While this deficiency is reasonably easy to correct, at least for those resources that have or can be assigned a market value, there is no substitute on the horizon for the use of short-term discount rates. Cost-benefit analyses are deeply affected by the choice of discount rate. Especially for policies that must consider the long term, any non-zero rate drastically undervalues the future consequences of present choices. This is not just an intergenerational issue. The effect is a powerful one over as short a time as ten or fifteen years, hardly longer than many international assistance projects. Rathjens rightly points out, however, that not only governments but also individuals heavily discount the future in their own behavior, so whatever substitute is used must reflect that reality. The needed change may therefore be as much cultural as methodological.

Other potent economic tools are *under*used. Several of our authors point to the role that the assignment of property rights can play in achieving sustainable environmental management. This applies to both real and intellectual property. Professor Tietenberg suggests that property rights should be treated as a fundamental principle of international cooperation on the environment. They are, he argues, a way to bridge the gap between local actions and global interests and to help ensure that international agreements are carried out. Kenton Miller and his colleagues note the role property rights could play in preserving biological diversity. Both Benedick and Cooper view the treatment of intellectual property rights as a crucial factor in the success or failure of technology transfer.

A vast amount can be achieved at little or no cost by correcting current policy failures. Low-cost, no-cost, and negative-cost improvements in the efficiency of resource use abound. Perhaps the greatest of these are the energy efficiency options Rathjens sketches. Replacing an inefficient policy with an efficient one, notes Tietenberg, "creates gains to be shared" that can lay the basis for international agreements. Other common policy failures—for example, in the management of tropical forests—are economically and environmentally counterproductive.

Tietenberg also argues that vast opportunities lie in more creatively harnessing the power of the marketplace. The implicit subsidies that cause high levels of pollution that later must be cleaned up at great cost can be rather painlessly removed. International cooperation can even be achieved through the appropriate use of market-based economic incentives. Cleverly enough handled, tools such as transferable emissions permits may also allow efficient cost sharing between rich and poor nations. Benedick points out that technological innovation can produce huge gains when stimulated to do so. A research and development (R&D) explosion followed on the heels of the Montreal Protocol, producing dozens of chlorofluorocarbon substitutes at a fraction of the expected cost.

This is intentionally not an exhaustive list of the views these chapters seem to hold in common. It is striking that in a young and swiftly developing field, a group of authors deliberately chosen for their diversity arrives at such broad common ground. There are important differences as well. Rathjens is far more pessimistic about the possibilities of near-term action to slow greenhouse warming, for example, than is Benedick. There are, inevitably, gaps. Each reader will reach his or her own assessment of the conclusions that are convincing and the areas that require further exploration. Everyone will certainly find a host of ideas and insights, far beyond what can be suggested here. Together the chapters lay a solid foundation on which sound policy and further scholarship can be built.

2

Population Growth Can Prevent the Development That Would Slow Population Growth

*Time as the crucial variable in the
population-development process*

NATHAN KEYFITZ

T he one thing that we know for sure about population is
that people in the developed condition do not have

NATHAN KEYFITZ has been leader of the Population Program of the International Institute for Applied Systems Analysis, Laxenburg, Austria, since 1984. Dr. Keyfitz is Andelot Professor of Sociology and Demography, Emeritus, at Harvard University, where he taught from 1972–83, climaxing a distinguished career as a research statistician for the Dominion Bureau of Statistics in Ottawa, and as professor of sociology at the Universities of Montreal, Toronto, Chicago, and California at Berkeley. He has lectured throughout the world, particularly in the Far East, and has advised the governments of Burma and Indonesia. Since 1986 Dr. Keyfitz has spent considerable time in Indonesia as a consultant for the Harvard Institute for International Development, Center for Policy and Implementation Studies (CPIS), with the Ministry of Finance in Jakarta. Author of numerous articles and books, Dr. Keyfitz is a fellow of the Royal Society of Canada and a member of the American Academy of Arts and Sciences and the National Academy of Sciences. Numbers in this chapter are mostly from the current assessment of world population by the UN, to whom the author is also grateful for advice on their interpretation. The author also would like to thank Anna Wils for making some charts and modifying others in the interest of clarity.

many children; whatever problems the rich countries face, rapid population growth is not one of them. Hence, all that is needed is for the poor countries to develop and they too will be spared the troubles arising from rapid population growth. Very true, except that their present rapid population growth, plus the corresponding damage to their ecological base, itself prevents the development that would be their salvation. Our task in this chapter will be to examine whether the circular chain of poverty–many children–poverty can be broken.

New obstacles are now appearing to what looked only a few years ago to be the prospect of an orderly process of universal development. The poorest countries are not the ones now securing the major share of economic advance. Leadership by the developed countries can increase the amount of development possible and distribute it where it will do most good. Yet our leadership is weakening, just at the moment when the world needs it most. With the whole planet under ecological pressure, the disaster that threatens through excessive population and excessive development of the wrong kind is not confined to the poor countries.

On this formulation, the time in which the chain can be broken is limited. To say "now or never" may seem too strong, but in fact a window now open could close within as little as a generation or two. That closing is determined by population growth plus the unwanted output of the economy, plus urbanization, plus the impatience of newly educated electorates, plus the sheer arithmetic of debt. But before taking these up I will consider how an ecological crisis can come on suddenly, like a point of singularity, when the underlying curves are smooth. That will be followed by some data on population and its growth.

The Apparent Innocuousness
of Population Growth

Population has been increasing slowly but steadily for a long time, and yet it is only in recent years that we have heard about the greenhouse effect, acid rain and forest dieback, pollution

of the oceans, and the decline of fish populations. The sudden-
ness of the appearance of these environmental phenomena,
contrasted with the gradualness of population increase, suggests that the latter can have no connection with the former,
and indeed this conclusion has been drawn. That population
has no part in causing the environmental damage is argued
from the fact that the worst of the damage has occurred since
population growth started to decelerate, i.e., during the 1970s
and 1980s. The world rate of growth was 2 percent twenty
years ago, and now it is down to 1.8 percent. If we got away
with a rate of 2 percent, how can a rate of 1.8 percent be
harming the planet? Writers adduce the fact that population
growth is slowing to show that population is no danger.

Such an argument on the innocuousness of population
growth has its complement on the economic side: *per capita*
incomes have been increasing steadily at 2 to 3 percent, and
motor vehicles at 4 percent, and they did no damage over several decades; why should anyone think that they do damage
now when their increase is no more rapid than in the past?

If one stays with the economics of the matter, the innocuousness of population is suggested in a different way. With the
shift from primary to secondary production, the law of diminishing returns ceases to operate, and increasing returns
become the rule. It costs less per television set to produce
2,000 than to produce 1,000; the major investment is in the
prototype, the first set produced. If primary production is responsible for only 10 percent of our income and expenditures,
why does it matter if land shortage doubles or trebles the unit
price of cereals? The reduced cost of the other 90 percent will
easily offset the rise, so that a larger population will be to our
overall advantage.

At one time the strongest case against population growth
was offered by nonrenewable resources, certain kinds of materials whose total supply is apparently fixed by nature: oil, met-
als, other commercial minerals. These were an important subject of classical economics; textbooks explained that the most
accessible sources were explored first, and that supplies would
become more and more costly. The same applied to land,

often given as the supreme example of the limits set by nature.

This argument has been rendered obsolete by the facility with which new supplies have been discovered; the apparent ease with which technical advance, spurred by price rises, has created substitutes; and more intensive use. The apparent overcoming of the classical "increasing marginal cost" has caused many of us to think that nature offers no further resistance to the expansion of population and economy.

Renewable and Nonrenewable Resources

These views cannot be corrected without consideration of the way that ecosystems work, including the relations of people and environment within them. Cases differ, of course— pollution of the oceans does not depend on population in the same way that forest dieback does, but a strong nonlinearity is common to all of them.

Biological systems, including soils, forests, animals in the wild, and especially fisheries, have been harvested from time immemorial and have been referred to as renewable resources. Wholly different rules apply to these from those governing minerals, and these rules have never been suitably incorporated in economics or other social sciences.

To anticipate what follows, there seem to be adequate amounts of the nonrenewable resources, and it is the renewable ones whose shortage will sink us. (Here is an example of how words coined in one time or context are self-contradictory in another.) It is an odd turn of language by which those resources called "nonrenewable" are the ones we will *not* run short of, while "renewable" resources like forests and water will be the ones whose shortage limits us.

Unreflective common sense tells us that since twice as many fish eaters, everything else constant, will eat twice as much fish, a doubling of population will double the stress on the aquatic system. The inference is correct only at low harvesting levels, the levels that existed through much of human history. Empirical study of the relation existing in the past between population and fish supplies can be totally misleading when the scale of exploitation has changed. No past data help unless they are incorporated into a model that takes account of the way that the biological system works.

The same fact can be described as a threshold above which further harvesting damages the resource. This change in the basic relations with change of scale means that special care is needed in handling empirical materials. Simply supposing that relations among past values of the variables will hold in the future can give absurd results.

Social and Biological Systems Interact

One or two people fishing in a lake are an easily assimilated element in the biosystem of the lake, the slightly greater mortality of mature fish being offset by better survivorship of the young. Let the fishers become dozens, and if the lake is not large they do affect the biosystem; as an added cause of mortality, they are comparable to a new disease in the fish population. But especially if their main incidence is on the mature individuals, they still need not interfere with the processes of reproduction. In fact, if the limiting factor is the supply of nutrients in the lake, such harvesting may not interfere at all; it takes away fish that have already reproduced, and the nutrients that these used are available to younger creatures. Thus up to a certain point, the harvesting leaves the resource intact. The contrast is with inanimate resources that do not regenerate themselves; oil taken out of the ground leaves less for later generations.

But the regenerative feature of natural systems—that up to a certain point they are not diminished by harvesting—turns to sharp disadvantage at a later stage. When those dozens of fishers increase to hundreds and thousands, there comes a point where the reproduction of fish is interfered with. Perhaps the nutrients are still there, the sun is still supplying energy to grow the plants on which the animal layers depend, but the nutrients cease to circulate through the fish because too many are removed prematurely. At some point in human population growth, the interaction between the natural system and the social system can become critical.

If the fishers can make and adhere to rules governing the

amount of fishing and the minimum size of fish allowed to be caught, then fishing can continue indefinitely—not in the sense that the population of fishers can increase at will, but rather that the maximum possible continuing catch can be worked out, and all the fish that the amount of sunlight and plant nutrients will permit are extracted, year by year indefinitely.

The perfect human institution implied in this is very different from actual institutions, especially as they function in international waters. Whether in a lake or in the oceans, unconstrained competition among fishers, in the context of a growing (or even constant, as we shall see) human population, will destroy the resource. Our main subject, if we are to deal effectively with ecological questions, has to be the interaction between the social system and the biological system. A social system of unrestrained competition, the most efficient for harvesting in the short run, can, just because of its efficiency, interact disastrously with the biological system.

A Competitive Economy in a Fragile Ecology

With given technology and given style of life the requirements from the environment are proportional to the number of people. Twice as many people cooking with the same wood stoves use up twice as much wood. Twice as many cars of a given kind and given condition of repair put twice as much carbon dioxide into the atmosphere. Twice as many fish eaters require twice as large a catch. With all else constant, the requirements are the simplest possible linear function of the number of people.

Consumption may be a linear function of population when technology and style of life are given, but the resulting strain on the environment is distinctly nonlinear. Once the woodcutting or fish consumption outpace the normal mortality of the trees or the reproductive capacity of the fish, then any increment of population (again with given technology and style of life) changes the ecology, and changes it permanently if populations do not decrease or, in some circumstances, even if they do subsequently decrease.

In the typical case there is no recovery, but at best a less productive resource from that time forward. An example is when a lake loses its ability to support commercially valuable fish, and they are replaced by worthless species, as in Lake Erie. A dry area kept fertile by artesian wells becomes desert when its fossil water is exhausted. These changes can take place suddenly and with no clear warning.

The situation can be much worse than just the output of the resource dropping to a lower level. Once the size of the human population has moved beyond what can be supported by the natural resource at equilibrium, a new feature of the interaction between the human population and the resource comes into play: less and less exploitation is possible. The less productive resource has to be harvested more intensively as people continue to depend on it: smaller trees are cut down for firewood, smaller fish are eaten. An intensive search goes on for any part of the resource that may be hidden in some kind of sanctuary. The response to a diminishing resource and a burgeoning market is higher prices and economic incentives to use even more ingenuity and more effective technology to hunt down and capture whatever of the resource remains. It may take more effort to catch smaller fish, but the effort still pays because of higher prices.

Thus we come into the epoch of those Korean trawlers pulling twenty-five-kilometer-long nets extending twelve meters down through the Mediterranean and picking up unnumbered marine creatures. Contrast the volume of water swept through per crew member per day with that for the Eskimo fisher spearing fish through a hole in the ice. A quick calculation shows that the first can easily be a million times as great as the second. What applies on a local scale to a lake or the Mediterranean applies on a world scale once markets have become larger than the sustainable catch. Even the vast Pacific will be turned into desert by super-efficient trawlers.

The important point here is that this occurs suddenly; once the market is even slightly too big, and the catch even slightly in excess of the equilibrium harvest, then further fishing that depletes the resource reduces the equilibrium catch. There follows a positive feedback that would lead to a crisis even if the human population stopped growing at this point and the technology did not become more intensive.

In different ways this nonlinear relation between population and the stress it causes applies to all resources, from agricultural land to disposal of dangerous waste. It applies on all levels, from the individual farm to the world stocks of fish, wood, and land. Striking environmental effects are reported in areas whose production has been quietly growing for thousands of years; we are noticing with alarm an activity that has been there all along, but now has just slightly passed the sustainable yield.

The fundamental relation in a competitive economy is that the catch effort can increase long after the sustainable yield has been passed. If the price elasticity is greater than unity, then it can become more and more profitable to invest in exploiting the resource once it starts to diminish. It is almost as though the market starts to present a bonus, an incentive to greater effort, in those very times, and for those very fish varieties, whose availability is diminishing. This is the kind of interaction between the social and the biological system that, if allowed to persist, ends with the destruction of both. The destruction can occur suddenly and at the end of thousands of years during which the population was small enough, and its technology harmless enough, that the social and biological systems could be in harmony.

Is It Population or Technology That Does the Damage?

Noted biologist Barry Commoner measures the factors that have broken up the harmony by decomposing the annual increase of pollution into three elements: increase of population, increase of income per head, and increase of polluting technology per unit of income. He is able to apply the decomposition numerically to individual countries with data based on postwar growth when all three of the factors have been increasing with unprecedented speed.

One of his examples is phosphate detergents in the United

States. Simplifying somewhat, over the period 1946–68 these increased 19.45 times; population increased in the ratio 1.42; by division we find that the pollutant per head of population increased in the ratio 13.78. There can be no question that the major effect was the amount of detergent used per person, rather than the number of people around to use it.

Yet to go from this unquestioned fact to what should be done about it is not straightforward. Some further information is indispensable: how difficult is it going to be to reduce population as against changing from phosphate detergents to something else? In this instance it would seem absurd to argue for reducing the population when it is technically straightforward to substitute for the phosphates and still get clean sheets.

But take another case, also from Barry Commoner's collection. In Pakistan, as his figures show, holding down the population would reduce the pollution of automobile exhausts about equally with reducing the number of automobiles. But what actually ought to be done involves something else as well: how easy it is to control population as against having people use other means of transport or against finding some way of burning gasoline with less exhaust fumes.

Of course decisions on the control of population depend on more than automobile emissions. One must take account of all the other unwanted outputs of the economy that are proportional to population.

In principle, whether we can get at the cause of the troubles in some deeper sense or not, what has to be done is plain. Effort along various lines—controlling population and inventing more benign technology, for instance—has to be directed where it will produce the largest results. In the language of economics: put effort into a variety of possible directions, always aiming to maximize the total return by equalizing the marginal return in reduced pollution per unit of effort. It is in such a context that human population numbers and their increase must be examined.

Population Numbers

The world population doubled between 1950 and 1985 and will add a further 50 percent by 2020 (Table 1 and Figure 1). This 50 percent may be a low estimate, since the United Nations supposed that there would be further success in the application of birth control. This would have lowered the birth rate below the projected value and so brought stability closer. In fact what has occurred since the estimates were published is the opposite: there has been a rise from 1.7 percent (1987) to 1.8 percent (1988) in the rate of world population increase.

But more important than the quality of estimate is the error in drawing conclusions from percentages. A 50 percent increase would have had no ecological significance when the population was as small as it was up to the eighteenth century, when much of Europe and practically all of North America was forest or uninhabited grassland. The current *percent* increases may seem innocuous, but the added *billions* can bring disaster.

TABLE 1. Population, Births, and Birth Rates, World and LDCs, 1950–2020 (Thousands)

	World			Less Developed Countries		
Year	Population	CBR	Births	Population	CBR	Births
Estimates based on data						
1950	2,515,652	37.33	93,902	1,683,796	44.39	74,749
1960	3,018,878	35.25	106,418	2,073,969	41.86	86,810
1970	3,693,221	31.65	116,879	2,645,829	37.23	98,510
1980	4,449,567	27.11	120,610	3,312,899	30.96	102,557
Projected						
1990	5,246,209	25.04	131,381	4,036,432	28.08	113,327
2000	6,121,813	22.25	136,223	4,845,166	24.41	118,261
2010	6,989,128	19.92	139,230	5,657,929	21.38	120,972
2020	7,822,193	17.72	138,570	6,445,508	18.61	119,957

Source: United Nations (1988).

FIGURE 1. Total population of the world, LDCs, and MDCs

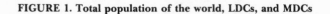

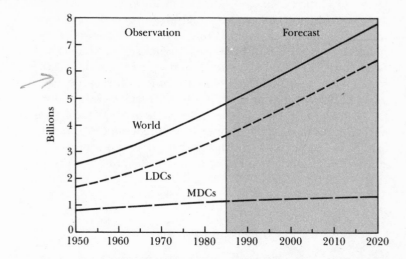

Here is a hazard for empirical analysis. Whoever wants to prove that the population danger is past points to the diminishing percent increase; whoever wants to prove the continued existence of the danger points to the growing number of billions.

Note the world crude birth rate (CBR) in Table 1. Much satisfaction is taken in its decline, from thirty-seven per thousand to the present twenty-five or so, with an even larger fall for the less developed countries (LDCs). But the table also shows that the absolute number of births is increasing and will continue to increase, both for the world as a whole and for the LDCs, at least to the year 2010, while the population increases to the end of the table in 2020 and well beyond.

The tree cutting and other demands on the environment are not related to the CBR but to the population, and the relation to population is not linear or proportional, but much more than proportional once a resource has become scarce. This is to emphasize again the distinction between demand on the environment and the stress on it discussed earlier.

The population growth is disproportionate in the LDCs

(Figure 1). In 1950 the LDCs had double the population of the more developed countries (MDCs); at the present time they are about three times, and by 2020 they are expected to be more than four and one-half times. (Here as elsewhere the definitions of MDC and LDC used by the United Nations will be followed.) This in itself need be no concern; in fact it restores the ratio that existed before the nineteenth century gave a large fillip to the population of Europe and America. It does mean, however, that those groups less able to support children and educate them are having most of them, and the sheerly arithmetic consequence of this is that poverty (as measured, say, by the absolute number of people who are hungry) is increasing in the world.

Increasing Poverty

To make the predicament clear, suppose that the world population of 5 billion includes 1 billion (most but not all in the MDCs) who have attained the developed condition, let us call it middle class when applied to individuals and families, and who are barely reproducing themselves. They share the planet with 4 billion (most but not all in the LDCs) who are poor and who are increasing at 2 percent per year, or in absolute numbers by 80 million per year. Economic progress is taking place; incomes are rising in both the rich and the poor countries, and some families are moving from poverty to the middle class where, among other things, they will have few children.

Suppose that the middle class 1 billion are increasing by 5 percent or 50 million per year, mostly through additions in the LDCs, leaving the number of poor people in the world going up by 80 − 50 = 30 million per year or ¾ percent. As long as this relation continues, poverty, and hence high fertility, in the world will continue to expand, and the poor, now growing by ¾ of a percent, or 30 million per year, will accelerate their increase.

The greatest intercontinental contrast overall is that between Europe and Africa (Table 2 and Figure 2). According to

TABLE 2. Contrast of Continents and Two Countries (Millions of Persons)

Year	Asia	Latin America	Europe	Africa	West Germany	Nigeria
Estimates from data						
1950	1376	165	392	224	50	33
1980	2584	361	485	479	62	81
Projections						
2000	3549	546	512	872	59	162
2020	4365	735	523	1468	55	302

FIGURE 2. Total population in four continents, 1950–2020

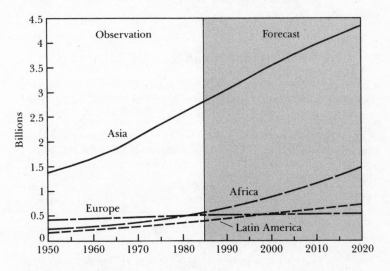

the projection Africa trebles over the coming forty years, while Europe's increase is a bare 7 percent. Nigeria's population started as two-thirds of West Germany and ends the seventy-year period five and one-half times as large. The contrast between Germany's throbbing economic growth and Nigeria's slow progress is not to be imputed to the populations they have to carry, for the causation is at least in part in the other direction: economic growth acts to slow births as well as the converse. The disentangling of the causal direction is a major subject of study and of controversy.

The Eleven Most Populous Countries

Table 3 shows those eleven countries that are expected to exceed 100 million by the year 2020. Their relative positions change greatly. Japan starts in 1950 larger than six of the others and ends as number eleven; Nigeria starts three-fifths as large as Brazil and ends 25 percent greater. The U.S. and USSR increase in about the same proportions; so do Brazil and Mexico. Among the less developed countries of Asia, China increases less than threefold over the seventy years; Indonesia a little more than threefold; Bangladesh and Pakistan nearly fivefold.

Births, Birth Rates, and the LDC-MDC Gap

Births for the world passed the 120 million mark in 1980 and continue to rise. It is hard to say when they will peak, but if we

TABLE 3. Countries Expected to Exceed 100 Million by 2020 (Millions of Persons). Number in Parenthesis Is the Ratio of Population in 2020 to That in 1950.

| Year | Japan | USA | USSR | Latin America | | Africa |
				Brazil	Mexico	Nigeria
1950	84	152	180	53	27	33
1980	117	228	265	121	69	81
2000	130	268	315	179	109	162
2020	133 (1.6)	304 (2.0)	358 (1.9)	234 (4.4)	146 (5.4)	302 (9.2)

Asia

Year	Bangladesh	China	India	Indonesia	Pakistan
1950	42	555	358	80	40
1980	88	996	689	151	86
2000	146	1256	964	211	141
2020	206 (4.9)	1436 (2.6)	1186 (3.3)	262 (3.3)	198 (5.0)

go along with the United Nations projection, as shown in Table 4 and Figure 3 (which shows births in five-year periods), we might extrapolate to something like 140 million per year by about 2030. After that they will presumably decline, so that by some time about the middle of the twenty-first century they may be back to the 120 million of 1980.

TABLE 4. Annual Births in the MDCs and LDCs, 1950–2020 (Thousands of Persons)

Year	World	MDCs	LDCs	LDC/MDC
1950	93,902	18,916	74,749	3.95
1980	120,610	17,597	102,557	5.83
2000	136,223	17,639	118,261	6.70
2020	138,570	18,493	119,957	6.49

FIGURE 3. Absolute number of births

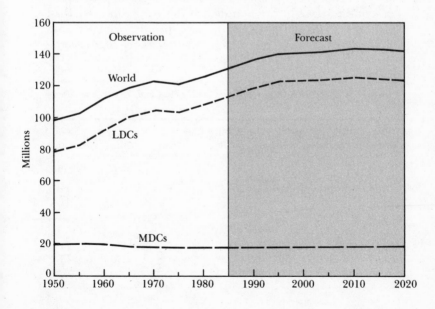

In contrast to the total for the world, the MDC births have apparently leveled off in the range of 17 to 19 million. Note that MDC births decline slightly between 1950 and 1980, then rise. But the rise is an assumption of the projection. There is little to tell us whether the MDCs are moving towards replacement fertility; however, unexpected and surprising changes have occurred in the past.

The LDC births, on the other hand, are nearly certain to increase in number, rising from over 100 million annually now to nearly 120 million by 2020. And of the increased number of births a larger fraction will survive, especially in the LDCs, and especially through the difficult years of infancy.

For the future, the fall in fertility is expected to accelerate and so to counter the further fall in mortality. From the viewpoint of the LDCs this is the optimistic assumption; we can only wait and see whether the decline of birth and death rates will materialize in the degree expected. I have nothing to offer that will improve on the United Nations projections presented in the tables of this article.

Crude birth rates are shown in Table 5 and Figure 4. For nearly all countries the birth rates decline; from 1950 up to the present the MDCs have fallen slightly more in proportion than the LDCs, so the ratio LDC/MDC rose from 1.95 to 2.00 from 1950 to 1980. On the other hand, the difference between the

TABLE 5. Crude Birth Rates in the World, LDCs and MDCs, and Three Continents

Year	World	LDCs	MDCs	Africa	Asia	Latin America
		Crude Birth Rate				
		Observed				
1950	37.4	44.6	22.6	48	43	42
1980	27.7	31.8	15.2	46	27	32
		Projected				
2000	22.9	25.3	13.1	40	20	24
2020	17.4	18.5	11.9	27	16	19

rates has been declining; per thousand population it was 44 − 23 = 21 in 1950, and by 1980 had fallen to 31 − 15 = 16. On this, as on many other "gaps," one can find the trend one wishes to find. By using ratios of birth rates one can argue that the gap is widening; by using differences of birth rates one can show that it is narrowing.

In 1950 birth rates in all three continents of the less developed world were well above forty per thousand (Table 5). Africa starts highest and falls most slowly. Asia's fall has been the greatest; it is heavily weighted by one country, China, whose success in family planning is well known, partly because of the criticism that it has aroused among those foreigners who do not like abortion. For the Chinese the choice is between abortion, always regrettable, and even more regrettable prospective unemployment of adults and hunger of entire communities.

FIGURE 4. Crude birth rates in the world, LDCs, and MDCs

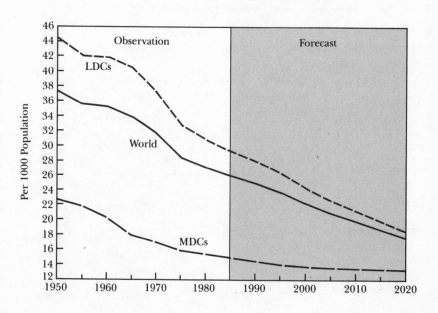

Deaths, Death Rates, and Longevity

Table 6 and Figure 5 show that deaths have stood at a level of about 45 million per year for the world as a whole up to now, but according to the projection used here deaths rise to about 63 million by 2020 as populations age. Despite the as-

TABLE 6. Absolute Deaths, Births, and Natural Increase in the World (Thousands)

Year	Deaths	Births	Natural Increase
		Observed	
1950	51,833	98,560	46,727
1980	48,560	128,735	80,175
		Projected	
2000	53,623	148,785	95,162
2020	63,394	143,865	80,471

FIGURE 5. Births, deaths, and natural increase in the world

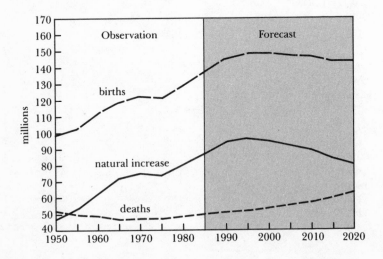

sumed continued decline in rates, the absolute number of deaths is bound to rise by virtue of changing age distribution. But the rise in deaths is not sufficient before 2020 to bring the annual natural increase down to where it was in 1980. By a rough extrapolation from the table, it appears that the natural increase will not be down to its 1950 level until about the middle of the twenty-first century, at which time the world population can be expected to be over 10 billion. The United Nations forecasts do not take into account the possibility that such dense populations as will then exist may be subject to increased mortality that could well enforce a density lower than the table implies. The UN projections are a judicious extrapolation of present trends, but they do not pretend to take account of economic or environmental constraints.

Decline of mortality rates in the postwar period has been dramatic, especially for the LDCs. In the space of thirty years the crude rate dropped by 55 percent, with a fall greater than this in Asia (see Table 7 and Figure 6). The assumptions of the projection were for a modest continuing fall in the age-specific rates; as was said, what turns this into a rise in the crude rate is shifting age distribution: all of the populations are getting older with the fall in mortality and especially in fertility, though Africa least so on the assumptions used.

Life expectancy, according to this projection based on recent trends, has very nearly reached a plateau in the MDCs, and the LDCs—those of Latin America and Africa in particu-

TABLE 7. Crude Death Rates in the World, LDCs, MDCs, Africa, Asia, and Latin America

Year	World	MDC	LDC	Africa	Asia	Latin America
			Crude death rate			
1950	19.62	10.07	24.24	27.06	23.97	15.40
1980	10.46	9.58	10.76	16.59	9.82	8.17
2000	8.52	9.83	8.19	11.08	7.75	6.62
2020	8.20	11.01	7.61	7.24	8.01	7.03

FIGURE 6. Crude death rates in the world, LDCs, and MDCs

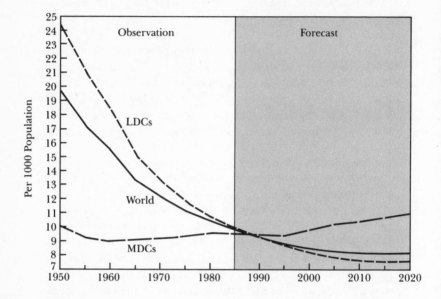

lar—will be coming up towards that same plateau by the year 2020 (Figure 7). The UN does not have any technique for projecting mortality beyond present ages; perhaps people will live to be 150 in the next century, but that cannot be inferred from existing statistical materials.

All forecasts are necessarily speculative in other ways. No one can guarantee that an epidemic—AIDS or some other— will not decimate the human population, or that some human-made disaster will not destroy the populations of large territories. If AIDS is not effectively contained within the present risk groups and escapes into the general population, the consequences could be truly catastrophic. A forecaster is almost bound to disregard such contingencies. But what about large-scale famine arising out of population growth itself? That should fall within the scope of the models used to project population, but in fact it does not.

FIGURE 7. Life expectancy at birth in the world, LDCs, and MDCs

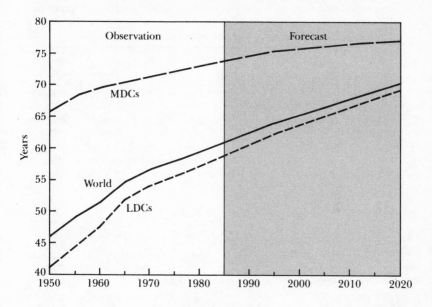

Infant Mortality

The demographic variable that has changed more than any other of the many shown in our tables is infant mortality. Table 8 permits us to examine its postwar variation for the world, LDCs, MDCs, three continents, and three developed and eight less developed countries, all having, or shortly to have, 100 million population or more. Japan's rate of fall is the most rapid (in the course of thirty years it dropped by seven-eighths) and its present level is the lowest. The USSR showed an enormous improvement during the 1950s, but much less thereafter.

But it is the less developed countries that draw most attention for persistent improvement, sometimes accompanying a fall in birth rates, sometimes not. China is the outstanding example of a country in which (with some ups and downs) the curves of infant mortality and of birth rates fell in parallel; the same applies also to Indonesia. On the other hand, the African

TABLE 8. Deaths Under One Year of Age per Thousand Live Births for the 6 Regions and 11 Countries Expected to Exceed 100 Million Population in 2000
Deaths Under One Year of Age per 1000 Births

Year	World	MDC	LDC	Africa	Asia	Latin America
1950	156	56	180	191	181	125
1980	78	16	88	112	83	62
2000	50	10	56	74	48	40
2020	30	7	33	45	26	27

Year	Japan	USA	USSR	Latin America Brazil	Mexico	Africa Nigeria
1950	51	28	73	135	114	207
1980	6	11	25	71	53	114
2000	5	7	15	45	33	79
2020	5	6	9	30	22	48

			Asia		
Year	Bangladesh	China	India	Indonesia	Pakistan
1950	180	195	190	160	190
1980	128	39	110	84	120
2000	85	20	67	46	79
2020	53	11	35	26	43

countries show an improvement in mortality not offset by a lowering of fertility.

Age Distributions and Dependency

The population of working age has declined as a fraction of the total for the world as a whole and is reaching a low point about now; from 1990 onwards it is expected to rise. Dependency ratios for the LDCs are attaining their peak and will decline. There will indeed be more old people as population ages, but their increase is more than offset by the declining proportion of children.

The fraction of the population under fifteen reflects preceding birth rates. The more developed countries have shown a considerable decline since the postwar baby boom; Asia and Latin America have shown slight declines, Africa an increase. From the viewpoint of the size of the upcoming generation, for the total of the LDCs, the improvement of mortality has more than offset any fall in fertility that may have so far occurred. It has been demonstrated that in some countries there has been an increase of fertility as a first consequence of modernization.

In the MDCs the increase of old people has not quite offset the decline of children, so there is a small fall in dependency from 1950 to 2000. The LDCs have had a balance in the opposite direction showing increasing dependency, but according to the projection this will reverse in the future; on the birth and death rates assumed, there will be increasing proportions of the population of working age, and the declining fraction of children will more than offset the increase of old people.

Conspicuous differences in the proportion of old people appear both through time and among continents. An actual decline in Africa over the thirty years since the war contrasts with increases elsewhere. By 2020 the MDCs, Asia, and Latin America will have more than double the proportion they showed in 1950; Africa barely comes back to the proportion shown in 1950.

Sudden Expansion of Education

The effect of increased proportions of young people is intensified, especially in the LDCs, by the way that education has proceeded. One can imagine a simultaneous expansion of education for young and old alike, but that is not the way things have happened. The expansion is essentially for those of school age, despite some attempts in the direction of adult literacy. Hence, superimposed on the shifts in age distribution, and greatly accentuating their effect, are very different proportions with middle school and college degrees at the several ages. The education explosion came close to coinciding in time with the total numbers explosion. A picture for the educated population would show a sharp division into young and old, with the young, aged twenty, say, as much as five to ten times the number aged sixty.

The sheer difficulty of providing jobs that would employ the large youth cohorts, in a situation where all jobs are centrally planned, is well known to the authorities in China. This is one of the main factors that have induced a freeing of the economy, so that people can make jobs for themselves and others. That or a severely repressive regime (which has also been tried and is now being tried again) would seem to be the only two ways of preserving political stability as the youth cohort emerges into adulthood. Of course politics is affected by many other circumstances, but the least one can say is that present changes toward the freeing of the Chinese economy are thoroughly in accord with the demographic exigencies. Whether similar associations of the massive increase of educated youth with high expectations will be found in other countries remains to be seen as their youth cohorts move forward in time, increasing in relative size and political weight.

Urbanization No Longer Depends on Industrial Advance

The locations and activities of population are as important as their numbers. While the world population in 2020 is given as three times the 1950 population, the urban total in 2020 is six times that of 1950.

It is in the nature of human settlements that their definition cannot easily be made uniform across countries. Cities, towns, and villages differ in many respects, including density, especially in the degree to which they are distinct from the surrounding countryside. The economic activities carried on by the urban inhabitants are not always clearly distinguishable from those of the rural inhabitants. Urban density is on the average much higher than rural, but the gradation from the center makes the boundary arbitrary. Even when the transition from rural to urban over space is sharp enough, there may be historical reasons why the point of transition is not used for statistical purposes; the legal and hence statistical boundary may be defined by articles of incorporation that are unrelated to any observable criterion. National cultures and traditions differ in their determination of what places are urban for statistical purposes. Our numbers are those of the United Nations, which is unable to collect data independently of national statistical sources and so must accept national definitions.

Urbanization was once mostly a feature of rich countries. Until very recently towns depended on an accessible hinterland with a surplus of foodstuffs. Provisioning of the city depended either on political domination of that hinterland or the economic capacity to provide goods and services needed by the peasantry. Cities grew with the increase of agricultural productivity and the simultaneous increase of urban goods and services.

A worldwide grain market was made possible by steam transport developed in the nineteenth century. Now there are European, American, and other surpluses, so that the link between the size of the city, on the one side, and its ability to dominate or serve an immediately accessible hinterland, on the other, has become weaker. At one time the countries that were richest could have the most and the largest cities, but that is decreasingly the case. The urban population of the LDCs passed that of the MDCs well before 1980, and by 2000 it is expected that there will be fully twice as many city inhabitants in the LDCs as in the MDCs, and by 2020 more than three times as many (Table 9 and Figure 8).

Percent urban as given in Table 10 shows the LDCs passing the point where they are half urban before the year 2020, while Latin America passed that point some years ago.

TABLE 9. Urban Populations of the MDCs and LDCs (Millions)

Year	World	MDC	LDC	LDC/MDC
1950	734	447	287	0.64
1980	1764	798	966	1.21
2000	2853	950	1903	2.00
2020	4488	1063	3425	3.22

FIGURE 8. Urban population of Asia, Africa, and Latin America

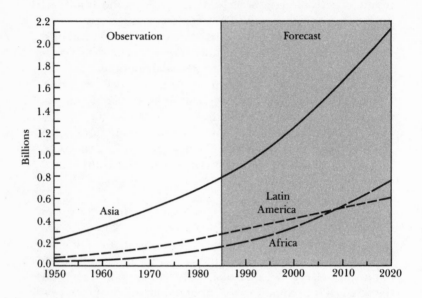

TABLE 10. Percent Urban Population of the MDCs and LDCs (Millions)

| Year | World | Percent Urban | | | | Latin America |
		MDC	LDC	Africa	Asia	
1950	29	54	17	16	16	41
1980	40	70	29	27	27	65
2000	47	74	39	39	35	77
2020	57	77	53	52	49	83

Do city populations press harder or less hard on the environment than rural ones? There is no single answer to this. Settling 20 million people in Mexico City could in principle reduce the amount of fuel needed for travel, or could use food raised in parts of the country or parts of the world that can ecologically afford to produce it. It is true that the air over the city is spectacularly bad, but the harm extends over a relatively small area. The economic effects of urbanization have been extensively discussed without any unanimous conclusions on the advantages or disadvantages; the literature investigating the ecological effects is small and even less conclusive.

The Dynamics of Urban Growth

Economic explanation of the growth of cities in poor countries is customarily in terms of the individual incentive to move; people will only come to the city if their prospective stream of income is greater there than it would be if they remained on the farm. There is a difference, of course. They can foresee with some precision their income on the farm; to the prospective migrant income in the city is a lottery. The migrant looks at the expected value of city income (suitably averaging what he would make collecting cigarette butts from the streets with what he would make if he got a factory job, and with what he would make if he got to be the owner of the factory). His calculation, like that of a casino *habitué*, tends to overweight the big prizes. Such a way of looking at the matter provides a useful explanation of individual migration at a given moment.

Yet this approach cannot by itself explain the seemingly indefinite growth of LDC cities. If conditions in the city were not altered by the migration, then after a certain number of migrants came in from the countryside, their competition would bring the expected return to labor down to the level at which it was in the countryside, and the equalization of expected returns to labor would halt further migration. It is not the spontaneous expansion of city economies that draws the migrants to Cairo, Calcutta, or Jakarta, as factories did in Adam Smith's day. Rather it is the systematic effort of national authorities to make life better for the urban dwellers than the natural movement of the economy would do. Political dynamics are the culprit.

The authorities center their own activities especially in the capital: they concentrate schools, especially of higher education, in cities; they accept investment in the city by domestic and foreign firms; they concern themselves with supplies of foodstuffs and the prices charged for them to city markets. Consider the last item alone. In a poor country where food is the largest part of nearly everyone's budget and practically the entire source of the farmer's income, an official order that lowers the price at which farmers can sell food lowers the living standard of the farmer and simultaneously raises that of the city person. The economic incentive to move to the city changes with each 1 percent adjustment on the price of foodstuffs. Assurance of supply is an even more important consideration. In hard times in the past depressed conditions pushed people out of the cities and onto the land; now it is the opposite: in a crisis the city is where food is to be found. The international trade in cereals, buttressed by foreign aid, means that the city no longer has to be supplied from its neighboring countryside.

Moreover, city crowds are dangerous. It was the Paris crowds (opposed by a countryside that was largely royalist) that unseated the royal government in the late eighteenth century. Contemporary rulers may never have heard of Louis XVI, but they have learned independently to fear crowds; whether democratically elected officials or self-appointed dictators, they are warily circumspect in dealing with the urban masses.

The larger the city population, the more governments have to be concerned about it and the more they must make concessions in setting prices and creating employment. And so they strain to provide low-priced food and adequate schools for the newcomers, not to mention streets, houses, clean water, and jobs. They know the political pressure, in the form of strikes and riots, that the concentrated millions can exert. At the same time they cannot improve conditions for the existing population without attracting further immigrants, and these increase further the pressure on governments.

Thus the political factor complements the economic incentive that attracts more individuals from the countryside and completes a circuit of positive feedback. The economic analysis is correct insofar as it goes, but only within a certain political context does it lead to the apparently indefinite growth of cities that we observe in the LDCs. This is one aspect only of the destabilization associated with incipient development.

FIGURE 9.

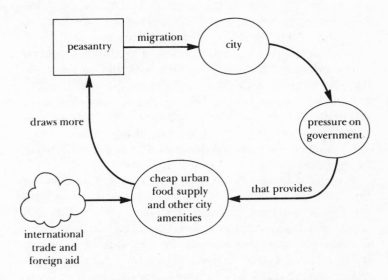

Destabilizing Effect of Partial Development

The world was relatively stable during many centuries. Birth and death numbers were on the average nearly equal; poverty was widespread, but it seemed to be borne with patience. Now we have economic progress nearly everywhere, which should make people more contented, and yet dissatisfaction has increased, along with potential and actual social and ecological instability. Some of the ways in which incipient progress is unsettling need to be noted.

When the population grows in Brazil it spreads over tropical forestland. In parts of Africa it is the need of the increased population for firewood for cooking that destructively interacts with the environment. Perhaps for a few years the added inhabitants can have employment cutting logs, panning for gold, or in other ways, but the logging soon ends for want of trees, and people turn to agriculture. Unfortunately for them, in tropical forests the nutrients are hardly at all in the soil, as they are in temperate forests; they are in the trees. When the trees are gone little is left, and that little is exhausted within two or three years of tilling or cattle raising.

It was said above that there could be a window of a generation or two after which more development may no longer be possible. But why is the time until the middle of the twenty-first century, say, so crucial? The answer has to be in terms of disturbance of an equilibrium existing over thousands of years. On the population side births and deaths were nearly equal; on the resource side techniques were aimed not at maximizing output so much as stabilizing it. The indians of the Amazon have always been relatively sparse; they are a part of the ecology. As for many other primitive peoples, traditional practices of birth restraint, including infanticide, together with natural mortality, prevent population from outgrowing its base, and economic practices aim not at wealth but at security against disaster. Left to themselves they could stay for geological eons in essentially their present condition.

Today no one is left to himself or herself. Logging companies buy cutting rights in the jungle, and they hire indians to do the cutting. When the logs are gone the indians try to plant crops on the cutover land that cannot sustain their agriculture. As in other parts of the world, development has tragic effects on native peoples whose traditional way of life is no longer possible and who do not fit easily into modern ways. Should the Canadian indians be kept as picturesque museum specimens within their ancient culture, or should they join the modern society? Current policy cannot avoid straddling the two possibilities.

A similar trend is evident in urban settings. In all countries, even the poorest, we see a process of convergence that is one of the most conspicuous marks of our times. We see movement toward a way of life characterized by supermarkets, homes with television and refrigerators, automobiles, a diet that includes meat at least once and often twice per day, and ultimately very few children. Perhaps the absence of children enables citizens to afford the multiplicity of goods; perhaps it is the plentiful goods that distract them from having children. What can be said is that the energy consumption, even the consumption of primary food calories, of the middle class family with one or two children is greater than the consumption of the peasant family with five or more children, and this unsettles traditional energy balances.

In a different way the education that becomes widespread in the early stages of development has an unsettling effect, as we have seen. Once young people become literate they are dissatisfied with traditional ways of living. East Javanese villagers whose schooling has gone beyond the elementary level almost never return to their native village. They are drawn to the city, and there they demand jobs and the benefits of modern life.

It is the destabilizing effects of partial development that insert the time constraint. That is expressed in the question: can Brazil develop fast enough that its population will be controlled at something like present levels, and while its environment continues capable of supporting human activity and its society holds together?

Development, Foreign Aid, and the Debt Crisis

This chapter does not concern foreign aid or loans, but these inevitably enter any discussion of development and especially of the capacity of the United States to influence policies in the LDCs.

As the flow of funds reverses direction, so that instead of our subsidizing the LDCs it is they who subsidize us, it is they who will influence our policies, not we theirs. Even if its foreign trade balance with other MDCs were healthier than it is, the United States would no longer be in a position to apply the brute force of money to influence countries to adopt sound policies.

Borrowing money had a relation to population, especially to the increasing number of young people. We have to see the use of foreign funds for development, and the repayment of loans, in relation to population growth and urbanization. In particular, the demand of large educated urban populations for employment has created an intensive search for new money and difficulty in repaying old debts. Even when net borrowing was at its height, the job seekers outnumbered the jobs that could be created at their level of education. Foreign private investment is of course the ideal, but for countries with large populations there has not been enough of it.

If the debts that have been incurred had all been spent optimally for development on the most useful elements of infrastructure, and other projects carried out with maximum efficiency, the money to service them could be readily available. In a well-run corporation the servicing of bonds and repayment of bank loans are provided for routinely out of the returns from the investment that they financed. There is no debt crisis when loans come due. But when loan proceeds are applied less than optimally, or eaten away by corruption, some money simply moving from a United States Treasury account to numbered Swiss bank accounts (some forty of them for the billions diverted by the Marcos family, according to current press reports), funds for service of the debt will not be available.

There are indeed many cases in which the money was handled honestly but incautiously invested in projects whose expected rate of return was lower than the rate of interest contracted for. The hope was that with development, Brazil could pay off such loans out of its increasing general financial resources, but now we know that development just does not proceed fast enough for that.

The debt crisis of the LDCs can be explained like that of a corner grocery store: money was borrowed for purposes, however worthy, whose financial return was not adequate for repayment of the loan with interest. Of course every specific project does not have to yield a return in international currency greater than the servicing requirements, but groups of projects, or else the general activities of the society, must be such as to yield the necessary amount of international funds. One is astonished in retrospect that lenders did not insist on a realistic plan of amortization that would show how the servicing would be accomplished. To the economic complexities of such a calculation must be added political problems.

Even disregarding the arithmetic of amortization, we cannot take it for granted that as long as the economy grows fast enough it will pay off its financial charges, for these are located amid a host of other claims. It is in this wider framework that population fits, in the form especially of the number of educated young people and their expectations of work and consumption.

It was a series of obligations and commitments that required the borrowing to begin with amid which repayment of financial obligations takes its place. These include the growth of population, especially of the youngest ages, that requires more schools, universities, and ultimately jobs. Making jobs requires capital, and much of the borrowing during the 1970s was for the declared purpose of making jobs. And as the population continues to grow and there are fresh waves of young people, the claims of the new youth for jobs join the competition with the claims of foreign lenders for repayment.

It was natural (but from our point of view naive) on the part of sophisticated bankers to have thought that foreign financial obligations would take precedence over political ones affecting the ability of the authorities to stay in power. If there is friction and violence then more military and police will be needed; skimping on these in order to meet the financial obligation is never to be contemplated. The importance of replanting forests is of course recognized, but it also is subordinated to the political calculus within the sovereign entity of the LDC.

City populations exert such pressures that food prices are kept artificially low, and this advantage to those peasants who come to the city brings more and more of them. Of course in principle the authorities could simply say no: we will service our foreign debts before any concessions are made, any food prices controlled, any housing projects completed in the cities. What that does is bring people out into the streets, as we have seen again and again over the last decade or two. We keep coming back to the fact that governments are disinclined to make choices that will lead to their own displacement.

The national plans placed much emphasis on how a loan was to be spent and gave only passing attention to how it was to be repaid. Would more careful planning for repayment have avoided the crisis? The social and ecological conditions that would have had to be incorporated in such repayment plans go far beyond the conventional categories of finance. I for one have no suggestions for a methodology to calculate loan servicing in a realistic economic-political context.

Such considerations have been regarded less than sympathetically by the MDCs, who react with a certain foreign aid weariness, including reluctance to make further loans. Like many other debtors, the LDCs were overoptimistic in their projections of net return, and now they need money even more than before; yet their credit rating is low.

Another factor in the declining enthusiasm for foreign aid may be a sense that environmental constraints, together with population growth, set limits on development. Given present technology and the style of life to which the whole world now aspires, the greenhouse effect and the disposal of waste are such serious problems that only a limited amount of development in the present style remains possible. Already there are 500 million automotive vehicles, operated by about one-fifth of the world population, and the effects in acid rain and terrestrial warming are ominous. Full development on the present pattern, with 2.5 billion vehicles, is inconceivable.

If only so much development is possible in the world then the question who will have it is going to dominate international politics in the short term. How much of it will Northern Americans have, how much Europeans, how much will be left for Turks, how much for Brazilians, how much for Nigerians? Such a zero-sum formulation could be based on the greenhouse effect alone, but this is reinforced by other limits.

If the total is limited then it would take an improbable

amount of altruism to provide foreign aid to the LDCs on a scale that would be decisive. Others becoming richer would still expand our markets, but would also increase warming and waste, so reducing our possibilities. One wonders whether the currently diminished scale of nonmilitary foreign aid is due to some sense of this. In accord with the smaller hopes for development, an increasing fraction of the foreign aid from all the MDCs is called humanitarian, which is to say it is to cover current emergencies and extreme poverty, satisfying what are called basic needs, without much pretense that it will be more than a palliative for the long-term state of underdevelopment.

New Conditions for United States Foreign Policy

In a world in which population is growing fast, the foreign aid enthusiasm of a few years back has waned, and disposable capital funds are short, so that the United States cannot count on buying the adherence of foreign countries to policies adapted to the general international welfare. What ought we to be doing? The need for leadership in the world is no less than it was just after World War II; in fact the need has increased with the internationalization of ecological constraints. The whole planet, the patrimony of humankind, is now threatened, not just the resources lying in individual countries. National sovereignty cannot cope with the greenhouse effect and consequent climate change, acid rain, pollution of the oceans and their overfishing, or nuclear contamination. The United States is the only power that can conceivably take the lead in protection of the ecosphere. With other rich countries waiting for us to act, and poor countries suspicious of our motives, what can we do? I have suggestions:

• Since World War II we have been the premier center of science, both theoretical and applied, in the world, and we ought to build on that and further extend our efforts and accomplishments. Technical advance could widen vastly the window for development. In due course a developed or middle class standard of living for 5 billion or more people will become technically possible: there will be fusion or other nonpolluting sources of power, stored as hydrogen, superconducting transmission of electricity, plants that can use sea water and so be cultivated in coastal deserts. No other country has equal educational and technical resources and is as capable as we of bringing closer these achievements, which will let more millions, indeed billions, of people enter the developed condition. Now neglected birth control is one of the techniques where American science can make a difference to the world.

- We ought somehow to counter the waning interest in science and attract more of our young people into engineering and scientific careers. In addition we should open the doors freely to those technicians of all kinds who want to leave their countries because they feel that they will be more effectively used in the United States.

- We will have more of the right kind of political influence the less political the motivation of our day-to-day activities. We cannot look statesmanlike when we are locked in a wrestling match with tiny Cuba and Nicaragua. Think of what we lost in world influence by the Vietnam war. We have to grant that there are intelligent foreigners—Swedes, French, Indians, Japanese—who act on different ideologies from ours. The physical problems of the planet cannot wait while we convert everyone to our general philosophy.

- We must recognize that countries are changing fast. The socialist 40 or so percent of the world is learning that their way will not work. From the beginning we kept telling them their system was morally evil, but we were as slow as they to recognize that it was unworkable and hence would change by itself. If we had seen this we would not have wasted so much in resources to fight it. We seem never to have had enough confidence in our market system to realize that it was bound to prevail. European observers have pointed out again and again how handicapped we Americans are in every policy field by the moralizing bent of our culture.

- Once we begin to act in a way that convinces others that we aim at the interests of the planet rather than promoting an ideology, we will be able to engage in the new kind of politics that the situation demands. We must act so that the Brazilians will understand that when we discuss their rainforest, we are not talking on behalf of the United States alone but for all of humanity. We are only slowly learning to separate the newly required world environmental politics from our own short-term economic interests as well as from our own ideology. The interests of the planet will often require individual countries, including ourselves, to act against their own interests on particular issues.

- Even though acting against our own immediate interests merely to set an example will sometimes be required, too much has been made of the conflict between ecological and economic objectives. Farm subsidies are wrong from both points of view, producing unsalable food as well as wasting the soil. We urge Europe to stop those farm subsidies; it would be better if we first eliminated ours, then spoke about theirs. We have done well in some fields: Europe is now following us in the use of catalytic converters and lead-free gasoline, an economic sacrifice, but an ultimately overall gain. On the other hand, we are doing badly by consuming as much gasoline as we do; a tax that would reduce its use is needed, and Europe is far ahead of us on that. Here as on many other fronts good economics is good ecology.

- The United States can take the lead in establishing a new rationale for foreign aid. With an armistice, if not permanent peace, in the cold war, with doubts on the benefit to us (in markets and sources of raw materials) of development of the LDCs, with the sense that more development along present lines means more pollution, and with the diversion of capital to Eastern Europe and the USSR, the old arguments for foreign aid will bring less and less of it to the LDCs. I know of only one rationale that can restore foreign aid, and that is also the only way to maintain the ecological patrimony of humankind.

Two conditions are to be satisfied: the polluter must pay, and the poor must not be asked to support the rich. Given the coal that China is burning, and the trees that Brazil is cutting, so that shifting to other fuels and replanting would be heavy costs, the two conditions look to be mutually contradicting. Yet they can both be fulfilled. Massive foreign aid would be transferred from the MDCs to the LDCs, and they would be subject to heavy fines for violating clean air, forestry management, and other standards. (Rights to pollute that could be bought and sold would reduce the overall cost.) The amount of transfer would have to be large enough (about 1 percent of gross national product [GNP] of the MDCs would do it) that no LDC could afford to stay out of the arrangement.

I have written extensively on this in other places, and the only point of bringing it in here is the opportunity it gives the United States to provide leadership.

• If the United States is to have the influence that is desirable, its science must be directed to needs rather than to spectacle. I recall that Indonesians were not thrilled when an American walked on the moon. They did not see it as a giant step for humankind; many thought it not merely unnecessary but downright offensive, almost as though we were ostentatiously appropriating a religious symbol that belongs to all.

Putting a man or woman on Mars will demonstrate even more the technological preeminence of the United States, and so be good domestic politics, but it will not help the hungry anywhere; the equivalent effort in such fields as genetic engineering could help them greatly. When we perform some very difficult feat for its own sake, we demonstrate that we are more than capable of devising technologies that the poor countries need, but that we prefer not to aim our effort in their direction. From the viewpoint of the world's poor, it is better to appear incompetent than to show competence and use it to some spectacular end that helps them not at all.

In 1950 the world contained 2.5 billion people, and there was little evidence of damage to the biosphere. Now with over

5 billion there is a great deal of evidence with another 2.5 billion and continuance of present trends of production and consumption, disaster faces us. The planet cannot over a long period support that many people; yet an even larger number is threatened.

In its best moments the United States gave the world leadership on population and many other matters. Renewing that leadership under today's different conditions is crucial for checking runaway population increase and substituting benign technologies for destructive ones.

3

Deforestation and Species Loss

Responding to the Crisis

KENTON R. MILLER
WALTER V. REID
CHARLES V. BARBER

I n the millennia since the world's forest mantle was first
breached to make way for systematic agriculture and
human settlement, it has changed markedly. While considera-

KENTON R. MILLER is director of the World Resources Institute's
Program in Forests and Biodiversity. Prior to joining WRI's staff in
1988, Dr. Miller served for five years as director general of the International Union for Conservation of Nature and Natural Resources
(IUCN). Before that, he was associate professor of natural resources
and director of the Center for Strategic Wildlife Management Studies, School of Natural Resources, University of Michigan.
WALTER V. REID is an associate with the WRI Program in Forests
and Biodiversity. Before joining WRI in June 1988, Dr. Reid was a
Gilbert White Fellow with Resources for the Future where he studied
the management of southern ocean fisheries and examined environmental issues related to sustainable development.
CHARLES V. BARBER is an associate in the Program in Forests and
Biological Diversity at the WRI. Formerly, he was an environmental
policy consultant in Indonesia for the World Bank, the United Nations Development Programme, the Food and Agriculture Organization, and other organizations. The authors would like to acknowledge
the substantial contributions of Peter Hazlewood to this chapter.

ble tracts of temperate forests in Europe, North Africa, North America, and the Orient long ago fell to the ax, until recently a vast reservoir of forested lands remained in most of the tropics. But today the erosion of forest ecosystems due to deforestation is rampant in tropical Asia, Africa, and America.

This rapid decline represents an unprecedented raid on the planet's biological wealth. Earth's tropical forests comprise a living treasurehouse—a trove of uncounted habitats and species as diverse and individual as snowflakes, linked in the complex webs of interaction that define local ecosystems. Researchers estimate that as many as 25 percent of all species inhabiting earth in the mid-1980s will have disappeared by 2015 if current deforestation trends hold. For this reason, tropical deforestation and species loss are indissolubly linked.

These forest communities and the diversity of life they harbor represent an irreplaceable asset to the biosphere and humankind. They are great engines of biological productivity, considerable sources of climatic stability, and home to at least 500 million people. They also contribute directly to human survival as sources of food, fiber, medicines, industrial products, and the genes needed to breed the improved crop varieties upon which the world's food security rests. Scientists believe that the wealth of the planet's forests has barely been tapped. Indeed, only a tiny fraction of the potentially useful species that reside in tropical rainforests has even been identified.

As the twenty-first century nears, we are "eating our seed corn," squandering in a heedless evolutionary moment the forest's genetic capital, evolved over billions of years. The price for doing so is biological impoverishment in the years ahead and a consequent ecological decline that will threaten the health, commerce, and quality of life enjoyed by developed and developing nations alike.

Tropical forest loss will also have serious impacts on global, regional, and local climate. The loss of forest cover reduces transpiration of water vapor into the atmosphere, changes the albedo (reflectivity) of the earth's surface, removes an important "sink" for ozone, and, through burning, contributes to the greenhouse effect through the release of carbon dioxide and other greenhouse gases into the atmosphere. At the same time, the essential services provided by intact forest ecosystems—such as watershed protection and regulation, the storage of carbon in plant tissues, or the absorption and breakdown of pollutants—are being degraded or destroyed.

In spite of these dangerous trends, it is not too late to address global forest decline. But the steps needed to prevent the loss of forests and the diversity they harbor will not be easy ones. They must address the combination of population pressures, migration of the rural poor, misguided government policies, and false economic premises that are the root causes of modern deforestation. Complemented by a well-managed system of critical forest preserves, strategies that combat these factors could allow realistic and sustainable development without plundering the forest resource and its genetic wealth.

Dimensions of the Problem

The Scope of Forest Loss

Since the dawn of agriculture about 10,000 years ago, when humans first began forest clearing in earnest, the world's forests have declined in area by about a fifth, from 50 to 40 million square kilometers (5 to 4 billion hectares). Until recently, temperate forests had suffered much of this loss, losing about a third of their area, and tropical evergreen rainforests—largely inaccessible—had suffered least, declining only about 4 to 6 percent. Today, forests and woods still cover two-fifths of the earth's land surface and account for about 60 percent of the net productivity of all terrestrial ecosystems (including agriculture) through biomass production—plant growth.

But the remaining forests are under increasing stress worldwide, of which the worst is outright deforestation, which is proceeding fastest in the tropics, where just over half the remaining forests are located. Together with the soil erosion, fuelwood loss, decline in agricultural productivity, and species extinction it causes, tropical deforestation can rightfully be considered the developing world's single worst environmental problem.

The extent of tropical deforestation and the area of remaining forests have not been accurately measured. The best available evidence indicates that these forests have lost from a quarter to a half of their former area. Most of this decline has taken place within the last forty years. Between 1950 and 1983, for example, forest and woodland areas dropped 38 percent in Central America and 24 percent in Africa. The rate of decline seems to be increasing.

The only worldwide estimates of the deforestation rate—calculated by the United Nations Food and Agriculture Organization (FAO) in 1980—showed an annual loss of some 11.3 million hectares worldwide. These numbers reflect only those areas completely cleared for other uses; they do not include the additional 10 million hectares grossly disrupted annually through logging or other activities that destroy the forest integrity and its habitat potential, even if what remains is nominally still called forest.

More recent studies using satellite data indicate that the widely cited FAO estimate is seriously understated. Brazil provides the most dramatic example. It has the largest remaining tracts of tropical forest and by far the greatest annual deforestation rate. Studies conducted by the National Space Research Institute of Brazil conclude that 8 million hectares of virgin rainforest—more than five times the official calculation—were burned and cleared in the Amazon region in 1987 alone.

These data are controversial, since they rely on satellite photos of the smoke that rises when the forest is cleared through burning. In addition, 1987 may have been an anomalously high year for deforestation because it was the last year tax credits were offered to Brazilian landholders who cleared their Amazon holdings. Follow-up studies showed a decline in the rate of clearing in 1988 and 1989, perhaps brought on by wetter weather and/or changes in government policy. Nonetheless, at least 7 percent of Amazon forests had been cleared by 1988.

Other recent studies also reveal sharply higher annual rates of deforestation in India (1.5 million hectares), Indonesia (900,000 hectares), Mayanmar (Burma) (667,000 hectares), the Philippines (143,000 hectares), Costa Rica (124,000 hectares), and Cameroon (100,000 hectares). Less recent statistics show high yearly losses in such nations as Colombia, Mexico, Ecuador, Peru, Malaysia, Thailand, Nigeria, Ivory Coast, and some thirty other countries in tropical Asia, Africa, and Latin America. Extrapolating from these data, two 1990 estimates of worldwide tropical forest loss put the total in the range of 20–25 million hectares annually—approximately double the FAO figure.

Since the data on deforestation rates and the amount of remaining forest area are sketchy at best, it is hard to make reliable predictions of how fast tropical forests will disappear. Nonetheless, it is evident that if present trends continue, significant—probably catastrophic—declines in tropical forest extent and quality will take place within thirty years, especially in accessible lowland forests.

In fact, the World Commission on Environment and Development concluded in 1987 that, given the current deforestation rate and the expected growth in world population and economic activity, little virgin rainforest would survive beyond the turn of the century outside of forest preserves, except in portions of the Zaire Basin, northeast Brazilian Amazonia, western Amazonia, the Guianan tract of forest in northern South America, and New Guinea. Even these tracts are not expected to last more than a few decades longer because their commodity value is soaring and pressures to cut or settle them are rising.

Such predictions do not ignore reforestation and natural regrowth. However, much tropical forestland, once converted to other uses, does not easily revert to healthy forest, even if such regrowth is allowed. Full forest regeneration requires almost one hundred years, even when pastures are only lightly used. If such pastures are more heavily used, or repeatedly burned over to stimulate grass growth, recovery time is much longer. As a practical matter, forest soils usually are seriously degraded after conversion. Moreover, studies have shown that the changes in regional climate following large-scale deforestation could make reestablishing the forest on any time scale even more difficult.

The Scope of Species Loss

Although closed tropical forests cover only 7 percent of the earth's land surface, they contain at least half—and possibly up to 90 percent—of the world's species. It is impossible to estimate the exact proportion of species that reside there, since so little is known about tropical organisms and ecosystems. Perhaps only 10 percent of all tropical species have been described to date. Current estimates place about half of all vascular plant and vertebrate species in tropical forests, and among invertebrates, the percentage may be considerably higher. Species diversity in temperate forests differs strikingly from that in tropical forests. Typically, forty to one hundred species of trees occur on a single hectare of tropical rainforest, compared to only ten to thirty on a hectare of forest in the eastern United States. Some 700 species of trees can be found in ten hectares in Borneo, the same as in all of North America. One tree in Peru may contain as many species of ants as occur in all of the British Isles.

With such exceptional species richness, tropical ecosystems (and a few others, such as coral reefs) lie at the heart of the world's biological diversity—or biodiversity, the blanket term for the variety of the world's organisms, including their genetic make-up and the communities and interrelationships they develop. Forest losses on the order of those occurring in the tropics—which radically modify or eliminate whole ecosystems—thus directly threaten the biodiversity that undergirds the well-being of the living earth.

Species loss through extinction is certainly not a new phenomenon in nature. The 10 million or so species that populate the earth today are the survivors of the several billion that evolution has produced since life began. Over the history of the planet, there have been several mass extinctions—relatively short periods when significant fractions of the world's species died out. The last such mass extinction was some 65 million years ago. Since then, global biodiversity has rebounded and is now close to its all-time high.

Humanity's impact on species extinction rates goes back thousands of years, but over the last century—especially over the last several decades—the human factor has increased dramatically. For instance, among all birds and mammals, we would expect an extinction only once every 100 to 1,000 years in the absence of humans. However, the actual extinction rate for birds and mammals between 1850 and 1950 was one per year—as much as 1,000 times greater than the background rate.

Predicting future extinction rates in response to the massive habitat disruption that accompanies deforestation is difficult at best. However, a useful rule of thumb is that if a habitat is reduced by 90 percent in area, roughly half of its species will be lost.

Between 1990 and 2020, tropical deforestation may extinguish 5 to 15 percent of the world's species. This percentage translates into an annual loss of 15,000 to 50,000 species— about 50 to 150 per day. According to another less conservative estimate, 5 to 10 percent of world species may be lost *per decade* over the next quarter century. In theory, if deforestation were to continue until all forests in the Amazon Basin were eliminated except those now legally protected from harvest, 66 percent of plant species and 69 percent of bird species in these forests would disappear.

Judging the effects of such massive losses on the functioning of the remaining species is difficult because of the complex dynamics among plant and animal species in even the simplest of ecosystems. In a given ecosystem, the extinction of certain key species may cause a cascade effect upon the populations of many other species. For example, during the dry season in Manu National Park in Peru, only 12 out of 2,000 plant species support as much as 80 percent of the park's mammals and a major fraction of the park's birds. Clearly, the loss of one or more of these key species would significantly affect a host of dependent species.

Habitat disruption through deforestation is not the only factor endangering biodiversity today. Overharvesting, ubiquitous chemical pollution, competition from introduced species, and climatic change also take a toll. Nor is outright extinction the only concern. Many species not in imminent danger of demise are nonetheless suffering from reduced populations and declining genetic variability that make them more vulnerable to disease, inbreeding, hunting, and other environmental stresses that can threaten their survival.

The Mechanisms of Tropical Deforestation

Tropical deforestation has four direct causes: slash-and-burn cultivation by a growing army of landless migrant poor; conversion of forests to cattle pastureland; wasteful and unsustainable commercial logging; and overharvesting of subsistence fuelwood and fodder. Often these factors work in concert to strip and degrade forest lands so that regrowth occurs slowly, if at all, even while the agricultural potential of the cleared land drops rapidly.

By far the most important source of forest loss is conversion for subsistence agriculture. Traditional "slash-and-burn" agriculture has been practiced for millennia by indigenous cultures in an environmentally sound fashion. Most tropical forest soils are not suited to continuous cultivation because of low fertility and other physical limitations, so forest dwellers have developed various systems of shifting cultivation.

In these traditional systems, most of the woody vegetation is cleared from a patch of land—usually by burning—and crops are planted for several years. Over time, declining soil organic matter, reduced nutrient levels, and competition from re-sprouting vegetation and weeds cause the farmer to move elsewhere, abandoning the plot to lie fallow. If the fallow time is long enough and the cultivated plot not overly degraded, the forest restores itself and replenishes soil productivity.

Unfortunately, this sustainable cycle has broken down in many forest areas because of population growth and a rapid influx of landless peasants. These displaced or "shifted" cultivators now far outnumber indigenous forest farmers in most

areas, and they bring with them dietary preferences and farming practices often ill-suited to the forest. Lacking an understanding of the traditional sustainable cycle and driven by
short-term needs, these forest settlers almost inevitably pur-
sue continuous cropping until soil fertility is lost and the land
fully degraded, before moving on to the next plot.

The Brazilian state of Rondonia in southern Amazonia exemplifies the impact of displaced cultivators. In 1975, when
the Brazilian government began encouraging the urban poor
to settle in Rondonia, the area's population stood at 110,000
and little forest was cleared. By 1986 the population had
reached more than 1 million and the cleared area had expanded to 2.8 million hectares, with smallholder clearings and
conversion to cattle ranches accounting for most of the loss.

Displaced rural farmers and urban poor are by no means
confined to Brazil. Slash-and-burn agriculture by displaced
peasants is also the primary agent of forest loss in the Philippines, Indonesia, Thailand, India, Madagascar, Tanzania,
Kenya, Nigeria, Ivory Coast, Colombia, Peru, Ecuador, and
Bolivia. The link between land degradation, burgeoning population growth, and rural poverty is incontrovertible, and can
only worsen unless current trends are reversed.

The conversion of forest to pastureland for cattle ranching
is a second major contributor to tropical deforestation, but
one that is confined almost entirely to Latin America. There,
more than 20 million hectares of rainforest have been converted to cattle pastures over the past twenty years. At least
half of this conversion has taken place in the Brazilian Amazon, about one-fourth in Mexico, and the rest in Colombia
(which contains about one-fourth of the Amazon Basin), Peru,
Venezuela, and Central America.

The cattle surge in the Brazilian Amazon began in the late
1960s, fueled by a growing network of paved roads, government tax incentives and subsidized credit, and land specula-
tion. By 1980 almost 9 million head of cattle grazed
Amazonian pastures, accounting for 72 percent of all forest
conversion in the region to that point. Although Brazil's government no longer subsidizes it, the conversion of forest to

pasture continues as a means of securing and retaining land title through "improvement" of the forest land.

In part, this emphasis on cattle raising stemmed from increased demand for cheap beef in North America—the infamous "hamburger connection." Ironically, while beef production in Central America more than tripled between 1955 and 1980, beef consumption among Central Americans actually fell during this period.

To form a pasture, forest cover is cut and burned, and African forage grasses are often planted. These usually flourish for a few years until soil nutrients wane and shrubs take over. Reburning the pasture revitalizes it for a time, but the response to successive fires diminishes until the soil is completely exhausted. In this manner, much of the converted pastureland has become degraded over the years.

Commercial logging operations are a third potent factor in forest loss. Logging is essentially a "mining" operation throughout the tropics: harvested timber is not replaced either by natural regeneration or forest plantations. A 1988 survey found that the amount of land under sustained yield management was negligible—only about 4.4 million hectares out of a total of 828 million hectares of exploitable forest.

Most tropical logging practices severely disrupt the forest's ecological integrity. Typically, commercially valuable species make up a small percentage of the stand. Only 10 to 20 percent of the trees are cut, but another 30 to 50 percent are destroyed or fatally injured, and the soil is disturbed enough to impede regeneration, even in the long run.

Some 4.4 million hectares of closed forest were logged annually between 1981 and 1985, mostly in Southeast Asia and West Africa. By 1985 about half of the productive closed forests in tropical Asia had been logged, and about one-fourth of tropical Africa's timber was gone. Countries such as the Philippines, once a leading exporter, have nearly exhausted their lowland forests. Indonesia, Malaysia, and the Philippines have all totally or partially banned log exports to reduce overharvesting and develop domestic processing facilities in order to capture more of the value of their timber.

The Amazonian region and Central Africa have been exploited significantly less, largely because of difficult access. However, logging is bound to accelerate in these regions as better roads and harvesting techniques become available and more accessible regions are cut over. Indeed, Latin America, where only 10 percent of exploitable forests have been logged, is expected to become the world's major source of tropical hardwoods within the next decade.

The impact of logging is greatly magnified by the subsequent conversion of forestland to agriculture. Logging roads open forest areas to subsequent encroachment. According to one 1982 report, nearly 70 percent of annual clearance of closed forests is in logged-over areas.

Overcutting of fuelwood, construction wood, and fodder is the fourth major source of deforestation. In open forests near population centers, these activities can destroy tree cover, especially if combined with overgrazing and repeated burning. About 80 percent of all wood harvested in developing countries is used for fuelwood and charcoal, and wood and other biomass fuels figure centrally in many countries' energy economies. Problems of woodfuel scarcity are most severe in densely populated portions of Africa and Asia, and severe land degradation is the common result.

The Root Causes of Deforestation
and Species Loss

Population Pressures and
Flawed Government Policies

A complex array of social, economic, and political forces is behind the present crisis of forest and species loss. These powerful forces are often deeply rooted in past development patterns and frequently reflect the imbalances that may exist within developing countries: rapid population growth that strikes hardest at those with fewest resources; concentration of land in the hands of a few, leaving millions landless; slow growth of job opportunities in both city and countryside that induces migration; and colonial patterns of resource exploitation that emphasize maximum short-term gain.

The rapid population increases typical of developing countries place ever greater demands on their resource bases and increase pressure to liquidate forest capital to finance immediate development needs. Since 1960 Brazil's population has climbed from 73 million to 147 million today; India's population from 442 million to 813 million, and Indonesia's from 96 million to 178 million, to cite just a few examples. Such population growth is already a prominent factor not only in the increase in landless forest settlers, but also in many government development policies that result in deforestation.

Flawed government management policies constitute a second major force in forest demise. Such policies include asserting government control over forest areas once governed—and protected—by local communities; establishing land tenure rules that encourage forest settlement, and clearing without providing the security that might encourage sustainable land use; building roads or making other improvements in forest areas aimed at extending government control into unsecured regions; and granting economic incentives that encourage forest exploitation.

Until relatively recently, most forestlands in developing countries were the communal property of local tribes, and farming and pastoral communities. These groups developed a diverse array of hunting and gathering, farming, and grazing practices based on traditional custom that effectively regulated forest access and use. However, in the past forty years, more than 80 percent of the world's tropical forests have been brought under government ownership, overruling traditional rights of forest control. Deprived of legal authority, tribal heads and community leaders no longer have a strong incentive to conserve the forest resource by, say, limiting shifting agriculture or timber operations. As customary conservation values erode, forests and wildlife have thus been put at greater risk.

For their part, governments have found themselves unable

to defend the rights they have asserted: the forest areas are too vast, most national forest agencies are underfunded and understaffed, and encroachment pressures are too strong. Yet having once asserted control, governments are reluctant to relinquish ownership and management rights to other parties. One exception is timber concessionaires, who are viewed as contractors able to generate much needed state revenue. As a result, no party with a vested interest in the long-term forest resource remains to regulate forest use.

The issue of land ownership—or tenure—is especially important in determining whether forestland use will be sustainable over the longer term. Under the rules of tenure in many countries, title to public domain lands is granted to those who "improve" it through conversion to another use. This arrangement has triggered deforestation in such regions as the Amazon Basin, the Philippines, and Malaysia, among others.

A corollary to this rule is that those who do not "improve" the land, such as many indigenous peoples who traditionally exercised communal ownership, are generally not granted direct title, though such ownership might be more conducive to sound forest management. Just as important, landless immigrants whose tenure is insecure are less likely than landowners to adopt sustainable practices, preferring instead to farm intensively for immediate gains in case they are forced to move on.

Governments often use the opening and development of forest areas to further their internal security and national defense goals. Such concerns have loomed large in the forest development policies of Brazil, Burma, Indonesia, Peru, Thailand, and Venezuela. Political insurgencies are often based in inaccessible forest areas. And since forest-dwelling peoples number among those least integrated into the social and political mainstream, governments seek to bring them into the fold by exerting political controls and extending government services to them.

External defense priorities also frequently motivate governments to open and secure the forest periphery. National borders in many tropical countries are ill-defined and frequently disputed because they lie in inaccessible forest areas. Building roads, railways, and other infrastructure elements near border areas tends to delineate and secure these areas.

In Brazil, Bolivia, Indonesia, and other countries, security concerns have also helped stimulate agricultural resettlement schemes in forest areas. While these projects are obviously intended to serve economic development goals as well, security concerns often shape their implementation.

Finally, many governments are directly or indirectly subsidizing forest exploitation through investment incentives, tax and revenue systems, and other policies that invite mismanagement. Generally, tropical timber harvesters work under regulatory regimes that provide incentives for the rapid exploitation of a few commercially valuable species and discourage investments in sustainable forestry.

Economic Factors

At the root of many flawed government policies are faulty economic analyses and unsupported economic assumptions about the use of forest resources. In essence, neither the true value of the forest—both its biological resources and the environmental services it renders—nor the true cost of exploiting it is accurately calculated. This pervasive misvaluation makes it hard to abandon abusive forest practices since their real costs remain hidden and the benefits of sustainable practices undervalued.

Typically, the value assigned to forests is limited to the "stumpage value" of their timber or the agricultural potential of the cleared lands. Even if their usefulness as watershed, tourist attractions, pollution removers, or repositories of biodiversity is recognized, it is difficult to assign a monetary value to these environmental services.

Biological diversity, for example, is a "public good" whose benefits are largely intangible but nonetheless essential to the enjoyment of various other products, including most of the world's major food crops and many pharmaceutical products. The costs of depleting biodiversity are equally diffuse and difficult to calculate, but very real. On the other hand, the immediate benefits of logging and other forms of forest exploitation are easily measurable and naturally weigh more heavily in land use decisions.

Often ignored in the forest planning of developing nations is the capacity of the intact forest to supply a perpetual stream of valuable non-wood products that can be harvested without cutting down the trees. Frequently, these wild foods and materials contribute greatly to rural livelihoods. Worldwide, there are more than 500 million forest dwellers (10 percent of global population), many of whom depend on nuts, berries, game, fish, honey, and other forest products to help them survive. The value of these products is largely ignored because they rarely reach the marketplace and mostly benefit weak minorities in the hinterlands.

However, resins, essential oils, medicinals, rattan, flowers, and other products do flow into commercial channels, producing considerable income for those who collect and trade them. Although they are usually considered "minor" products, their aggregate value can be quite large. For instance, by the early 1980s Indonesia exported $125 million worth of such products annually. These products constitute a small fraction of the *potential* sustainable yield of tropical forests. Indeed, in some cases, the value of non-timber forest products may greatly exceed the value of a one-time timber harvest. One study in Peru found that the net revenue obtained from harvesting fruit and latex from the forest was thirteen times greater than the revenue that could be obtained by using the forest for timber production.

Even as many forest resources are undervalued, all too often the anticipated benefits of forest exploitation—especially the expected agricultural yields of converted forestland—are overvalued. The soils underlying 95 percent of the remaining tropical forests are infertile and easily degraded through erosion, laterization, or other processes once the vegetative cover is stripped. Unlike temperate forests, where organic matter can build up in the soil, copious rains and high temperatures quickly leach nutrients from tropical soils. In the intact tropical

forest, most of the nutrients are held in the plant tissues themselves and efficiently recycled before they can be lost. Most
agricultural systems cannot duplicate the rainforest's complex
recycling ability, so the few nutrients in the soil are lost to
leaching and erosion within a few years, and agricultural productivity drops rapidly.

The economic benefits of timber harvests are also widely
overstated because the costs of logging—to the environment
and to forest dwellers—are rarely included in economic
evaluations. In addition, most of the profits from timber harvests have gone to private logging companies—many of them
foreign—and the politicians and military officers who are often
their silent partners. Government treasuries realize a surprisingly small net gain from depleting their forest base, often less
than the administrative and infrastructure costs of the timber
harvest (a situation paralleled in many U.S. national forests,
where "below-cost" timber sales are common and quite controversial). Even the employment benefits of logging enterprises have usually failed to live up to expectations, and local
communities are often left with little to show for the destruction of the nearby forest.

Finally, since the costs of unsustainable forest practices such
as watershed degradation or species loss are not explicitly recognized, those who benefit from such practices are seldom the
ones to pay these costs. Instead, they are passed on to inno-
cent parties or to the society as a whole—often to future generations. For example, the logging company does not bear the
cost of the siltation it causes; that is borne by downstream
farmers or communities whose use of the waterway is compro-
mised. Likewise, the cattle rancher does not have to concern
himself with the species he wipes out to clear his pasture; that
cost is borne by the nation or the world at large. If the costs of
these inadvertent losses fell to the parties that caused them, a
much different forest economy would emerge as the value of
sustainable practices took on tangible dimensions.

International Factors

Among international economic factors that play a major role in forest and species declines, the crushing debt load carried by many developing countries is the most important. Half of the Third World external debt and over two-thirds of global deforestation occur in the same fourteen developing countries. These nations owe some $800 billion to public and private banks, and much of their working capital goes to service this debt. This burden operates as a powerful inducement to liquidate forest capital since it is one of the only resources readily convertible to much needed cash. The need for foreign exchange also stimulates the planting of cash crops for export, often grown on converted forestland.

Most countries cannot hope to halt and reverse deforestation and other environmental problems as long as a significant portion of their financial resources is siphoned off to repay foreign debt. Forestry and other low-priority sectors are often hardest hit by cutbacks in staff and expenditures imposed by economic austerity programs, and these programs, combined with economic stagnation, also intensify pressures on forests through their impacts on the poor. The economic adjustment process almost invariably hits the poor hardest as unemployment increases and incomes decline. This forces people back into subsistence agriculture and the conditions of poverty that lead to migration and forest degradation.

A second important international factor is the high demand in industrialized nations for tropical timber and other commodities grown at the expense of forests. Roughly half of all tropical hardwood timber produced is exported to the developed world, with a net worth of some $7 billion annually. Japan, in particular, has been a major tropical timber importer, accounting for nearly one-third of the world trade. Exports of pasture-fed beef to North America and plantation-grown cassava (commonly used as a cheap and nutritious animal feed) to Europe are also important influences in tropical forest conversion.

The Implications of Forest
and Species Decline

National Implications

Forests and their biological wealth are among the most valu-able productive assets that developing countries possess. They contribute to many sectors of the national economy and pro-vide vital sources of food, fuel, fodder, medicines, building materials, and many other necessities for hundreds of millions of people in developing nations. They help make farming and pastoral systems stable and provide a major source of income to those who gather and process forest products.

Extensive deforestation and species loss thus represent a serious threat to the economies of many nations. In essence, the net income derived from exploiting forest resources dis-guises the actual loss of real wealth. Even as gross national product (GNP) increases, total assets of the economy are de-clining. The estimated economic costs of unsustainable forest depletion range from 4 to 6 percent of the GNP in major tropi-cal hardwood-exporting countries—clearly, enough to offset any economic growth that exploitation might allow.

Growth built on such resource depletion is almost certain to be unsustainable. While international trade in hardwoods is expected to double by the year 2000 as the timber boom reaches its peak, an even more precipitous decline is antici-pated thereafter. By 2020 exports will likely be only 70 percent of their 1980 level and declining.

Once depleted, biological wealth (especially biodiversity) is all but impossible to recapture. Its loss will leave developing countries asset poor precisely when their resource needs are rapidly accelerating. This progressive impoverishment has im-plications in every sector of government—from national secu-rity to energy policy and environmental protection.

The potential for societal upheaval is also profound. Indige-nous peoples will suffer greatly as traditional sources of wild food, fodder, and building materials dwindle and the mainstays of social and spiritual life unravel. Forest immigrants will also be squeezed as soil fertility on converted ground is lost and forest areas available for new settlement shrink.

Forest dwellers will be the first to bear the brunt of the degradation of environmental services. Local erosion, flooding, siltation, susceptibility to fire, and even desertification in some places will render forest areas less hospitable and less able to support increasing populations. But these impacts will not be locally confined. The creation of a class of environmental refugees is already well advanced in some Asian and African nations, and will increase pressures on remaining undisturbed forests and reserves, international borders notwithstanding.

The prospects for energy security in developing countries will also dim as forest areas disappear, because wood is such a large component of these nations' budgets. In Africa, for example, 76 percent of the energy consumed for all purposes is supplied by wood. Scarcity of woodfuel is already a problem of major dimensions and a potent force in forest decline. According to the FAO, 1.5 billion of the 2 billion people who rely on wood for fuel are cutting wood faster than it is growing back, a figure that is projected to double in less than a decade.

The implications for national security are also sobering. Deforestation directly erodes a nation's productive capacity as surely as the occupation of a foreign power does. Impoverished governments will be less able to provide even basic services to the growing ranks of landless rural and urban poor, with increasing discontent the inevitable result.

Many countries use forests as "safety valves" to cope with demographic and economic pressures. Promoting migration to forest areas relieves overcrowding and landlessness in prime agricultural regions, and is considerably easier than creating jobs, ameliorating rural poverty, or pushing for land reform. As deforestation proceeds, forest areas will be less able to serve this function, thus perhaps exacerbating internal frictions and inciting international ones as well.

All these facets of deforestation and species loss will probably take place on a regional basis too. Although the severity of their effects will vary from country to country, they will likely exact a cumulative, regional toll far beyond that felt by individual nations. Environmental degradation may proceed synergistically as ecosystem services erode over ever wider areas and spillover effects begin to accumulate.

On a hopeful note, the prospect of a regional threat also brings the possibility of regional response, which may be far more effective than unilateral efforts in meeting the common challenge of deforestation. The development of common approaches and policies that reach beyond country borders could help stretch limited conservation budgets and could lend credibility and momentum to national programs.

Global Implications

Tropical forests provide goods and services whose loss will have global repercussions. As one example, these forests contain genetic material that plant breeders use to confer resistance to disease and pests on some of the world's most important food crops, such as rice and cassava, as well as on such other important commodity crops as coffee, cocoa, bananas, and pineapples. In addition, many natural insecticides (such as pyrethrins and rotenoids) derive from tropical plants, and insect predators and parasites found in tropical forests control at least 250 kinds of agricultural pests. The wholesale loss of species due to deforestation thus puts global food security at risk, as well as the international commerce based on the trade of agricultural commodities.

Tropical plants also represent a veritable pharmacopeia. Indians dwelling in the Amazon Basin make use of some 1,300 medicinal plants, including antibiotics, narcotics, abortifacients, contraceptives, antidiarrheal agents, fungicides, anesthetics, muscle relaxants, and many others—most of which have not yet been investigated by researchers. As it is, one-fourth of all prescription drugs sold in the United States originate in wild plants and animals, and 70 percent of the more than 3,000 plant species known to produce anticancer agents are found in tropical plants. Obviously, current uses of tropical species represent only a small fraction of their potential uses.

The loss will not be confined to useful products. Such environmental services as primary production of food, fuel, and fiber; decomposition; nutrient and water cycling; soil generation; erosion control; pest control; and climate regulation have a global reach—some directly, like climate regulation, and others indirectly through their contribution to the smooth functioning of the biosphere.

In this regard, perhaps the most serious global threat that deforestation poses is its contribution to the greenhouse effect and global warming. Deforestation is second only to fossil fuel combustion as a human source of atmospheric carbon dioxide, currently the most important heat-trapping, or greenhouse, gas. (It is also a substantial contributor to methane and tropospheric ozone concentrations: two other important greenhouse gases.) According to the most recent estimates of deforestation, forest clearing accounts for the release of some 2.8 million metric tons of carbon dioxide per year—about a third of the total annual carbon dioxide emissions caused by humans—and almost all of this load originates in the tropics.

In 1987 eleven countries were responsible for 82 percent of this net carbon release: Brazil, Indonesia, Colombia, Ivory Coast, Thailand, Laos, Nigeria, Viet Nam, Philippines, Burma, and India. During that year, when land clearing by fire peaked in the Amazon Basin, more than 1.2 million metric tons of carbon are believed to have been released. By comparison, the United States, by far the world's largest greenhouse emitter, released 1.2 million metric tons of carbon in 1987 through fossil fuel combustion and cement plant emissions.

Although uncertainties abound related to the timing, intensity, and distribution of the effects of global warming, its disruptive potential is generally accepted. Climate change could alter the constitution and functioning of ecosystems worldwide, with consequences for agriculture, marine and forest productivity, and the survival of native flora and fauna. In turn, these changes pose fundamental threats to the economic and environmental security of all nations, north and south.

In light of these many impacts, a good deal of international attention has been focused on deforestation and species loss in the last decade. Vigorously stated international concern evoked a cool response at first from many governments in the tropics, which expressed irritation that northern politicians and nongovernmental organizations should tell them to preserve forests instead of developing as temperate countries have. But international concern has generally echoed and strengthened national concerns with forest and development policies that were being voiced both within and outside of governments, and many developing nations now embrace the concept of minimizing damage to forests—even if strong programs to address the problem are not yet in place—so their economies can grow more sustainably.

The debate over the fate of tropical forests has become a topic of fruitful discussion and the subject of possible global cooperation in the future, including the funding of critical conservation programs through international development aid, and the establishment of demonstration projects based on sustainable agricultural and forestry methods. Likewise, the development of strategies to combat the greenhouse effect has already become an international priority, with some developing nations as active participants.

Addressing the Loss: Policies for Change

Since 1980 some encouraging progress has been made in informing world opinion about the dangers of forest and species decline, and convincing tropical nations to reexamine their forest resources. A global poll commissioned by the United Nations Environment Programme (UNEP) in 1988 to gauge environmental attitudes found considerable concern over deforestation in the developing countries. In Latin America and the Caribbean, 78 percent of those polled expressed concern; in Asia, 73 percent; and in Africa, 77 percent.

Many national governments and international aid agencies have publicly recognized the threat of deforestation. The Tropical Forestry Action Plan (TFAP) is one manifestation of this recognition. The plan was designed in 1985 by the FAO, The United Nations Development Programme, the World

Bank, and the World Resources Institute to mobilize the political will and the human and financial resources needed to arrest deforestation and promote sustainable forest management.

The plan has already helped stimulate an increase in investment in tropical forestry from $500 million in 1985 to $1 billion in 1989, and it has improved development assistance coordination. However, some of its most innovative recommendations are not yet being implemented. The plan attempted to provide a mechanism for reorienting government and development assistance policies, and for dealing not only with deforestation, but also with forest degradation, with an emphasis on agroforestry, fuelwood production, ecosystem conservation, and other forms of forest management that can provide goods and services to rural people and national economies. Reviews of the more than sixty national forest planning efforts inspired by the plan have revealed that policy reform has rarely been given priority, and that the bulk of increased donor support has gone to traditional forestry programs. Efforts are now under way to reorient the TFAP so that it can achieve its initial aims and incorporate the lessons learned since 1985.

In a similar vein, the creation of the International Tropical Timber Organization (ITTO) several years ago has provided a forum for dialogue among the major tropical forest producing and consuming countries on conservation and sustainable development issues. ITTO has sponsored research on techniques for sustainable timber harvest, and has initiated several pilot projects to experiment with promising approaches to forest management.

As encouraging as these initiatives are, they do not go far enough. Moving from uncontrolled deforestation and species loss to sustainable forestland use requires a major rethinking of prevailing forest development strategies. Past efforts to cope with deforestation have focused largely on remedial efforts rather than preventive measures, treating symptoms rather than underlying causes. Greater emphasis must now be placed on broad-based policy and institutional reform aimed at addressing the social, economic, and political forces behind deforestation. Success in forging these reformed policies and putting them into action will require new forms of cooperation and collaboration within and among governments, local communities, nongovernmental organizations, industry, and development agencies.

Reforming Government Policies

Honest Economic Accounting of Biological Resources. A key to making the conservation of forest ecosystems a development priority is accurately reflecting their full value and the full costs of losing them. National accounts cannot provide a true reflection of net national productivity unless such natural resources as forests and species diversity are treated as capital assets, thus allowing capital increases or depreciation to be fairly represented as the resource is either maintained or exploited.

The misvaluation of biological wealth results in part from the longstanding perception of forests and the diversity of living things as a free and unlimited resource, rather than a capital asset. Depreciation of the forest resource base has been ignored, and the loss of forests registers as a contribution to national income rather than a loss of capital stock. As a result, the depletion of valuable capital assets is confused with the generation of income.

Of course, some of the problem lies in the difficulty of putting a dollar figure on biological resources. How much is biological diversity worth? What is the value of watershed protection or climate stabilization? Just this kind of evaluation must be made, or the value of intact forests will be understated relative to logging or agricultural conversion when governments make land use decisions.

Integrated Land Use Planning. Current land use patterns in developing countries are the cumulative result of centuries of human occupation, and often they do not represent optimum use. Consequently, the country's land base does not produce as much as it could, and more land is cleared than might otherwise be needed. Often, fragile ecosystems such as steep upland slopes, humid forests, and semiarid woodlands are exploited beyond their carrying capacity and degraded, effectively shrinking the productive land base and putting pressure on remaining forests.

Land use planning can improve forest conditions in several ways. Most directly, a good land use plan that allocates large areas for sustainable forest uses provides the legal and institutional basis for effective forest management. In addition, land use planning that preserves prime agricultural lands and the watershed areas that sustain them helps maintain agricultural carrying capacity. The more people who can be supported on existing agricultural land, the fewer who will turn to the forest frontier.

In most tropical forest countries, land use decisions tend to be made incrementally by a patchwork of sectoral agencies with little coordination and active competition among them. Basic data on soil, water, slope, vegetative cover, biological resources, critical ecosystems, and indigenous inhabitants are often lacking. What information there is varies among agencies and rarely reflects systematic field surveys.

Today's dysfunctional planning process must be replaced by one that reflects both the scientific and technical basis of modern planning, and the inherent conflicts between competing government sectors. Even more important, the planning process must involve a true cross section of society by ensuring the participation of local community groups, forest dwellers, and others affected by forest policies.

Effective land use planning requires that legal, fiscal, and operational authority be centralized under one agency or interagency working group. The lead agency must also have the funding and capability to carry out a systematic land resource inventory that includes valuation of forest goods and services. Without accurate and complete data, the exercise has little point. It must also have the power to override various government agencies when the inevitable disputes arise.

In planning land uses to minimize forest impact, the role of such large infrastructure projects as dams, mines, and roads must be kept in mind. In particular, the effects of road building on deforestation cannot be overestimated, though roads are essential elements of all other infrastructure projects. Quite simply, governments that want to limit deforestation in particular forest regions should not build roads there for any purpose, since they inevitably bring on deforestation.

Modifying Rural Land Tenure Systems. Establishing property rights for traditional forest dwellers and new forest immigrants is essential to encouraging sustainable subsistence agriculture that protects forest resources from ever-deepening degradation. If forest cultivators are to make the long-term investments of capital and labor in land (through, say, terracing and tree planting), they must hold a clearly defined bundle of rights—land tenure—that provides security for investment, sale, or other options. Evidence from many developing countries indicates that security of tenure increases long-term investment in land and increases per unit productivity.

The response throughout most of the world to the need for secure tenure has been to establish systems for land documentation, registration, and titling. Such proof of land ownership provides a legal basis for repulsing encroachment. In many countries, it also broadens access to credit because it can serve as collateral with official lending institutions.

But land tenure systems in most tropical forest countries do not reflect actual patterns of land occupancy; indeed, they neither recognize the traditional ownership customs of indigenous peoples nor provide for farmers who have settled on public land. For example, in many countries title will not be granted unless the land is "actively" worked. This stipulation obviously excludes forest areas and the traditional "low-impact" management practices needed to maintain the sustainable character of traditional agriculture.

Titling agencies generally work on a reactive basis, providing land registration and titling when people ask (and pay) for it. A more activist approach is required for the rural poor; legal land security must be brought to them, at a cost they can afford, and through unintimidating procedures. In some cases, local nongovernmental organizations (NGOs) may be effective as intermediaries to explain and help people take advantage of land registration.

As for immigration onto public land, governments must assess these occupied lands and regularize their status. The broad choices are simple: governments can issue land titles and take the land out of the public domain, establish a long-term lease system in which occupation—but not ownership—is legalized, or resettle the occupants. Strategies and solutions will vary; what is important is that governments recognize that choices must be made and actions taken.

Of course, provision of land rights is only one element of what should be an integrated strategy to provide small farmers with enough resources and security to allow for a longer-term view of land management. Access to credit, fertilizers, markets for their products, improved agricultural extension services, and opportunities to participate in local decision making are essential as well. Satisfaction of short-term subsistence needs is the most fundamental prerequisite to land stewardship over time. Quite simply, if today's basic needs are not met, management of the land for tomorrow has little meaning.

Encouraging Sustainable Systems of Land Management and Agriculture. Indigenous systems of forest agriculture and land management have much to teach us, and have great potential value for use by new forest immigrants if they are to take up the challenge of land stewardship. Yet shifting cultivation by forest settlers receives the least government support of any agricultural system in developing countries because it is looked upon as an illegitimate use of public forestland.

Once they have located in the forest, settlers would be dramatically less destructive if they were provided with sustainable alternatives to farming for short-term gains. The Kayapo people in southern Para in Brazil, for example, manage to farm sustainably in the tropical forest using traditional methods of soil enrichment and cropping that allow them to cultivate cleared plots for eleven years with a fallow period as short as five years. In contrast, most forest colonists in the Amazon who have not had long experience with farming find cleared plots unusable after two to three years.

Evidence from the Peruvian Amazon also shows that the acidic soil under the forest can be stabilized enough to provide for sustainable agriculture. A variety of sustainable management options with varying levels of agricultural inputs has been tested and experimentally proven. For every hectare farmed in such highly productive environmentally benign ways, between five and ten hectares per year of rainforest could be saved.

These technologies and techniques help make it possible to stabilize shifting cultivation systems, but the move from demonstration plots to wide-scale adoption by farmers is a difficult one. Shifting cultivators must be given incentives to adopt new technologies, and institutions must be devised to support their decisions. For example, the granting of land titles to public forest could be made contingent on participation in government agricultural extension programs that teach sustainable farming systems.

Of course, policies that subsidize farming of any sort at the forest frontier may backfire if pursued in isolation, actually increasing incentives for migration to the forest. Thus government policies must simultaneously focus on reducing the pressures that drive people to the forest in the first place.

Ending Government-sponsored Resettlement in Forest Areas.
Many governments of tropical forest countries continue to support the colonization of their forests and adjacent areas by farmers despite ample evidence that these communities are neither sustainable nor cost effective. The largest such resettlement schemes have been carried out in Brazil and Indonesia, but Peru, Bolivia, Malaysia, and a number of other countries have orchestrated similar colonization programs.

Between 1950 and 1984, Indonesia's "transmigration" program resettled some 2.3 million people from the populated inner islands of Java and Bali to the densely forested outer islands. But soils on the outer islands were so poor that settlers could not use rice cultivation systems patterned after those found viable on the fertile volcanic soils of the inner islands. Many of the colonists subsequently abandoned the settlements, and international donor support for the program eventually dissipated in light of its limited success.

Brazil's resettlement efforts along the Transamazon Highway have faced similar difficulties. The widespread movement of settlers into unsustainable shifting cultivation—often followed by unsustainable cattle grazing—has been widely documented. These settlers are eventually forced to move on to the expanding agricultural frontier as the productivity of the land declines.

The official price tag of such settlements is high—nearly $10,000 per family in Indonesia. If the real costs in terms of forest destruction and the loss of environmental services were considered, the figure would soar far higher. Halting sponsored settlements and redirecting funds into stabilizing the agricultural systems of both existing settlements, as well as those of spontaneous shifting migrants, would be far more sustainable and cost effective.

Promoting Compatible Human Uses of Forest Preserves. Forest parks and preserves play a vital role in preserving biological diversity by safeguarding critical forest habitat from the ravages of deforestation. But while tropical forest nations have increasingly embraced the idea of national parks and preserves and have set aside considerable acreage in recent decades, conservation efforts cannot succeed unless far greater areas are removed from direct production than modern societies will ever willingly accept.

The solution to this dilemma is to supplement the network of strictly protected areas (such as national parks) with protected areas designed and managed to permit and even encourage compatible human uses. These include limited collection of fuelwood, rattan, resins, nuts, honey, flowers, and game—all the products that indigenous peoples have exploited for millennia. With this approach, local communities become partners in the conservation effort, rather than illegal poachers with no stake in preserving the forest.

The management of strictly protected areas should also be changed to ensure that surrounding communities, which often bear the opportunity cost of the lost access to the land, benefit from the new park either through employment or through receipt of a portion of park revenues. All too often, park managers have an adversarial relationship with the residents surrounding the parks. While the forest policeman is feared, he is rarely present, so resentful rural residents whose activities may defy park preservation goals basically have unregulated access.

A wiser and more comprehensive strategy would be to institute mega-reserves where core areas of more restricted-access lands of highest conservation value would be surrounded by buffer areas of limited protection where compatible multiple use activities would be allowed.

Something very like this system has evolved in Costa Rica, where a new land use program places the various parks, forests, and other reserves—which together make up 27 percent of the country's area—under seven regional authorities that report to the minister of natural resources, energy, and mines. All agricultural, forest, and grazing lands, as well as villages and towns found within each region, are under the jurisdiction of each regional unit. These units work both with managers of protected areas and with community-oriented development programs in which conservation figures centrally. As a result, conservation goals are served over the entire area.

International Action

Perhaps the most fruitful area for international action to arrest deforestation and species loss lies with the bilateral and multilateral development assistance agencies. While national governments make the policy decisions that most directly affect pace of deforestation, international lenders exert significant influence on those decisions. Development aid provides the funding, technical assistance, and expertise that allow certain projects to proceed, and it affects the balance of investment between different sectors.

Until quite recently, the impacts of development assistance programs on deforestation were largely ignored. But this critical relationship has earned more attention in the past few years as the negative environmental effects of many development projects—from dams in India to livestock schemes in Africa—have been widely publicized and the major development agencies have come under increasing criticism. A fairly strong policy commitment and institutional framework to ensure that development assistance protects or enhances tropical forests have now been established, but translating these policies into programs in the field is a difficult and nascent process.

In several ways, development assistance support could help halt deforestation and preserve species diversity.

Natural Resource Inventories. Basic physical, biological, and socioeconomic data on tropical forests are currently inadequate for evaluating forest resources, and tropical forest countries rarely have the funds and trained personnel needed to gather this data. Support for natural resource inventories, baseline studies, and environmental sector reviews would thus promote sound land use that minimizes forest disturbance.

Recent advances in resource assessment—among them, remote sensing, geographical information systems, rapid rural appraisal, and biological resource inventories—make it feasible for tropical forest countries to assess their natural resource bases fairly rapidly. The development community possesses the financial resources, expertise, and technological access to bring these technologies to bear. If it uses them to help build national capacity to undertake such inventories, it can both meet immediate information needs and strengthen local institutions.

Preservation of Critical Tropical Forest Areas. Conservation of critical forest ecosystems is the most direct use to which natural resource inventory data can be put. Development assistance can not only contribute to government plans for new reserves; it can also materially improve these reserves' prospects by supporting initial infrastructure (for example, guard posts, light planes, and tourist facilities). Most important, such assistance can help tropical countries meet recurrent costs, such as for salaries, equipment, and fuel.

Promotion of Sustainable Forestland Use. Sustainable agroforestry—forest farming techniques—is an important part of any scheme to reduce deforestation and species loss. Research on agroforestry has come a long way in the last decade, but the design of systems tailored to local communities is a painstaking process of assessing community needs against the backdrop of local ecological conditions. In many cases, major donors with large budgets find it administratively difficult to give small grants or loans. One solution is support for national research institutions and local nongovernmental organizations. Block grants to small donors with expert local staff in particular countries is another solution.

Support of Sustainable Timber Harvesting Methods. Forest production policies in many nations are patently unsound; yet levels of donor support for such projects are actually growing. Donors must cease funding nonsustainable forestry practices and support research and action aimed at making timber harvesting and production more profitable, efficient, and sustainable. As part of this effort, donors should pay increased attention to developing such "minor" forest products as rattan, various tropical fruits and nuts, and latex.

Support of Local and International Nongovernmental Organizations. Assistance should not be confined to national governments. Many nongovernmental organizations are active at the grassroots level where government officials are rarely seen. Many act at the national level as well. Several have helped engineer "debt for nature" swaps in Latin America—one of several innovative schemes to finance conservation goals. Donors can provide direct support to these groups and, just as important, serve as a bridge to build trust and cooperation between governments and the NGO community. Many university and other research institutions also need support so they can be more effective in national conservation efforts.

Other actions are needed to provide the international legal

framework for preserving biodiversity and to develop the political will to do so. Work has commenced on a Biological Diversity Convention that would spell out conservation goals and create an international fund to support conservation projects in developing countries. Under this convention, the primary approach to conservation would be through habitat protection—preserving the biological integrity of forests, both tropical and temperate.

Another fund has been established by the FAO as part of its "International Undertaking on Plant Genetic Resources" to address the need for increased financial support for the conservation of crop genetic resources. However this voluntary fund has not received enough contributions to enable it to meet its goals. A key element of the proposed Biodiversity Convention will thus be the establishment of a mechanism whereby significant financial resources can be mobilized to support conservation. Among those currently under consideration are taxes on certain commodities, on industries benefiting directly from genetic resources, and on emissions of various atmospheric pollutants (such as carbon dioxide).

Still other international agreements are in the initial stages of discussion. Some thought has been given to the possible advantages of a Tropical Forest Convention targeted specifically at the need for forest conservation and the needs of forest dwellers in these ecosystems. Others have suggested that tropical deforestation should be viewed in the context of other global environmental problems, such as global warming, and that decision makers should consider a "global bargain" in which nations agree to address their local contributions to global problems, knowing that other nations would be taking equally significant, and costly, steps.

Although various international agreements and the numerous international lenders and donors can play significant roles in reversing tropical deforestation, numerous other opportunities exist at national and local levels. Often, the individuals, community groups, and organizations that are most effective in slowing forest loss while meeting human needs operate on scales far too small to be compatible with typical donor programs. Moreover, though increased financial support is clearly needed, other initiatives, such as providing greater access to information or to research and technical expertise, may do even more to foster changes in resource management and government policies.

As a senior partner in the development community, the United States has an important part to play in tropical conservation. The U.S. Agency for International Development (AID) is the world's largest bilateral forestry donor. In recent years, it has increased its commitment to tropical forest and biological diversity conservation, and it increasingly stresses projects that contribute to sustainable forestry, farming, and range management. The United States is also a major contributor to the multilateral banks, and it has recently pressed the banks to incorporate environmental considerations into development projects.

The United States could be doing much more to promote sustainable forest utilization, however. Its trade policies may have far greater impact on tropical forest resources than any number of development projects; yet, environmental considerations are rarely incorporated into bilateral trade negotiations or into those under the General Agreement on Tariffs and Trade (GATT). The United States should also be setting a better example in its own back yard on how to manage forest resources. Currently, the United States provides many of the same incentives and subsidies to promote unsustainable logging practices at home that it is criticizing abroad.

The United States must also unequivocally support conservation goals by explicitly recognizing international conservation law, and actively participating in a global convention on biodiversity. Another action that would count heavily in the eyes of tropical forest nations would be the assumption of a leadership role in reducing global greenhouse gas emissions, thus demonstrating a national willingness to abide by the same sustainable development criteria we urge on the developing world.

4

Protecting the Ozone Layer: New Directions in Diplomacy

RICHARD ELLIOT BENEDICK

O zone has been characterized as "the single most important chemically active trace gas in the earth's atmosphere."[1] Two singular characteristics of this remote, unstable, and toxic gas make it so critical. First, certain wavelengths of ultraviolet radiation (UV-B) that can damage and cause mutations in animal and plant cells are absorbed by the extraordinarily thin layer of ozone molecules dispersed throughout the atmosphere, particularly in the stratosphere six to thirty

RICHARD ELLIOT BENEDICK, as deputy assistant secretary of state, was the chief U.S. negotiator for the ozone protection treaties. He is currently on assignment from the State Department as senior fellow of The Conservation Foundation/World Wildlife Fund. A career diplomat, he has served in several countries and has headed numerous U.S. delegations. Ambassador Benedick recently received the highest presidential career public service award. His work on economic, environmental, and population issues has been published in the U.S. and abroad. This chapter is adapted from *Ozone Diplomacy: New Directions in Safeguarding the Planet,* by Richard E. Benedick, Cambridge, Mass.: Harvard University Press, © 1991 by World Wildlife Fund & The Conservation Foundation and Institute for the Study of Diplomacy, Georgetown University.

miles in altitude, and thereby prevented from reaching the earth's surface; and second, differing quantities of ozone at different altitudes can have major implications for global climate. Indeed, the ozone layer, as currently constituted, is essential to life as it has evolved on earth.

Disturbing Theories

In 1973 two University of Michigan scientists, Richard Stolarski and Ralph Cicerone, while exploring the possible effects of chemical emissions from National Aeronautics and Space Administration (NASA) rockets, theorized that chlorine in the stratosphere could unleash a complicated chain reaction that would continually destroy ozone for decades. A year later, Mario Molina and Sherwood Rowland at the University of California, Irvine, became intrigued with some peculiar properties of human-made chlorofluorocarbons (CFCs). Molina and Rowland discovered that, unlike most other gases, CFCs were not chemically destroyed or rained out quickly in the lower atmosphere, but rather migrated slowly up to the stratosphere. There they remained intact for many decades—sometimes for more than a century. The two researchers concluded that the CFCs, which are not naturally present in the stratosphere, are eventually broken down by radiation and thereby release large quantities of chlorine.

The combined implication of these two hypotheses was that CFCs might cause significant depletion of the ozone layer. The enhanced levels of ultraviolet radiation that would then reach the earth's surface could have potentially disastrous impacts on human health and the environment. Researchers projected millions of future deaths from skin cancer, millions of cases of eye cataracts and blindness, suppression of the human immune system, losses in food production and fisheries, damage to plastics and other materials, and intensification of the greenhouse heat-trap effect.

Amazingly, the research paths that led to the suspicion that the stratospheric ozone layer was in jeopardy had been serendipitous. For decades, CFCs had been widely used without fear that they were in any way harmful to the environment. Indeed, following their invention in the 1930s, CFCs had been thoroughly tested by customary standards and found to be completely safe. Possible effects high above the earth simply never came under consideration.

CFCs are stable, nonflammable, nontoxic, and noncorrosive—qualities that make them extremely useful in many applications. Since they vaporize at low temperatures, they are highly efficient coolants for refrigerators and air conditioners, as well as excellent propellants in spray containers for cosmetics, household products, pharmaceuticals, and cleaners. They make energy-efficient insulators and have found use in the manufacture of a wide range of rigid and flexible plastic-foam materials. Their nonreactive properties make them seemingly perfect solvents for cleaning microchips and telecommunications equipment and for a myriad of other industrial applications. As an added bonus, CFCs are inexpensive to produce. A related family of bromine compounds, the halons, which have been unsurpassed fire extinguishants in the defense, oil, aircraft, electronics, and other industries, was produced in much smaller quantities, but molecule-for-molecule posed an even greater threat to ozone.

The ozone depletion hypothesis stimulated a great wave of scientific research over the following years. It would be difficult to exaggerate the complexities involved. To understand what was happening to the ozone layer, researchers needed to go far beyond atmospheric chemistry. They had to bridge disciplines, examining the earth as an interrelated system of physical, chemical, and biological processes taking place on land, in water, and in the atmosphere, and influenced by economic, political, and social forces. Scientists developed ever more sophisticated computer models simulating, for decades into the future, the stratospheric interplay between radiative, chemical, and physical processes, and utilized balloons, rockets, and satellites to track remote gases measured in parts per trillion of volume.

Ozone itself amounts to considerably less than one part per million of the total atmosphere. Intrinsically unstable ozone molecules are constantly created and destroyed by complex natural forces involving solar radiation and interactions with even more minute quantities of other gases. Ozone concentrations fluctuate naturally on a daily, seasonal, and solar-cyclical basis: indeed, during the 1960s they had actually increased on average. Ozone abundance also varies significantly over different latitudes and at different altitudes in the atmosphere. Scientists thus faced an enormous challenge in attempting to detect a minuscule "signal" of the beginnings of the postulated long-term downward trend in stratospheric ozone concentrations.

Transatlantic Differences

The United States and the twelve-nation European Community (EC) dominated the market for CFCs, together accounting for over 80 percent of the world's output in 1974. Notwithstanding their shared political, economic, and environmental orientation, critical differences marked their approach to the potential threat to the ozone layer.

The ozone depletion theory seemed to capture the imagination of an American public that was, perhaps because of U.S. journeys into space, more sensitized than Europeans to events in the stratosphere. Concern over the ozone layer figured more prominently in the United States than in Europe in media coverage, in congressional debates, and in the activities of environmental organizations. In contrast, for many years there was no countervailing power in Europe to the voice of the chemical industry. The otherwise environmentally conscious European public was long indifferent to the ozone issue, mainly because it accorded higher priority to such closer-to-home problems as acid rain and chemical spills.

The chemical industry on both sides of the Atlantic vigorously denied any linkage between the health of the ozone layer and the growing sales of CFCs. Industrialists mobilized research and public relations efforts to stress the scientific uncertainties, the necessity of CFCs for modern lifestyles, the infeasibility of substitutes, and the alleged high costs and economic dislocations associated with controls on these chemicals.

Differences emerged, however, between American and European industrialists, probably reflecting the relative strength of U.S. public concern. Millions of independent decisions by worried American consumers cut the U.S. market for spray cans by two-thirds by 1977 even in the absence of governmental regulation. The threat of a patchwork of varying state regulations made U.S. industry favor uniform and therefore less disruptive federal controls.

Responding to public reaction, the U.S. Congress passed landmark legislation in 1977's Clean Air Act authorizing the administrator of the Environmental Protection Agency (EPA) to regulate "any substance . . . which in his judgment *may reasonably be anticipated* to affect the stratosphere, especially ozone in the stratosphere, if such effect *may reasonably be anticipated* to endanger public health or welfare" (emphasis added). This law attempted to balance the considerable scientific uncertainties with the enormous risks of inaction. And it opted for a low threshold to justify intervention: the government was not obligated to prove conclusively that a suspected substance could modify the stratosphere or endanger health and environment. All that was required was a standard of reasonable expectation.

Following this legislation, the United States banned CFCs as propellants for nonessential aerosol sprays in early 1978, affecting nearly $3 billion worth of sales in a wide range of products. This action was followed by Canada (a small producer), and by Sweden, Norway, Denmark, and Finland (all importing countries).

Under heavy pressure from the European chemical industry, the EC waited until 1980 before following suit. It then enacted a 30 percent CFC aerosol cutback from 1976 levels, together with a "cap" on production capacity. These actions seemed almost disingenuous: European sales of CFCs for aerosols had already declined by over 28 percent since 1976, while capacity was deliberately defined as a twenty-four hour operation, which would enable output to increase by over 60 percent. The EC measures were clearly dictated more by commercial than by environmental concerns. They were painless actions, fully supported by European industry, which gave an appearance of control while permitting unhampered expansion for two more decades.

The divergent U.S. and EC official actions were reflected in economic developments. The year that the CFC-ozone connection was hypothesized, 1974, coincidentally represented a historic peak for CFC production and use—which had been growing by 13 percent per year on average since 1960. The United States was by far the major producer, with nearly half of the global total, while all EC countries together accounted for under 40 percent; Germany was the largest European producer, followed by the United Kingdom, France, and Italy.

After the aerosol ban, the United States never regained its former market preeminence. By 1986 world output, which had fallen in the late 1970s, had recovered and exceeded the 1974 peak. The EC dominated the market with an estimated 43 to 45 percent, while the United States had dropped to about 30 percent. Meanwhile, other countries had increased their shares over the years, especially Japan (11–12 percent) and the Soviet Union (9–10 percent), with smaller amounts for Canada, China, Australia, Brazil, Mexico, Argentina, Venezuela, and India. The European Community also supplied CFCs to the rest of the world, particularly the growing markets of developing countries. EC exports rose by 43 percent from 1976 to 1985 and averaged almost one-third of its production. In contrast, the United States consumed virtually all it produced.

Europolitics

International discussions on possible actions to protect the ozone layer were strongly influenced by the political evolution of the twelve-nation European Community. Responsibility for environmental matters was gradually being transferred from the sovereign member states to the EC Commission in Brussels. Consequently, substantial ambiguities surrounded the commission's actual authority. The EC's centralized enforcement powers were weak and the commission lacked both money and staff. Indeed, in its approach to CFC regulation throughout much of this period, the EC Commission seemed to many observers often more concerned about European economic union than about protecting the ozone layer. In the words of one respected German political scientist, "The motivation behind EC environmental policy . . . is not so much a common interest in environmental protection (even though this is, naturally, continually and solemnly asserted), but rather the harmonization of the conditions of production within the Common Market."

The EC Commission long based its position on ozone largely on the self-serving data and contentions of a few big companies. European industry's primary objective was to preserve market dominance and to avoid the costs of switching to alternative products for as long as possible. Both industry and government officials felt that panic had driven Americans into the aerosol ban in 1978 and that the United States had only itself to blame for any market losses. Epitomizing the close industry-government linkages, company executives represented European governments on official delegations at negotiations—in contrast to their American counterparts, who came as unofficial observers.

The Vienna Convention

The United Nations Environment Programme (UNEP), under the strong leadership of Mostafa Tolba, sought from the start a global approach to ozone protection. It began by sensitizing governments and vigorously promoting research and data collection. The question of international controls, which Tolba (himself a scientist) believed essential, was first raised in an April 1977 intergovernmental meeting hosted by the United States. At a German-sponsored meeting the following year, governments could not agree even on voluntary coordinated CFC reductions because the United Kingdom and France blocked consensus within the EC, which voted as a unit. (See Appendix A for a chronology of key events in the ozone history.)

By the early 1980s, the sense of urgency for new regulatory

action had diminished considerably. Changing understanding of the stratospheric chemical reactions, together with refinements in computer modeling, led many politicians as well as scientists to believe that the original ozone-depletion hypotheses had been overstated. In addition, CFC production had declined due to the world economic slowdown.

Had not Mostafa Tolba and UNEP pushed persistently ahead with their mission, the ozone issue might have died at this stage. Even as it was, negotiations convened by UNEP in 1982 over a global agreement on protecting the ozone layer dragged on for three years. Most governments had envisaged such a convention to cover only cooperative research but not international regulation. However, in 1983 the "Toronto Group," comprising Canada, Finland, Norway, Sweden, Switzerland, and the United States, proposed to supplement the convention with a worldwide agreement to eliminate CFCs in nonessential aerosols. They maintained that an aerosol ban was clearly feasible, as the United States had already introduced economical substitutes. Eliminating CFCs in spray cans would yield immediate and important benefits to the ozone layer: it would reduce CFC emissions by about a third and thereby buy time for the still-evolving science to provide clearer guidance to policy makers on the need for additional controls.

The EC rejected this proposal, and countered with their capacity cap concept. Correctly, EC representatives pointed out that growing nonaerosol uses could eventually cancel out aerosol reductions. The Toronto Group responded that while the EC proposal was theoretically elegant, it was practically ineffectual: under the EC cap, unutilized European capacity would allow millions of additional tons of CFCs to be released over the next twenty years. Moreover, the cap would lock in existing market shares, and was therefore biased against countries with little or no surplus capacity, such as the United States.

Whatever the intrinsic merits of the respective proposals, each of the two contending blocs backed a protocol that would require no new controls for itself and considerable adjustment for the other. Faced with this stalemate over regulatory strategies, the negotiators decided to return to the original concept of a research convention, which would at least provide a frame-

work for future protocols to control ozone-modifying substances.

The Vienna Convention on Protection of the Ozone Layer,
signed in March 1985, represented the first international effort
to deal formally with an environmental danger before it
erupted. Its signatories accepted a general obligation to take
"appropriate measures" to protect the ozone layer. The convention specifically established mechanisms for international
cooperation in research, monitoring, and the exchange of data
on the state of the stratospheric ozone layer and on emissions
and concentrations of CFCs and other relevant chemicals;
these provisions were significant because, before Vienna, the
USSR and some other countries had refused to provide CFC
production data.

Over initial European objections, the United States and its
allies pushed through a resolution at the Vienna meeting that
directed UNEP to reopen diplomatic negotiations with a 1987
target date for a binding CFC control protocol. This resolution also launched an innovative fact-gathering and consen-
sus-building process, in the form of informal workshops under
UNEP sponsorship, that proved critical to the future formal
negotiations.

Models of Uncertainty

In the years following the first scientific hypotheses, various
computer model predictions of the impacts of CFC emissions
fluctuated widely. Projections of global average ozone depletion fifty to one hundred years in the future began at about 15
percent in 1974, fell to around 8 percent in 1976, climbed
again to nearly 19 percent in 1979, and then dropped steadily
to approximately 3 percent by 1983 (see Figure 1). These
swings tended to dampen public and official concern.

In late 1984 a remarkable cooperative international scientific venture was launched to analyze and reassess all available
evidence on the present and prospective state of the ozone
layer. Under the cosponsorship of UNEP, the World Meteorological Organization (WMO), three U.S. government agencies, the West German Ministry for Research and Technology,

and the European Commission, approximately 150 scientists of various nationalities worked under NASA's leadership for over a year. The resultant study, *Atmospheric Ozone 1985,* was the most ambitious analysis of the stratosphere ever undertaken: three volumes containing nearly 1,100 pages of text, plus eighty-six pages of references.

This comprehensive WMO/UNEP assessment supported, but could not prove, the ozone destruction hypotheses of 1973–74. It revealed that accumulations of CFCs in the atmosphere had nearly doubled between 1975 and 1985. Because these stable chemicals have such long atmospheric lifetimes, millions of tons of prior-year CFC production were still en route to their fatal stratospheric rendezvous with ozone. Even if CFC emissions were to level off or decline, chlorine would continue to accumulate in the stratosphere for many decades, and some future depletion of the ozone layer seemed inescapable. The scientific consensus was that continued CFC emissions at the 1980 rate could reduce global average ozone by

FIGURE 1. Models of Uncertainty—Various Predictions of Ozone Layer Depletion, 1974–85

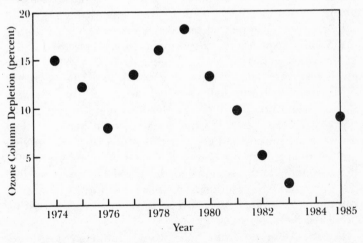

Sources: Adapted from National Research Council, *Causes and Effects of Changes in Stratospheric Ozone: Update 1983.* Washington: National Academy Press, 1984; and World Meteorological Organization, *Atmospheric Ozone 1985.* Geneva: WMO, 1986.

about 9 percent by the last half of the twenty-first century, with even greater seasonal and latitudinal decreases.

Despite this progress in theoretical understanding, the uncertainties were still great in 1986 as diplomats began to debate the need for international controls on CFCs. Thirty years of measurements had not demonstrated any statistically significant loss of total ozone (apart from an Antarctic anomaly, discussed below). Nor did the models predict any global depletion, at existing levels of emissions, for at least the next two decades. Not only was there no indication of increased levels of UV-B radiation reaching the earth's surface, but such measurements as existed showed *reduced* radiation. The WMO/UNEP report itself noted many knowledge gaps, inadequacies in the models, and data inconsistencies. Writing in *American Scientist* in 1989, Sherwood Rowland observed that "statistical evaluation through 1986 gave no indication of any trend in global ozone significantly different from no change at all."

The Antarctic Ozone Hole

Too late in 1985 for analysis under the WMO/UNEP assessment, British scientists published unexpected findings based on ozone measurements made at their Halley Bay station in the Antarctic. It appeared that ozone levels recorded during the Antarctic springtime (September–November) were about 40 percent lower than they had been in the 1960s. While ozone levels recovered toward the end of each spring, the degree of the seasonal ozone collapse had apparently accelerated sharply beginning in 1979. The "ozone hole" (that is, a portion of the stratosphere in which greatly diminished ozone levels were measured) had expanded by 1985 to cover an area greater in size than the continental United States. Ironically, U.S. satellites had not signaled the trend because they had been programed to automatically reject such low ozone measurements as anomalies far beyond the error range of existing predictive models.

Did the Antarctic ozone hole strongly influence the subsequent negotiations and make agreement on international controls inevitable? While plausible in hindsight, this popular misconception overlooks how little was known about this phenomenon during the negotiations. There was no proof at the time that CFCs had affected Antarctica; it was possible that the hole was a localized and natural phenomenon born of unusual polar conditions. In 1986 springtime Antarctic ozone levels had actually improved. Rowland admitted in 1986, just before the negotiations began, that "the causes of the massive seasonal loss of ozone over Antarctica are not yet fully understood, and its implications for the ozone layer above the rest of the earth are also uncertain."[2] Even after the international CFC control agreement was signed a year later, EPA concluded that "the Antarctic ozone hole cannot yet serve as a guide for policy decisions."[3]

Negotiating for International Controls

Despite the remaining uncertainties, the scientific activities of 1984–86 had contributed to a growing consensus that some international regulation of CFCs was desirable.

The evolving understanding, together with mounting domestic pressures for new controls, also influenced U.S. industry. American companies had long resented the competitive advantage that their European rivals had achieved by escaping regulation in the late 1970s. Not surprisingly, American industry did not want any further U.S. regulatory action that was not also binding on the other major producer countries. Hence in September 1986, the Alliance for Responsible CFC Policy, a coalition of about 500 U.S. producer and user companies, announced its support for *international* controls on CFCs.

This unexpected development broke industry's united front practically on the eve of international negotiations and caused consternation in Europe. Some European industrialists had suspected all along that the United States was using the ozone scare to cloak commercial motivations. They now believed that American companies had endorsed CFC controls in order to enter the profitable EC export markets with substitute products that they had secretly developed. But this suspicion was unfounded: to the dismay of environmentalists, du Pont had admitted in 1986 that it had ceased research on CFC alternatives in 1981.

Partly because the preparatory work, in particular the informal UNEP-sponsored workshops mentioned above, had been so extensive, it took only nine months to negotiate a formal control protocol. The negotiations were launched in Geneva in December 1986 and continued in three further week-long plenary sessions plus several supplementary bilateral and multilateral consultations. Despite their relative brevity, the negotiations were difficult and sometimes heated. The United States and the European Community remained the principal protagonists, differing over nearly every issue at every step of the way.

The EC, still dominated by the chemical industries and the governments of the United Kingdom, France, and Italy, argued that there was time to delay stringent production cuts and wait for more evidence since the scientific models projected no significant ozone depletion for at least two decades. Initially, the USSR and Japan shared this perspective. Within the EC, however, deep internal divisions developed as the negotiations wore on, with the Federal Republic of Germany, the Netherlands, Belgium, and Denmark increasingly favoring stronger measures.

The United States, together with Canada, Norway, Sweden, Finland, Switzerland, and New Zealand, endorsed major cutbacks. These nations argued that, because of the century-long lifetimes of CFCs, action had to be taken well before critical levels of chlorine accumulated. Further delay of meaningful action, they maintained, would increase the health and environmental risks unacceptably, thereby necessitating even more costly future measures.

To persuade other governments of the need for strong controls, the U.S. Department of State designed a multifaceted diplomatic strategy. Over the next several months, it provided about sixty U.S. embassies with material intended to help them engage their host governments in a continuous dialogue on ozone protection. Through a steady stream of cables between Washington and the embassies, the State Department kept abreast of subtle changes in foreign attitudes and provided new information in response to other governments' concerns. Special policy and science missions visited West European capitals, Moscow, and Tokyo. U.S. officials influenced foreign public opinion in Europe, Asia, and Latin America through speeches, press conferences, radio, and television. At the June 1987 Venice Economic Summit, a U.S. initiative made ozone the priority environmental issue.

The Montreal Protocol

The provisions of the agreement that was finally reached on controlling CFCs and halons (see Appendix B) represented creative solutions to difficult technical, economic, and equity problems. The heart of the protocol negotiations, and the most fiercely contested issues, were the interrelated questions of (a) which chemicals would be regulated; (b) what parameters would be controlled (i.e., production or consumption of the substances); and (c) to what extent and how early would they be phased down.

With respect to chemical coverage, the EC long opposed a U.S. proposal to control *all* major ozone-destroying substances, rather than only CFCs 11 and 12, which had been the original focus. A critical scientific meeting in 1987 influenced many governments to support the U.S. position, as the scientists concluded that unless rapidly growing CFC 113 and the highly potent halons were also included, their emissions would lead to major losses of stratospheric ozone.

The scientists also agreed to assign a weight to each individual chemical according to its ozone-depleting potency. Using this weighting system, the negotiators formulated a protocol provision that allowed the chemicals to be controlled as a combined "basket" rather than individually. This ingenious formulation gave countries an incentive to impose greater reductions on those substances that were relatively more harmful to the ozone layer and/or whose uses were less essential to them. The flexibility offered by this provision was instrumental in gaining the support of many governments for strong controls, mostly notably Japan, which had long opposed limits on CFC 113 because of its importance for the Japanese electronics industry.

The issue of whether restrictions should be applied to the production or the consumption of controlled substances proved extremely difficult to resolve because of its commercial implications. On grounds of administrative simplicity, the EC argued for production limits since there were only a few producers, as opposed to countless points of consumption. But a production limit would essentially lock in the Europeans' export markets, since other producers could supply importers only by starving their own domestic consumption. Moreover, if growth in European demand for CFCs tempted EC countries to scale back on exports so as to serve home markets, importing countries would have neither access to other suppliers nor treaty authority to expand their own production. In this situation, they would have to bear a disproportionate share of CFC reductions; because of this vulnerability, importers might choose to remain outside the protocol and build their own CFC capacity.

Since the great majority of countries were importers rather than producers, a formula had to be devised to prevent the proportion of world output devoted to the export market from being reduced even as total production was phased down. The solution at Montreal was a surrogate for consumption, defined as production *plus* imports *minus* exports to other protocol signatories. Under this concept, if an importing country's traditional supplier either raised prices excessively or cut back on exports, the importing nation could meet the shortfall either by substituting its own production or by turning to another producer from among the protocol parties. In turn, a producing country could increase its production (and exports) to meet such needs without having to reduce its domestic consumption. Only exports to those countries that were outside the treaty would have to be counted against domestic consumption, and this prospect would serve as an added incentive for importing countries to join the protocol, lest they lose access to suppliers.

The most visible and contentious aspect of the protocol negotiations was the stringency and timing of cutbacks. Most participating governments were deeply influenced by a scientific finding, developed midway through the negotiations, that significant damage to the ozone layer would occur under the weaker control options being considered. But the EC moved only slowly and reluctantly away from its original position of minimal controls. The final success on this issue at Montreal was attributable to a combination of factors: the U.S. diplomatic and information campaign, which prompted Japan and the Soviet Union, among others, to agree on the need for strong controls; the personal efforts of UNEP's executive director at the negotiating table and behind the scenes with key developing country governments; and the growing influence of the Federal Republic of Germany within EC councils.

The protocol text (see Appendix B) provided for a freeze on CFCs at 1986 levels within one year after the treaty entered into force, followed by a 20 percent reduction in 1993–94, and a further cut to 50 percent in 1998–99. These fixed anchor dates for the reductions removed any temptation for governments to stall the protocol's enactment in hopes of delaying the cutbacks; they also provided industry with firm dates upon which to base planning.

Another innovative feature of the Montreal Protocol was the system designed for the treaty's entry into force and for future decisions of the parties. Disillusioned with one nation/one vote procedures in UN bodies, the U.S. government persuaded other parties that the protocol would be ineffective unless major stockholders had a corresponding influence in the collective decision-making process. A related concern was that the United States could find itself obligated to an "international" protocol while its major competitors were not. Both potential problems were neatly circumvented by a unique two-stage voting procedure. The United States obtained agreement at Montreal that the protocol would not take effect until it was ratified by at least eleven parties that together constituted at least two-thirds of estimated global consumption of controlled substances. In practice, the United States plus at least four of the six other large consumer countries—France, the Federal Republic of Germany, Italy, Japan, the Soviet Union, and the United Kingdom—would have to ratify the protocol for it to enter into force. Similar two-stage voting procedures applied to revisions to the reduction schedule and other provisions.

In order to strengthen the treaty's effectiveness and to discourage the movement of CFC production facilities to countries outside the protocol, the United States and other governments argued for restricting trade in controlled substances with nonparties. Initially, the EC wanted only to study the feasibility of trade restrictions. But once it was established that the General Agreement on Tariffs and Trade (GATT) permitted such measures if necessary for protecting health and the environment, a consensus grew in their favor. These clauses, summarized in Appendix B, provided a warning that it would be difficult for nonparties to profit from international trade in the controlled substances.

The European Community added an extra complication to the protocol negotiations by demanding special treatment for its twelve member countries because of their growing economic union. This issue almost scuttled the 1985 Vienna Convention, and the commission again raised it at the eleventh hour in Montreal. EC representatives insisted that the community be treated as a single unit in determining compliance with control obligations, even though all member governments would be separate voting parties under the protocol. The EC Commission was unable, however, to tell its negotiating partners whether it had full authority ("exclusive competence") to enforce any given provision of the treaty or whether power was shared with member countries ("mixed competence"). Other governments could thus not be certain whether, under some unforeseen circumstances, a treaty obligation could fall *between* the commission's purview and member states' responsibility.

The United States and other governments, therefore, opposed the EC demand. If the community were treated as a unit, they argued, already planned German reductions could offset unchanged or even expanded output by other EC members. Moreover, if the EC submitted aggregated rather than country-by-country data, monitoring the compliance of individual EC member states would be impossible.

Compromise was reached, but this was the final issue to be settled at Montreal and impasse was only narrowly averted. The European Community was allowed to be treated as a unit with respect to the consumption targets, but EC member countries had to meet the production limits on an individual basis and submit data accordingly.

After these and other issues were resolved at the final session, the Montreal Protocol on Substances that Deplete the Ozone Layer was signed on September 16, 1987, by representatives of twenty-four nations plus the EC Commission. In his closing address to the plenipotentiaries, Mostafa Tolba summed up the process and its probable impact: witnessing the fruition of twelve years of personal struggle, he declared that the agreement had shown "that the environment can be a bridge between the worlds of East and West, and of North and South." "As a scientist," he continued, "I salute you: for with this agreement, the worlds of science and public affairs have taken a step closer together. . . . a union which must guide the affairs of the world into the next century." "And," he concluded, prophetically, "This Protocol is a point of departure. . . . the beginning of the real work to come."[4]

The treaty signing attracted worldwide media attention, and it was hailed as "the most significant international environmental agreement in history," "a monumental achievement," and "unparalleled as a global effort."[5] Perhaps the most extraordinary aspect of the Montreal Protocol was that it imposed substantial short-term economic costs in order to protect human health and the environment against speculative future dangers—dangers that rested on scientific theories rather than on proven facts. Unlike environmental agreements of the past, this was not a response to harmful developments or events, but rather *preventive* action on a global scale.

A unique strength of the treaty was that the timing and extent of reductions, as well as the list of chemicals to be reduced, could be changed by the parties to the agreement without extensive formal renegotiation. The protocol was deliberately designed to be reopened and amended as needed through regularly scheduled scientific, environmental, economic, and technological assessments. These provisions not only reflected the scientific uncertainties at the time of the negotiations, but also bridged the differences between those governments demanding strong controls and those who were less convinced, since the controls could be either relaxed or strengthened as new evidence accumulated.

Ratification of the Protocol

Many additional governments were to sign and ratify the protocol over the ensuing months. In March 1988 Mexico became the first to ratify, followed three weeks later by the United States. By midyear, however, only three other countries—Norway, Sweden, and Canada, all relatively small consumers—had joined them. By the end of November, sixteen countries had ratified; despite initial apprehensions by some environmentalists, Japan and the Soviet Union were among them. In all, however, the ratifying countries still accounted for only about half of global CFC consumption, and two-thirds was needed to trigger entry into force. With one month to go, the major EC countries were conspicuously missing.

Growing fears that the protocol might not enter into force on the targeted date of January 1, 1989, were fueled by the EC Commission's insistence that all member states, plus the commission, ratify the protocol *simultaneously.* This departure from customary practice, which seemed primarily designed to demonstrate the commission's expanding authority, effectively tied the entire EC accession to the pace of its slowest member. (Nations normally adhered to international treaties as soon as they completed their respective internal ratification processes, which might vary considerably in duration.) The commission's position prevented the larger EC countries, whose ratification was essential if the treaty were to become operational, from joining when they were ready.

At the last possible moment to avoid delaying the protocol's entry into force, the EC Commission ratified in mid-December together with only eight of its twelve member governments. Two states, Luxembourg and Portugal, had inadvertently ratified two months earlier, while two others, Belgium and France, were unable to complete their internal approval process until the last days of the year.

With this ultimately meaningless delay past, the Montreal Protocol entered into force on January 1, 1989, ratified by twenty-nine sovereign nations and the European Commission, together accounting for an estimated 83 percent of global consumption of CFCs and halons. Fifteen months later, by April 2, 1990, a total of fifty-five governments had ratified.

As Mostafa Tolba had predicted, however, the work was far from finished. Once formal negotiation of the protocol was concluded, three issues came to the fore: (1) new scientific evidence, (2) the drive for stronger controls, and (3) North-South differences.

Alarming New Scientific Findings

Even as the negotiators were hammering out the final compromises in Montreal, an unprecedented international scientific expedition was taking place in Antarctica. Using specially designed equipment placed in balloons, satellites, a DC-8 flying laboratory, and a converted high-altitude U-2 aircraft, the scientists tracked stratospheric chemical reactions and minute concentrations of gases. Preliminary results of these measurements, announced about two weeks after the protocol's signing, indicated high stratospheric chlorine presence and the worst-ever seasonal drop in Antarctic ozone; until these data could be more completely evaluated, however, scientists remained unable definitively to link CFCs to the ozone hole.

Six months later, in March 1988, a joint NASA-NOAA press conference released the Ozone Trends Panel Report, a new comprehensive international scientific assessment of all previous air- and ground-based stratospheric trace gas measurements, including those from the 1987 Antarctic expedition. The conclusions were sensational: no longer a theory, ozone layer depletion had at last been substantiated by hard evidence. The analysis established that between 1969 and 1986, stratospheric ozone over heavily populated regions of the northern hemisphere, including North America, Europe, and the Soviet Union, China, and Japan, had diminished by small but significant amounts. And CFCs and halons were now implicated beyond dispute—including responsibility for the ozone collapse over Antarctica.

The new scientific findings were profoundly disquieting. The models on which the Montreal Protocol was based had proven incapable of predicting either the chlorine-induced Antarctic phenomenon or the extent of ozone depletion elsewhere. Most probably, therefore, they were *underestimating* future ozone losses.

Following the Ozone Trends Panel Report, a worldwide consensus for a phase-out of the ozone-destroying chemicals began to gather momentum. Calls for the elimination of CFCs took on added urgency because of growing public concern, exacerbated by the long, sweltering summer of 1988, about the prospect of rapid climate warming. That the CFCs were greenhouse gases was bad enough. But since several greenhouse gases—carbon dioxide, methane, and others—partially offset the effect of CFCs on stratospheric ozone, any measures to reduce emissions of these gases in order to mitigate global warming would actually *aggravate* ozone destruction unless CFC concentrations were substantially reduced.

New studies during 1989 revealed additional grounds for concern. It appeared that emissions of methyl chloroform and carbon tetrachloride, both widely used solvents, could significantly increase stratospheric chlorine concentrations—even if CFCs were eliminated. Moreover, it was discovered that hydrochlorofluorocarbons (HCFCs), under development as promising substitutes for CFCs because of their lower ozone-depletion potential, could damage the ozone layer if their use were greatly expanded. A related chemical family, the hydrofluorocarbons (HFCs), also being studied as CFC alternatives, contained no chlorine to harm the ozone layer but did have a greenhouse effect. Thus, in the eyes of many observers, all of these chemicals could no longer be considered more than interim solutions.

Political discussions during late 1989 were dominated by the new scientific findings. A 1989 scientific report to the protocol parties summarized the concerns: unexpectedly large ozone losses over northern latitudes; the possible dilution effect on ozone over southern populated latitudes caused by the recurring Antarctic ozone hole; the potential for serious ozone loss over the Arctic; and an ominous new hypothesis that a large volcanic eruption could propel minute sulfate particles into the stratosphere, which could intensify chlorine's ozone-destroying effect over other heavily populated regions.

Scientific analyses indicated that if existing atmospheric concentrations of chlorine and bromine were merely stabilized, the Antarctic ozone loss would be perpetual. In order for ozone levels over Antarctica gradually to recover, and to avoid possibly crossing similar unforeseen atmospheric thresholds in the future, it would be necessary to restore atmospheric chlorine concentrations (then at three parts per billion and rising) to levels at least as low as those prevailing in the early 1970s—or two parts per billion. And to bring about this gradual recuperation—a process that would in any event take decades—would require eliminating all CFCs, halons, methyl chloroform, and carbon tetrachloride, as well as strictly limiting reliance on the HCFCs.

Many scientists were anxious about the uncertain consequences of delaying a return of the atmosphere to its previous state. The 1989 scientific report to the parties declared that a complete and global phase-out is "of paramount importance in protecting the ozone layer." The longer the delay in implementing a phase-out, the longer the recovery time for the ozone layer.

Prospects for Early Phase-Out

The signatories at Montreal sounded the death knell for an important part of the international chemical industry, with implications for billions of dollars in investment and hundreds of thousands of jobs in related sectors. The protocol did not simply prescribe reductions based on "best available technology," which had been a traditional accommodation to economic interests. Rather, the negotiators boldly established target dates for replacing products that had become synonymous with modern standards of living, in full knowledge that the technologies for accomplishing this did not then exist.

Industry's initial reactions were mixed. The CFC Alliance expressed concern in a September 1987 public statement that the treaty's reduction schedule "attempts to go too far, too fast, and far beyond that which is necessary based on current scientific understanding." The alliance initially estimated that implementing the protocol in the United States alone would cost $5–10 billion. In late 1987 and early 1988, evidence suggested that a few companies in Europe and the United States might be attempting to circumvent the treaty before it entered into force by establishing CFC production facilities in developing countries.

In general, however, it became evident even in the early months after Montreal that the protocol was moving industry in directions that two years earlier had been considered impossible. By providing CFC producers with the certainty that their market was destined to decline, the protocol unleashed the creative energy and considerable resources of the private sector to find alternatives. Significantly, du Pont had announced in 1986 that it could develop substitutes within about five years, but that "neither the marketplace nor regulatory policy . . . has provided the needed incentives" to justify the required investments.[6]

Following the treaty's signing, the chemical industry began the race for substitutes. Four months after the Montreal conference, several hundred industry representatives participated in a CFC trade fair in Washington. In cooperation with a small Florida company, AT&T announced a substitute for CFC 113, derived from citrus fruit, for cleaning electronic circuit boards. Du Pont unveiled plans to construct a pilot plant for a new generation of refrigerants. Du Pont also announced that it would build a facility in Britain to provide European markets with the CFC-free aerosols that had been standard in the United States for a decade. At the initiative of American companies, an international consortium was established to test

CFC substitutes for toxicity; the multimillion dollar cooperative program would soon include fourteen chemical companies from the United States, Europe, Japan, and South Korea.

The Montreal accord was clearly functioning as its designers
had intended: none of these actions would have occurred in
the absence of the protocol. However, with the release of the
alarming new scientific evidence in March 1988, the pace
quickened further. Perhaps the most dramatic immediate reaction came from du Pont—the world's largest producer of
CFCs—which announced that it would halt production of all
CFCs and halons by the end of the century.

As calls to eliminate CFCs multiplied in parliaments and the
media, the international chemical and related industries intensified efforts to adapt to the evolving situation. In September
1988 the CFC Alliance declared its support for a phase-out.
Following du Pont, other major U.S. and European companies
stated they would cease producing CFCs. Food-packaging industries announced plans to stop using CFCs in the manufacture of disposable plastic containers. American automakers
voluntarily accepted new EPA standards to permit increased
use of recycled CFCs in automobile air conditioners. British
plastic foam insulation manufacturers agreed to an early
phase-out. Similar developments were reported from other
major producing and consuming countries.

As time passed, it became clear that industry's claims regarding the costs and difficulties of adapting to new regulations had been greatly overstated. Stimulated by the market
incentives furnished by the new protocol, industry began de-
ploying its technical resources to find solutions rather than to
obstruct action. Before long, entrepreneurs were coming forth
with previously unanticipated technologies. Even by late 1988,
most observers agreed that a substantial reduction in *combined*
CFC and halon use—at least 50 percent—could be accomplished relatively quickly and at little cost.

Aerosols, which still accounted for about a third of global
CFC consumption, were obvious candidates for early elimination. Ironically, consistent with its perception of the mounting
danger to the ozone layer, the U.S. government had promoted

large production cuts for the protocol knowing that it would
be much harder for American industry than for the EC to comply. Since aerosols still comprised over half of European CFC
production, EC chemical companies could easily attain the
protocol's 50 percent reduction goal far in advance of the
1998–99 treaty timetable. And that is precisely what happened: the European chemical companies, which for over a
decade had been informing their governments that CFCs were
indispensable in spray cans, discovered after Montreal that an
American-style aerosol ban made sense after all.

Emissions from CFC 113 solvents in the electronics and
other industries, which had grown to about 16 percent of
global consumption, could be cut substantially by a combination of substitutes and better containment and recycling practices. Similarly, reductions in CFC use for plastic foam production, which amounted to about one-fourth of global
consumption, appeared technically feasible through recycling
and substitution.

For refrigeration and air conditioning, however, which absorbed 25 percent of the world's CFC consumption, practical
replacements were not yet obvious—and this was the fastest
growing sector. There were also no alternatives to halons, although confining them to their most essential uses, and eliminating such wasteful practices as spraying areas purely for test
purposes, could bring some reductions.

Although substantial cutbacks in the treaty-controlled substances appeared feasible to most observers, prospects for
total elimination aroused more controversy. Environmental
groups minimized the costs and difficulties of a rapid phase-
out. Other analysts, noting that CFCs were employed in hundreds of manufacturing processes, raised concerns that replacements represented a major technological challenge and
might be both less effective and more expensive.

Initial research indicated, for example, that replacing CFCs
with substitute technologies would in some cases, particularly
refrigeration, consume more energy—which would conflict
with the energy conservation needed to counteract greenhouse warming. Another major problem was servicing existing

equipment designed to use CFCs: in the United States alone, an estimated 100 million refrigerators, 90 million air-conditioned cars and trucks, and tens of thousands of large air-conditioned commercial buildings could be replaced only gradually.

By mid-1989 a special technology assessment panel, convened by UNEP and consisting of experts from governments, industry, and research institutions, concluded that it was at least "technically feasible" to substantially phase out CFCs, methyl chloroform, and carbon tetrachloride by the end of the century; the panel could not agree on a phase-out date for halons because of the continued unavailability of prospective substitutes. The costs of phase-out would include research and development, safety and toxicity testing, new capital investment, and new operational costs. The expert panel concluded that very rapid phase-out (much less than ten years) would cost substantially more than a slower schedule, mainly due to premature abandonment of capital goods. On the other hand, based on past experience, continuing rapid innovation could mean that any cost projections based on existing technologies were likely to be overestimated.

In any event, based on intergovernmental discussions held under UNEP auspices, it was clear that the Montreal Protocol would be substantially strengthened at the 1990 Meeting of Parties. The originally controlled CFCs and halons would be phased out more rapidly than any of the Montreal negotiators had dreamed possible. And new chemicals would be added to the regulatory list, reflecting the greater scientific understanding that had developed since the treaty's signing in 1987.

Developing Countries—An Unfair Burden?

One of the premises of the Montreal Protocol was that developing countries would be encouraged to join if they were permitted a modest increase in use of CFCs and halons during the transition to new technologies. The protocol provided a ten-year grace period, during which any developing country with per capita annual consumption below 0.3 kilograms would be permitted to rise to this level "in order to meet its basic domestic needs." This quantity represented approximately one-third of the existing per capita consumption in Europe and the United States, or about two-thirds of the targeted level in the industrialized countries after their own cutbacks were made.

Both during and after the negotiations, a number of developing countries had been at the forefront in demonstrating commitment to protecting the ozone layer. Mexico, the first nation to ratify the protocol, had moved quickly to reduce imports and production. Venezuela convened a conference of Latin American countries to promote implementation of the treaty. Egypt announced that its only CFC-using factory would switch to other products. In Indonesia, the environment minister blocked an application for the country's first CFC facility. Kenya and Thailand announced plans to limit imports.

By 1989, however, many developing countries appeared to be having second thoughts about the equity of the treaty's arrangements. Industrialized countries, with less than 25 percent of the world's population, were consuming close to 85 percent of CFCs. On average, their per capita consumption was nearly twenty times greater than that of the developing nations. For China, the world's most populous country, the disparity was even greater: its per capita CFC consumption was only one-fortieth that of the EC and the United States. In effect, use of these chemicals for decades had made the industrialized countries wealthier while inadvertently building up an environmental threat to the entire planet.

In the developing countries, products made with or containing CFCs, especially refrigeration and air conditioning, were now considered essential to raising living standards. These countries wanted assurances that their populations would neither be deprived of the benefits of these chemicals nor have to pay more for equivalent substances and technologies— thereby enriching the very chemical industries that had created the ozone problem in the first place. Governments of developing countries expressed growing anxiety that the drive toward a phase-out of CFCs would take a toll on their standards of living and economic prospects. They argued that additional technical and financial assistance would be needed to enable them to implement the protocol's obligations.

Potential incremental burdens to developing countries for participating in the global effort to repair the ozone layer fell into several categories. One concern was that low-cost supplies of CFCs might not continue to be available to developing countries during the transitional period in which they were allowed to expand their use of these substances. Other additional costs might include new technology (patents and royalties); conversion of existing CFC facilities to new processes; and prices of CFC substitutes, products, and associated capital equipment. Some developing countries also felt that the protocol unfairly excluded them from possibly lucrative trade in products made with or containing CFCs.

To what extent were these concerns realistic? On the question of CFC prices, it seemed logical that unless substitutes were developed soon, rising demand in the industrialized countries would push short-term prices higher as they became scarcer due to the treaty-imposed reductions in output. Offsetting this, however, would be the effect of the protocol's provision forcing consumption in the industrialized countries to decline at a faster pace than production, thereby creating excess capacity to supply the relatively small transitional needs of developing nations. Further, as research costs were recovered and economies of scale and competition had their effect, the prices of substitute products and technologies would probably drop by the time developing countries needed them in quantity. Indeed, substitutes and new technologies might even turn out to be cheaper and more efficient than CFCs, as had been the case with aerosol sprays.

How much damage potential demand for CFCs and halons in the developing countries might cause was also uncertain. If all developing countries were to expand consumption in ten years from existing insignificant levels to the treaty-imposed ceiling of 0.3 kilograms per capita, the resultant increase could dwarf cutbacks in the industrialized countries. But it was questionable whether the economic realities in the developing nations would allow such an enormous growth in CFC demand over the foreseeable future.

In 1989 the technology assessment panel established by the parties to the protocol concluded that the growing refrigeration needs in developing countries would require less CFCs than had been originally feared. Domestic refrigeration was only 1 percent of global CFC consumption, and developing countries accounted for only a small fraction of that. Therefore, even if household refrigerator use in all developing countries were to grow by 30 percent annually, the panel estimated that this use would amount by the year 2000 to a demand for CFCs equivalent to under 2 percent of global 1986 consumption.

This new assessment notwithstanding, the longer-term potential for developing countries to undermine the effectiveness of the Montreal Protocol could not be dismissed. Their proportion of the world's population was over 75 percent and growing, and CFC technology was inexpensive and uncomplicated. As factories could be small in scale, rapidly constructed, and enjoy a relatively fast payback, some developing nations might be tempted to build their own plants rather than purchase more expensive substitute technology or products. The treaty's trade sanctions were an irrelevant impediment for countries with large potential domestic markets. Moreover, if many of these nations stayed outside the protocol (and therefore were not bound by the trade restrictions), new producers in other developing countries could enter the export markets in Africa, Asia, and Latin America currently dominated by European producers and du Pont overseas affiliates.

Developing countries, however, could not themselves regard continued emissions of CFCs and halons with indifference: they also had a stake in protecting the ozone layer. Even though harmful ultraviolet radiation would cause greater incidence of skin cancer among lightly pigmented populations, all peoples are susceptible to suppression of the immune response system and to eye cataracts. Indeed, developing-country populations faced increased risks because of their poorer general health conditions and less adequate medical facilities.

Possible declines in agricultural and fisheries productivity would also have a disproportionate impact on the developing world, where poverty and food shortages were already common. Similarly, as more ultraviolet radiation reaches the tropics than elsewhere, increased levels could inflict relatively more severe damage to materials, plastics, paints, and buildings.

A 1987 RAND Corporation study predicted that the thirteen developing countries with the largest demand for CFCs by the year 2000 would be, in order of potential use: China, India, Brazil, Saudi Arabia, South Korea, Indonesia, Nigeria, Mexico, Turkey, Argentina, Venezuela, Algeria, and Iran. As of April 2, 1990, fifteen months after the Montreal Protocol entered into force, only three of the thirteen had ratified: Mexico, Nigeria, and Venezuela. In all, twenty-four developing nations were parties to the protocol by that date, and an additional seven had signed but not yet ratified.

If some reasonable accommodation could be found to allay the anxieties of developing nations concerning likely additional burdens to their economies, it is probable that most, if not all, potentially large users of CFCs would join the protocol. This economic issue was clearly at the heart of the developing nations' concerns. Led by Mexico, they proposed during intergovernmental discussions in late 1989 a binding mechanism that would ensure compulsory contributions by industrialized nations to finance technology transfer and cover any incremental costs of phasing out ozone-depleting substances. This assistance, they argued, should be additional to, and not a diversion of, existing aid flows.

The industrialized countries acknowledged that the arguments had merit on equity grounds. They also recognized that their own efforts to protect the ozone layer could be jeopardized in the long run if the developing world did not, or could not, cooperate. Assisting the poorer countries to by-pass CFC technology would be a good investment when measured against the probable costs of major damage to the ozone layer.

But parties to the debate had no idea how much money would be necessary. Some activists in developing countries apparently hoped to use the ozone layer—and, by extension, the climate change issue—as a lever for redressing North-South economic inequalities. Enormous resource transfers were suggested by some quarters as the price for enlisting developing nation cooperation in protecting the global environment.

In a more pragmatic spirit, the parties to the protocol commissioned specific country case studies to identify the actual needs and costs of technology transfer and other adjustment factors. Donor governments wanted assurances that additional financial aid would be used to meet the protocol's objectives. They also mistrusted the idea of creating new institutions outside their control, preferring instead to channel assistance through bilateral aid programs or existing multilateral institutions such as the World Bank.

There was no denying the potential conflict between the aim of broad participation by developing nations in the Montreal Protocol and the need to maintain incentives for the private sector to undertake research and development of new products and technologies. Ways had to be found to compensate for intellectual property rights, and to enable industry to recoup its costs without monopolistically exploiting developing countries. Direct compensatory aid to developing nations, technical training, joint business ventures, direct investment, subsidized licensing, tax relief for companies working with developing countries—all of these were possible options that were being explored. What was clear was that resolving this issue was essential to bringing the major developing nations under the protocol's regime—and that doing so would require new forms of cooperation among governments, industry, and the international aid community. The intergovernmental talks sponsored by UNEP, which also involved the World Bank, UN Development Program, and other multilateral institutions, argued well for progress also on this front.

Lessons for a New Global Diplomacy

The problem of protecting the stratospheric ozone layer presented an unusual challenge to diplomacy. Military power was irrelevant. Economic might was not decisive either: it did not take great wealth or sophisticated technology to produce large quantities of ozone-destroying chemicals. Traditional notions of national sovereignty became questionable because local decisions and activities could affect the well-being of the entire planet. The very nature of ozone depletion meant that no single country or group of countries, however powerful, could effectively solve the problem. Without far-ranging cooperation, the efforts of some nations to protect the ozone layer would be vitiated.

The Montreal Protocol was by no means inevitable; knowledgeable observers had long believed it would be impossible to achieve. The ozone negotiators confronted formidable political, economic, and psychological obstacles. The dangers of ozone depletion could touch every nation and all life on earth over periods far beyond politicians' normal time horizons. But although the potential consequences were grave, they could, at the time, neither be measured nor predicted with certitude. The concept was not obvious: a perfume spray in Paris destroyed an invisible gas in the stratosphere and thereby contributed to skin cancer deaths and species extinction half a world distant and several generations in the future.

Against this background, entrenched industrial interests claimed that new regulations would cause immense economic dislocations. Some governments allowed commercial self-interest to influence their scientific positions, and the scientific uncertainty was used as an excuse for delaying hard decisions. Technological solutions were either nonexistent or were considered unacceptable by most major governments.

Thus many political leaders were prepared to accept potential long-term environmental risks rather than to impose the certain short-term costs entailed in limiting products seen as important for modern standards of living. Short-range political and economic concerns were formidable obstacles to cooperative international action based upon the ozone-depletion theory.

Nevertheless, the international community was ultimately successful in its approach to the problem of the stratospheric ozone layer. This experience suggests several elements of a new kind of diplomacy that is needed to address such similar global ecological threats as greenhouse warming.

First, scientists must assume an unaccustomed but critical role in international negotiations. Without modern science and technology, the world would have remained unaware of an ozone problem until it was too late. Science became the driving force behind ozone policy. The formation of a commonly accepted body of data and analyses and the narrowing of the ranges of uncertainty were prerequisites to a political solution among negotiating parties initially far apart. In effect, a community of scientists from many nations, dedicated to scientific objectivity, developed through their research an interest in protecting the planet's ozone layer that transcended divergent national interests. In this process, the scientists had to assume some responsibility for analyzing the implications of their findings for alternative regulatory strategies. Close collaboration between scientists and key government officials who became convinced of the long-term dangers ultimately prevailed over more parochial and short-run interests of national politicians.

Second, the ozone history demonstrates the importance of political leaders taking action while there are still scientific uncertainties, based on a responsible balancing of the risks and costs of acting or not acting. Unfortunately, current tools of economic analysis are not adequate for this task and are in urgent need of reform: the customary methods of measuring national income and growth do not satisfactorily reflect ecological costs—especially those in the future. Politicians need to resist a tendency to assign excessive credibility to self-serving economic interests that demand scientific certainty and insist that dangers are remote and, therefore, unlikely. By the time the evidence on such issues as the ozone layer and climate change is beyond dispute, the damage may be irreversible and it may be too late to avoid serious harm to human life and draconian future costs to society. The signatories at Montreal imposed substantial short-run economic dislocations even though the evidence was incomplete; the prudence of their decision was demonstrated when the scientists' models turned out to have underestimated prospective ozone losses.

Third, educating and mobilizing public opinion can be a powerful force to generate pressure for action on often hesitant politicians. The interest of the media in the ozone issue and the use of television and press by U.S. diplomats, environmental groups, and legislators greatly influenced governmental decisions. Aroused consumers brought about the collapse of the CFC aerosol market. In their educational efforts, it is worth noting that the proponents of ozone layer protection generally avoided invoking apocalypse, resisting temptations to overstate their case in order to capture public attention. Exaggerated pronouncements could have damaged credibility and provided ammunition to those interest groups that wanted to delay action.

Fourth, leadership by UNEP and the U.S. government proved critical in mobilizing an international consensus. UNEP was indispensable in coordinating research efforts and informing world public opinion, and played a crucial catalytic and mediating role during the negotiating and implementation phases of the protocol. UNEP provided an objective international forum, free of the time-consuming debates on extraneous political issues that have too often marred the work of other UN bodies. For its part, the U.S. government financed major American and international scientific research; it then developed a comprehensive strategy for protecting the ozone layer and promoted its international acceptance with ingenuity and tenacity. As the largest emitter of both ozone-destroying chemicals and greenhouse gases, the United States has enormous influence on the policy considerations of other governments on these issues.

Fifth, it may be desirable for a leading country or group of countries to take preemptive environmental protection measures, even in advance of a global agreement. Such action can slow dangerous trends and thereby buy time for future negotiations and for development of technological solutions. Preemptive actions can serve to legitimize change and also set an example for possibly recalcitrant nations. Early adoption by the key industrialized nations of measures to mandate energy conservation and lower carbon dioxide emissions, for example, without waiting for prolonged negotiations on a global climate convention, could have a powerful impact in delaying greenhouse warming. The 1978 U.S. ban on aerosols relieved pressure on the ozone layer and lent greater credibility to the U.S. government when it later campaigned for even more stringent global controls. Although unilateral environmental protection might, in the short run, adversely affect a country's international competitiveness, it could also, through stimulating research into alternative technologies, give that country's industry a head start on the future. Moreover, short-term negative impacts could, if necessary, be offset by trade restrictions against products of trading partners that are not subject to comparable environmental controls. During the ozone protocol negotiations, the U.S. Congress threatened such action, which is permissible under the General Agreement on Tariffs and Trade if related to protection of health and the environment.

Sixth, environmental organizations and industry are important participants in the new diplomacy. The activities of both industry and citizens' groups in research, publicizing data, and lobbying governments influenced the international debate on the ozone problem. Environmental organizations can also play a future role as informal watchdogs over compliance by industry with international accords. Industry's involvement and cooperation is essential, since society ultimately depends on it to provide the technical solutions. It should also not be overlooked that individuals can make a surprisingly significant difference. From the overall leadership on ozone provided by UNEP's Mostafa Tolba, to the roles of individual scientists, negotiators, environmentalists, and industrialists, it was personal ideas, decisions, and actions that often proved critical to the successful outcome.

Seventh, a regulatory agreement works best when it employs realistic market incentives to encourage technological innovation. Technology is dynamic, and not, as implied by those who resist change, a static element. But left completely on its own, the market may not necessarily bring forth the right technologies for environmental protection. The ozone protocol set targets that initially appeared difficult but were in fact achievable for most of industry—thereby averting monolithic industrial opposition that might have delayed international action. By getting the protocol on the books with a goal of 50 percent reductions, the negotiators effectively signaled the market that research into solutions would now be profitable. Competitive forces then took over, and the later phase-out decisions became technically easier.

Eighth, economic and structural inequalities among countries must be adequately reflected in any international regulatory regime. In the longer run, the developing countries, with their huge and growing populations, could undermine efforts both to protect the ozone layer and to forestall greenhouse warming. They did not cause these problems, and the rich nations that were responsible must now help them to implement the necessary environmental policies without sacrificing their hopes for improved standards of living. Under the leadership of UNEP, the parties to the Montreal Protocol were actively exploring ways of transferring the needed technology while preserving intellectual property rights and incentives for private entrepreneurship to develop new technologies.

Ninth, an international environmental agreement must strive for a "level playing field" among competing nations. While each country's specific regulatory strategies need not be identical, the economic effects should be equivalent. The debates involving the United States, the European Community, and importing nations over whether to control production or consumption of CFCs, described above, illustrated the importance of commercial considerations; the eventual compromise represented an effective balancing of interests. Other provisions of the protocol required initial CFC reductions that would be easier for European than for American producers (who had already eliminated aerosols ten years earlier); nevertheless, U.S. industry could accept this disadvantage because it was reasonably confident that its research superiority would develop substitutes for other CFC uses. Another example of the importance of commercial equity was the treaty's trade restrictions, which would make it difficult for countries to profit by not joining the protocol.

Tenth, the signing of a treaty is not necessarily the decisive event in a negotiation; the Montreal Protocol also broke new ground in its planning process. The complicated ozone protection issue was separated into manageable components, and informal collaborative efforts—workshops, conferences, consultations—laid the foundation for the eventual international consensus. Extensive scientific and diplomatic groundwork thus enabled the subsequent formal negotiations to move forward relatively rapidly.

And finally, unlike traditional international treaties that attempt to cement a status quo, the Montreal Protocol was deliberately designed as a dynamic and flexible instrument. The proponents of strong controls were pragmatic: they did not insist on a perhaps-optimal solution that might have unnecessarily prolonged the negotiations. Instead, they emphasized getting a reasonable agreement in place that could serve as a springboard for future action. By providing for periodic integrated scientific, environmental, economic, and technological assessments—the first of which was advanced in date to 1989 in response to the rapidly changing science—the negotiators made the treaty readily adaptable to evolving conditions. Indeed, the essence of the Montreal Protocol is that, far from being a static solution, it constitutes an *ongoing process.*

UNEP's Mostafa Tolba has observed: "The mechanisms we design for the [Montreal] Protocol will—very likely—become the blueprint for the institutional apparatus designed to control greenhouse gases and adaptation to climate change."[7] In fact, this appears to be happening. The Intergovernmental Panel on Climate Change—established in late 1988 with participation from both public and private sectors and multiple scientific, economic, and policy workshops—is analogous to the fact-gathering phase before the Montreal Protocol. And an international consensus has developed for work to proceed toward a framework climate convention and implementing protocols aimed at mitigating and adapting to the effects of greenhouse warming. In this work, precedents from the successful ozone experience will be relevant. Indeed, the Montreal Protocol itself exemplifies how interim progress can be made on the climate problem by means of a constituent protocol; the potential significance of such partial steps can be gauged from a NASA estimate that if CFCs had continued to increase at the growth rates of the 1970s, they would by 1989 have surpassed the greenhouse impact of carbon dioxide.

In conclusion, in the realm of international relations there will always be resistance to change and there will always be uncertainties—political, economic, scientific, psychological. Faced with a new generation of global environmental threats, governments must act while some major questions remain unresolved. The story of the ozone treaty may signal a fundamental shift in attitude among critical segments of society when confronted with uncertain but potentially grave threats that require coordinated international action. In achieving the Montreal accord, consensus was forged and decisions were made on a balancing of probabilities—and the risks of waiting for more complete evidence were finally deemed to be too great. In the real world of ambiguity and imperfect knowledge, the Montreal Protocol may thus be the forerunner of an evolving global diplomacy, as sovereign nations seek ways of dealing with uncertain dangers and accepting common responsibility for stewardship of the planet.

Summary

In 1974 scientists theorized that the remote layer of unstable ozone molecules that protects all life from harmful ultraviolet radiation could be depleted by a family of anthropogenic chemicals with growing uses in many products synonymous with modern standards of living. Over strong opposition from entrenched economic interests, an international treaty was forged that imposed substantial short-term costs in order to protect human health and the environment against speculative future dangers—dangers that rested on theories rather than proven facts. This landmark achievement offers insights for addressing other global environmental challenges where co-operative action is necessary before complete scientific evidence is at hand. The ozone issue reflected the critical contributions that can be made by national leadership and multilateral diplomacy in mobilizing an international consensus. The accord broke new ground in its treatment of scientific uncertainties, long-term risks, commercial rivalries, and North-South relations. The treaty's innovative negotiating process and its creative provisions, emphasizing market incentives and flexibility, were useful precedents. The ozone history also demonstrated the importance of an educated media and public opinion, the growing role of environmental and industry groups, and, perhaps most crucial for the future, the need for closer links between scientists and policy makers.

Appendix A

Protection of the Ozone Layer

Chronology of Key Events

Late 1974   Theories of CFC/chlorine-induced ozone layer depletion published.

March 1977   Washington: U.S. hosts UNEP meeting that recommends "World Plan of Action on the Ozone Layer" and establishes annual science review.

1977   Ozone protection amendment to U.S. Clean Air Act.

March 1978   U.S. bans use of CFCs in nonessential aerosols, followed by Canada, Denmark, Finland, Norway, and Sweden.

1980   European Community reduces aerosol use by 30 percent and enacts capacity cap.

March 1985   Vienna: *Convention for the Protection of the Ozone Layer* adopted. Covers research, monitoring, and data exchange, but negotiators fail to complete protocol on CFC controls.

May 1985   British scientists publish data showing seasonal Antarctic ozone hole.

July 1986   WMO/UNEP assessment, *Atmospheric Ozone 1985,* published.

Dec. 1986   Geneva: first round of negotiations on ozone control protocol; subsequent sessions in February, April, June, and September 1987.

June 1987   Venice Economic Summit declaration lists stratospheric ozone depletion first among environmental concerns.

Sept. 1987   Montreal: final round of negotiations—*Protocol on Substances that Deplete the Ozone Layer* adopted.

Jan. 1988   Washington: trade fair on CFC substitutes.

March 1988   Washington: Ozone Trends Panel releases new evidence that CFCs are causing both global ozone depletion and the Antarctic ozone hole.

March 1988   Du Pont announces phase-out of CFCs.

April 1988   U.S. ratifies Montreal Protocol.

Sept. 1988   Vienna Convention enters into force.

Dec. 1988   Commission of the European Communities together with eight of twelve member countries ratifies Montreal Protocol. (Other four members ratify separately.)

Jan. 1, 1989 Montreal Protocol enters into force.

May 1989   Helsinki: First Meeting of Parties to Vienna Convention and Montreal Protocol. Declaration calls for complete phase-out of CFCs and halons.

Aug. 1989–May 1990   Nairobi, Geneva: meetings of working groups to consider revisions to protocol.

June 1990   London: Second Meeting of Parties to Vienna Convention and Montreal Protocol.

Appendix B

Montreal Protocol on Substances That Deplete the Ozone Layer

Summary of Provisions
(as signed on September 16, 1987)

- Controlled substances include CFCs 11, 12, 113, 114, and 115, and halons 1211, 1301, and 2402. (For purposes of calculating control levels, the production, imports, and exports of each chemical are weighted by an individual ozone depletion potential estimated for each chemical.)

- Entry into force (EIF) requires at least eleven signatory nations representing at least two-thirds of estimated 1986 global consumption of controlled substances.

- Consumption and production of CFCs will be frozen at 1986 levels beginning six months after the date of EIF. (Consumption is defined as production *plus* imports *minus* exports to parties.)

- Consumption and production of halons will be frozen at 1986 levels beginning three years after EIF.

- Consumption and production of CFCs will be reduced to 80 percent of 1986 levels beginning in the period July 1993 to June 1994.

- Consumption and production of CFCs will be further reduced to 50 percent of 1986 levels beginning in the period July 1998 to June 1999.

- An additional 10 percent of production will be allowed for purposes of supplying developing nations until June 30, 1998; On July 1, 1998, this percentage increases to 15 percent.

- Low-consuming developing nations are allowed to increase consumption up to 0.3 kilograms per capita for a period of ten years in order to meet "basic domestic needs." After ten years, the developing nations must follow the reduction schedule.

- Scientific, environmental, economic, and technological assessments will be made beginning in 1990 and at least every four years thereafter.

- Import of any controlled substance in bulk from nonparty states is prohibited beginning one year after EIF.

• Import from nonparty states of products containing CFCs is banned beginning four years after EIF.

• Within five years after EIF, parties will determine the feasibility of banning or restricting trade in products made with CFCs.

• Canceling the 50 percent reduction step would require a vote of two-thirds of parties representing two-thirds of the calculated level of consumption of all parties to the protocol.

• Other adjustments and reductions require a vote of two-thirds of parties representing 50 percent of consumption.

• Addition of new controlled substances to the agreement requires a simple majority of two-thirds of the parties.

Notes

[1]Albritton, D. L., et. al., *Stratospheric Ozone: The State of the Science and NOAA's Current and Future Research,* Washington, DC: NOAA (1987), p. 1.

[2]Rowland, F. S., "A Threat to Earth's Protective Shield," *EPA Journal* 12: 10 (December 1986), 4.

[3]U.S. Environmental Protection Agency, "Protection of Stratospheric Ozone," *Federal Register* 52:239 (December 14, 1987), 47492.

[4]Tolba, M.K., "Facing a Distant Threat," Nairobi: United Nations Environment Programme (UNEP), Information 87/21, October 5, 1987.

[5]U.S. Senate, Committee on Foreign Relations, *Ozone Protocol,* Executive Report 100-14, Feb. 19, 1988, Statement of Lee M. Thomas, Administrator, U.S. EPA, p. 61; "President Signs Protocol on Ozone-Depleting Substances," Text of President Reagan's Statement, April 5, 1988, cited in *Department of State Bulletin,* June 1988, p. 30; U.S. Senate, *ibid.,* Statement of Senator George Mitchell, p. 53.

[6]"Du Pont Position Statement on the Chlorofluorocarbon-Ozone-Greenhouse Issues," *Environmental Conservation* 13:4 (Winter 1986), 363.

[7]Tolba, M.K., "The Tools to Build a Global Response," statement to meeting of the Working Group of Parties to the Montreal Protocol, UNEP Press Release, Nairobi, August 21, 1989.

5

Energy and Climate Change

GEORGE W. RATHJENS

An Introduction to the Greenhouse Problem

W ith the oil shocks of the 1970s, energy policy became an important issue in the United States and most other developed countries, and there developed an impetus to reduce dependence on imported oil through conservation and emphasis on alternative means of energy supply and use. In

GEORGE W. RATHJENS is a professor of political science at the Massachusetts Institute of Technology, where he has taught and conducted research since 1968. He has been much involved in arms control and defense policy since 1953 and in energy and environmental policy since the mid-1970s, serving with the president's science adviser, as chief scientist and deputy director of the Defense Advanced Research Projects Agency, as special assistant to the director of the United States Arms Control and Disarmament Agency, director of the Systems Evaluation Division of the Institute for Defense Analysis, and on special assignment in the Department of State. He is chair of the Council for a Livable World, past chair of the Federation of American Scientists, and a fellow of the American Academy of Arts and Sciences.

the trade-off studies that followed, and in debate and legislation, much attention was given to the undesirable effects of burning coal: the emission of sulfur and nitrogen oxides and their destructive effects on ecology and health. There were also references to the fact that the carbon dioxide (CO_2) content of the atmosphere would be increased by such combustion, and that of other carbonaceous materials, and that this could lead to a change in world climate, a global warming. When, during the 1980s, summer temperatures, at least in the United States, were noticeably warmer than people were used to, concern about a causal linkage between energy use and climate change increased. Study efforts accelerated and the results got widespread attention. Most of the serious analytical work and a spate of popular articles suggested that if man's consumption of fossil fuels has not already committed us to significant climatic change, continued use of such fuels and changes in the amounts of some other trace gases in the atmosphere will.

This is not a new thesis. It has long been realized that were the earth not endowed with an atmosphere containing a substantial amount of carbon dioxide it would be covered with ice, and be about 34 degrees C. colder. That it is, on average, as warm as it is, is due to the so-called greenhouse effect. This arises because CO_2 and water vapor, along with some other trace gases in the atmosphere, are nearly transparent to light in the visible part of the electromagnetic spectrum, where solar radiation peaks, but are strongly absorbing in some parts of the infrared spectrum. Because an atmosphere containing these greenhouse gases (GHGs) envelopes the earth, absorbing some of the infrared radiation from it, the earth's surface is heated to a significantly higher temperature than would be the case for a planet without such an atmosphere. This is essential for the maintenance of thermal equilibrium,[1] i.e., so that the net outward heat flux from the earth-atmosphere system will balance the heat flux from the sun.

If the amount of CO_2 in the atmosphere were to change, one would expect the equilibrium temperature of the earth to change with it. Although it is by no means obvious that relatively low CO_2 concentrations led to the ice ages, or were even important causal factors, there is a strong correlation between atmospheric CO_2 levels and global average temperatures in ice ages and interglacial periods[2] (see Figure 1). Measurements of the surface temperatures of Mars and Venus, where the concentrations of CO_2 are much lower and much higher respectively than in the case of the earth, are also consistent

FIGURE 1.

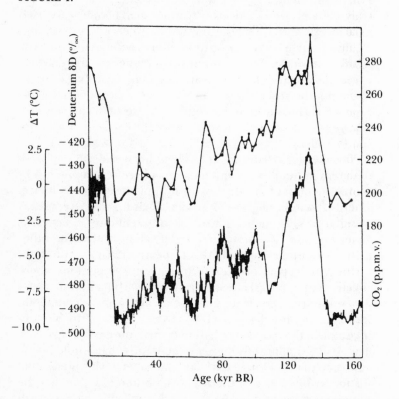

Carbon dioxide levels and temperatures over the last 160,000 years from Vostok 5 Ice Core in Antarctica. The temperature scale is for Antarctica; the corresponding amplitude of global temperatures swings is thought to be about five degrees Centigrade.

with the greenhouse theory. Even after allowing for the differences in the intensity of radiant energy from the sun due to their different distances from it, Mars is colder and Venus much hotter than would be the case were their atmospheres similar to that enveloping the earth.

But change in average temperatures is only the beginning of the story as regards the impact of GHG loading on climate. The second-order effects—patterns of cloud cover, precipitation, winds, ocean currents, and glaciation—depend sensitively on average surface temperatures and, notably, on seasonal and geographic *differences* in temperatures.

Until the industrial revolution, the composition of the earth's atmosphere changed slowly—the CO_2 concentration increased from about 195 parts per million (ppm) during the last ice age, 18,000 years ago, to 280 ppm in the late 1700s; but it has been increasing at an accelerating rate since then. It is now at about 352 ppm and increasing at about 1.2 ppm per year (see Figure 2). Additionally, other greenhouse gases arising from human industrial and agricultural activities—notably methane, nitrous oxide, tropospheric ozone, and chlorofluorocarbons (CFCs)—are being added to the earth's atmosphere at accelerating rates, and are now estimated to be about as significant in their collective impact on climate as the changes in CO_2 composition that have occurred in the last century.

Most of the change in atmospheric GHG concentrations is directly attributable to energy use. Perhaps 80 percent of the CO_2 increase is due to the burning of fossil fuels (the remainder, mostly to the burning of tropical forests and production of cement); some of the methane increase is due to mining of coal, leakage from gas pipelines, wells, and refineries; the tropospheric ozone is due mainly to the use of internal combustion engines, which are major factors in the creation of photochemical smog; and some of the CFC loading is due to leakage from refrigerating and air conditioning equipment. Thus the "greenhouse problem" is seen as largely one of energy use. And if one is concerned about the possible effects of energy use on *global* climate, the greenhouse issue *is* the prob-

FIGURE 2. Carbon Dioxide Concentrations at Mauna Loa and Fossil CO₂ Emissions

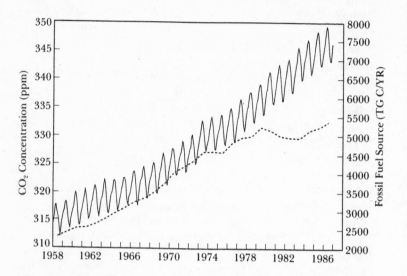

The solid line depicts monthly concentrations of atmospheric CO₂ at Mauna Loa Observatory, Hawaii. The yearly oscillation is explained mainly by the annual cycle of photosynthesis and respiration of plants in the northern hemisphere. The steadily increasing concentration of atmospheric CO₂ at Mauna Loa since the 1950s is caused primarily by the CO₂ inputs from fossil fuel combustion (dashed line). Note that CO₂ concentrations have continued to increase since 1979, despite relatively constant emissions; this is because emissions have remained substantially larger than net removal, which is primarily by ocean uptake.

lem. (Local climate can be affected by the diversion of rivers and creation of reservoirs for hydroelectric power generation, and by high power output in urban areas.)

What are likely to be the climatic effects of changing GHG loading of the atmosphere? What might be the effects of the consequent climatic changes on humans? What can be done, what is likely to be done, and what should be done to mitigate adverse effects and/or to adapt to them? All these questions demand serious attention by scientists and policy makers, now that it seems likely that human activities, including particularly the use of energy, will lead to significant changes in climate some time in the next century.

But there is still considerable doubt about how large and serious the effects might be. Although substantial efforts have been made to model climate, the problems are formidable, and the results so far are anything but definitive. There are many nonlinear processes, competing effects, and feedback loops involved, so that great uncertainty attaches to attempts to estimate the magnitude of effects and, in some instances, even the sign.

The problem is particularly complicated because so much of the earth's surface is covered by water and because, at the temperatures that obtain on the earth, water is present in significant quantities in all three phases: gas, liquid, and solid. The formation, dissipation, and characteristics of clouds are consequently important determinants of climate and so, too, is the transfer of heat and CO_2 within the oceans, and between the oceans and the atmosphere. Unfortunately, some of the processes are poorly understood. For example, it is not yet clear whether clouds have a net heating or cooling effect. They reflect short wave solar radiation, tending to cool the earth, but they also absorb longer wave radiation, thereby acting as GHGs do, warming it. In trying to estimate the effects on climate of clouds, one must then try to estimate the difference between two large quantities, which difference is likely to be much more significant than the *direct* effects of the GHGs. Since the distribution of clouds is likely to depend in very complicated ways on temperatures at the earth's surface and in the atmosphere, there is the possibility of feedback effects of GHG-induced warming being either positive or negative; in fact, of both occurring simultaneously, varying regionally. There are many other complicating effects. To give one other example, again relating to the special role of water on our planet, warming will tend to melt ice and snow cover, reducing the earth's albedo, causing the earth to absorb more solar energy, hence causing more warming. Thus there is a positive feedback effect. But warming may also lead to increased evaporation of water from both land surfaces and the sea, and consequently to increased precipitation and greater snow accretion in polar regions, and with that, to an increase in albedo and negative feedback.

There are other great difficulties in modeling, arising from a paucity of observations in some parts of the world, and from the fact that capabilities of presently available computers are so limited that it is not possible even to attempt estimation of global climatic variation on grid scales of less than a few hundred kilometers. Yet we know that the variations on scales smaller than this can be dramatic. No "average" climate for a region like California can be very meaningful. Consider, for example, the great variation in going from the Pacific coast to the agricultural Central Valley and then on to the Sierra Nevada mountains, a distance of less than 300 kilometers.

From this very limited discussion, it should be clear that the state of the art in modeling climate does not now permit confident prediction of the likely consequences of increases in GHG loading for climate on a global scale, much less on regional bases. Having said this, there is agreement among those engaged in climate modeling on at least two important points, in addition to acceptance of the fact of increasing atmospheric GHG concentrations since the industrial revolution, and of a correlation between atmospheric CO_2 concentration and global temperatures on *geologic* time scales.

a) There is a significant disparity between, on the one hand, the amounts of CO_2 that are released to the atmosphere through combustion of fuels and the burning and decay of vegetation and, on the other, the increases that are measured in the atmosphere. Apparently, about half of the amounts released are removed through photosynthesis and absorption in sea water (and possibly by other mechanisms, unknown).

b) The ocean-atmosphere system is not now at anything like equilibrium. Of major importance is the fact that the heat capacity of the oceans—even of just the upper layers, where mixing time is of the order of a decade or two—is enormous. Accordingly, the oceans can act as a great "sink" for heat, which means that, on a global scale, the full heating effects of increasing levels of GHGs will be much delayed. Additionally, the removal of CO_2 by absorption in the oceans may also be delayed because of the long time constants for mixing of the surface and deeper layers. Because of these phenomena, it could be anywhere from one to several decades before the effects of recent releases of GHGs are fully reflected in climate change.

There seems, in addition, to be consensus, but by no means unanimity in the community, on the following:

c) Although comparison of satellite and surface-based measurements of temperatures over the last decade raise some doubts about the adequacy of the latter as a basis for reaching conclusions about long-term temperature trends, the average temperature of the earth *appears* to have increased by about 0.5 degrees C. over the last century (see Figure 3).

d) It will not likely be possible before the first decade of the next century to make meaningful estimates of regional climatic change with a resolution of better than a few hundred kilometers.

e) It now appears likely that an increase in CO_2 content to twice its preindustrial levels—or the equivalent in total increase in GHG accumulation—will result in an increase in average temperature of 1.5 to 4.5 degrees C. for the earth as a whole. Current trends in emission suggest that this loading may be realized by about 2035. (Dissenters suggest that the range of temperative increase could be an order of magnitude smaller, significantly because changes in cloud cover and characteristics may dwarf the *direct* effects of changes in GHG levels. On the other hand, increases in atmospheric water content with increasing temperature, not fully reflected in most modeling so far, could mean that warming could well be greater than the 1.5–4.5 degree estimate.)

FIGURE 3. Surface Air Temperature (Degrees Celsius)

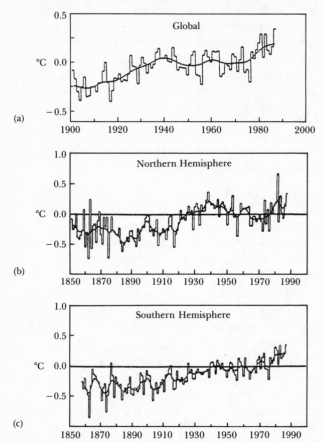

(a) Global surface air temperature, 1901–1987. This record incorporates measurements made both over land and from ships. The smooth curve shows ten-year Gaussian filtered values. The gradual warming during this period is not inconsistent with the increasing greenhouse gases during this period, but the large interannual variations and the relatively flat curve from 1940 to 1975 show that there are also other important causes of climate change.

(b,c) Land surface air temperatures, 1851–1987 for the northern hemisphere and 1857–1987 for the southern hemisphere. Note the larger interannual variability before 1900, when data coverage was much more sparse.

f) It is probable that however great the average increase, it will be several times as large in the polar regions and correspondingly less in the tropics.

g) With a doubling of the GHG loading, average sea level is likely to rise by 0.2 to 0.5 meters.

h) With such doubling, annual precipitation would likely increase overall by a few percent, but there would be marked changes in precipitation patterns. There would likely be increases in high latitudes and the coastal regions of the temperate zones. In the interior regions of the temperate zones, there would likely be a decrease in moisture content in soils and possibly in precipitation.

Projecting Energy Use

All this suggests that there is a very broad consensus in the geophysical community that continuing increases in GHG content of the atmosphere will likely lead to climate change that will at least be noticeable sometime in the next century and that may have great impact on humans and their environment, but that there is great uncertainty about the magnitude of change as a function of the level, and the rate of increase, of GHGs. There is also great uncertainty about future patterns of energy use, and other factors that determine GHG levels, and projecting those factors over decades, which is what is desired for policy prescription, turns out to be of about the same order of difficulty and the results, so far, about as uncertain, as attempting to forecast climate as a function of GHG loading.

Until the oil shocks of 1973, one might have had a more sanguine view of energy forecasting, at least as regards the United States. Electricity use increased at a nearly constant rate of 6.9 percent per year from 1920 until the early 1970s (5.5 percent per capita per year), something quite remarkable considering that the period included the Great Depression and World War II. And, utilities came to accept this rate of increase as a basis for planning. More significantly for our purposes, the elasticity of energy use with respect to growth in the gross national product (GNP) was stable from the early 1940s until the early 1970s: with each increase of 1 percent in GNP, energy use increased by about 0.9 percent. From this—and from crossnational comparisons of the ratios of energy use to GNP (see Table 1)—there developed a fairly widespread view that the two were inherently tightly coupled: increase in energy use was seen as essential to economic growth, including notably for societies making the transition from poverty to affluence.

But in all of the Organization for Economic Cooperation and Development (OECD) countries, both the trend in electricity use as a function of time and the correlation between growth in energy use and GNP broke after 1973. The rate of increase in use of electricity in the American economy has been about one-third since then of what it had been (and the rate per capita, about one-quarter); and the rate of increase in energy use with increasing GNP has dropped by a factor of about ten. It is noteworthy that corresponding changes did not occur in the centrally planned economies. The energy elasticity to GNP remained at about 1.25 for the Soviet Union, just about the same value that obtained from 1960 to the mid-1970s, and for Eastern Europe, the elasticity actually increased slightly.

Why the energy to GNP elasticity for Western economies has dropped so dramatically is not entirely clear. Three factors, all largely absent in the case of the centrally planned economies, have presumably been important: structural changes, i.e., increases in services relative to energy-intensive industries; legislative and regulatory actions designed to reduce energy use, e.g., the establishment of corporate automobile fuel economy (CAFE) standards; and consumer and industrial responsiveness to increasing costs of energy. (The short-term responsiveness of industry, in particular, seems to have been much greater than many analysts expected.) Whatever the explanation, a consequence has been that nearly all forecasts of energy use in Western economies made before about 1975 now seem much inflated. Thus projections for U.S. energy requirements for the year 1985 that were made in 1972

TABLE 1. Energy Intensity

**1986 Energy Consumption per $ (1980) of GNP
(kilojoules)**

Switzerland	6.389
France	8,719
Sweden	8,871
Japan	9,797
Austria	10,544
Italy	10,989
Germany (Fed Rep)	11,304
United Kingdom	14,591
United States	20,664
USSR	24,400
Canada	24,454
India	26,348
Egypt	34,372
China	43,394
Hungary	49,655
Poland	88,255

and 1973 generally turned out to be about 60 percent too high; and projections made in 1972–73 for the year 2000 roughly twice those made a decade later.

The dramatic drop in the elasticity of energy use to GNP is especially noteworthy for it lends substantial weight to the thesis of many environmentalists that material well-being need not imply profligate use of energy, and that attempting to reduce energy-related environmental insults through conservation may be less costly than many had thought likely as recently as ten or fifteen years ago.

The breakdown in historic trends in energy use has challenged the energy-modeling community, and led to the development of models that are quite complex, involving many variables. With great differences in structure and in parameters considered, these have led to a range of recently made projections that is enormous. This is reflected in a survey by Bill Keepin (*Ann. Rev. Energy,* 1986), wherein the estimates for global primary energy consumption for 2050 range from about one-third to about five times present levels (see Figure

4). When one compounds this uncertainty with that in climate change, *given* a specified level of energy use, it will be apparent that no one should have *any* confidence in a forecast of climate change for, say, 2020, much less for more remote periods. One should not conclude from this, however, that modeling efforts are worthless. They can be useful for sensitivity analysis, e.g., for estimating how CO_2 emissions, if not climate, might *change* with, say, increased use of nuclear power or electrically powered automobiles.

It would be unrealistic to discount totally the possibility of

FIGURE 4.

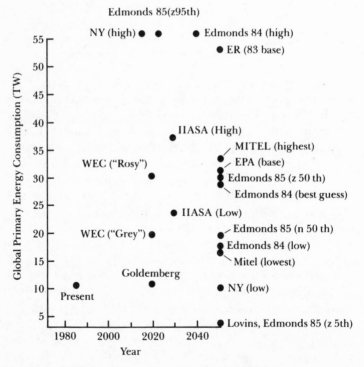

Projections of global primary energy consumption to 2050.

energy use being influenced by deliberate policy decisions—indeed, a number of such decisions have been taken and more can be expected and should be considered—and so it is not surprising that within the range of models that have been run, a number have involved exogenous assumptions about measures that might be deliberately implemented to subsidize technologies that are relatively benign from an environmental perspective, and to "internalize" the environmental costs of others, i.e., to cost energy inputs at levels that would reflect not just resource value, cost of extraction, transportation, and so on, but also the costs to the environment.

Speculations on the Ecological and Human Consequences of Climatic Change

With the world probably committed to a more rapid rate of temperature increase than has ever occurred in the past, based on GHG emissions that have occurred during this century and those that can be reasonably projected for the next decade or two,[3] a question arises as to whether humankind, its institutions, and other biological species will be able to adapt readily. A highly differentiated conclusion is almost certainly in order.

Natural species, particularly those unique to particular islands and other isolated regions, may simply die out, and even in the case of those that are found over much larger geographical ranges, there could be massive reductions in, and in some cases, increases in populations. Considering the interdependence of biological species, whole ecological systems could be destroyed or transformed, especially with the destruction of wetlands, estuaries, and barrier islands. The possibility of dramatic changes in ocean currents—of which recent variations in El Niño provide an example—could have catastrophic effects on fisheries and local climates.

At the other extreme, many humans, particularly those in modern industrial societies, are not likely to face unusual problems of adjustment. As people have moved from one place to another, they have experienced and adapted to far greater changes in climate than are likely to occur in any one region in a single generation. Particularly in the United States, with its unusually mobile population, people have moved readily in response to economic pressures and opportunities. So has industry; witness the displacement of the textile industry from New England to the South. Moreover, movement has become easier than at an earlier time in our history when a large fraction of our population was engaged in agriculture, or even a generation ago when heavy industry, with its dependence on easy access to raw materials, power, and transportation, played a larger part in our economy. For such industries as information processing and light electronics, location is essentially irrelevant except insofar as the environment, including availability of housing, cultural opportunities, and so on must be attractive to workers.

One can imagine, in the event of gradual warming, movement of both people and industry from regions that become climatically less attractive to those that become more so, at no great *collective*[4] cost. There could well be some reversal, or at least attenuation, of population movement from our northern states to Florida and the Southwest. Presumably fuel bills for most people in the advanced industrial countries would decrease and sales of air conditioners and the cost of running them would increase, including, remotely perhaps, even in northern Europe. We would likely see increased squabbling over water rights in our western states—something that is likely to occur even absent climatic change, given population pressures in the Southwest. But the prospect of such changes is not likely to get most people really very excited about GHG emissions.

For agriculture, adaptation to climatic changes can be expected to be more difficult, but with time scales measured in decades, one can imagine changes in agricultural practices— growing wheat in regions formerly used for corn, developing new strains of plants better adapted to a changed climate, abandoning some farms and opening up other areas to agriculture—that would not seem traumatic, much less impossible, for world agriculture in the aggregate, or even for any of the world's major diversified agricultural producers. It is perhaps worth noting that although the United States is one of the world's great agricultural producers, the direct contribution of its farms to GNP is only 2 percent. Obviously, substantial decreases or increases in its agricultural productivity would have little impact on the standard of living of most Americans.

For many in the developing world, adjustment to climatic change may be much more difficult; indeed, for some, impossible. Poverty implies less mobility and less flexibility to otherwise adapt to change. For the Dutch, building higher dikes as a hedge against rising sea levels and greater frequency of storms is a realistic possibility. Not so for the Bangladeshis. Their choices are likely to be between attempting migration to an already overpopulated, and hence a probably resistant, India or death by drowning or starvation—not all at once or suddenly, for there is no basis for projecting a sudden, dramatic rise in sea level—but as a result of intermittent flooding of increasing severity and perhaps frequency.

But it is perhaps worth noting here that the rates of increase in sea level and of other adverse manifestations of global warming are likely to be very low compared to the rates of population increase for most of the world's nations that are likely to be most vulnerable to climatic change. While ultimately global warming could mean the death of Bangladesh, for many years, for it and most other poor countries, rapid population growth will be a far more serious problem—and one more susceptible of mitigation.

While it is hard—probably impossible—to make much of a case to the effect that the world's present climate is optimal in any absolute sense, it is commonly argued that change would be *generally* undesirable because biological species, agricultural practices, human settlement patterns, and individuals have adapted to what we have. On balance, the benefits of change, it is claimed, would likely be exceeded, indeed perhaps be dwarfed, by the costs.

But it is conceivable that, with improvement in climate modeling capabilities, some nations—and interest groups—will conclude that they will likely be "winners" in the event of global warming, and if this turns out to be the case, they can hardly be expected to do much in support of mitigation efforts. In fact, there are already reports suggesting beneficial effects. Even aside from questions of whether one should have much confidence in such judgments, and the virtual certainty of unanticipated and very possibly offsetting adverse effects,[5] "intuition" about possible advantageous effects may carry some weight in the development of public opinion and in decision making. So too will cultural and experiential factors.

The case of the Soviet Union is perhaps instructive and important. At first blush, one might expect that it could benefit substantially from global warming. Winters would be less severe; it quite plausibly would gain more in productive agricultural land than it would lose, particularly since the northern parts of the country were not stripped of top soil by glaciation in the last ice age, as was the case in much of Canada; access to ice-free waters, both ports and the Northeast Passage, would be improved; and any increases in sea level would be proportionately less troublesome than in the case of most other industrial nations. Moreover, although attitudes may be changing after such experiences as Chernobyl, the pollution of Lake Baikal, and the despoliation of the Aral Sea, the history of the Soviet Union, and of the post–World War II Communist regimes of Eastern Europe, suggests a generally callous and, indeed, shocking disregard for maintenance of environmental quality.

To the extent that the foregoing speculations are borne out, the poor are more likely to suffer, and likely to suffer more, from climatic change than the rich. Inasmuch as a fair case can be made that the latter, including the Soviets, will have been disproportionately responsible, one must expect that climatic change, and even projections of it, will be a source of increased North-South tension.

Problems and Opportunities in Mitigation

The greenhouse/climate problem is sometimes characterized as one of choice between adaptation or abatement, but the reader should not be misled into believing that abatement (in Webster's first sense, meaning "to put an end to") can be a realistic near- or medium-term hope. It will be years before the effects of increased GHG levels of the last few decades will be fully realized and, more significantly, it is a virtual certainty that GHG levels will continue to increase for some decades. Thus the most that can be hoped for is mitigation, (or abatement in Webster's second sense, "to reduce to a degree") and, to whatever extent this may occur, individuals, institutions, and societies will have to adapt as best they can to some degree of change.

It should be understood that global warming is not just a question of energy use, although that is the subject of this chapter. Clearing of tropical forests for agricultural and other purposes, agricultural practices that are major factors in the production of nitrous oxide (N_2O) and methane, and the production of CFCs and other halogen-containing small organic molecules for other than energy related purposes will also be important, so much so that they could become the dominant factors in changing GHG loading if the burning of carbonaceous fuels is severely reduced. Much of what follows pertaining to the possibilities, problems, and likelihood of limiting climatic change by affecting energy use would carry over to agriculture as well. The problems of the CFCs and other troublesome industrial gases would, however, seem much less severe. Acceptable alternatives are, or are likely to be, available at comparatively modest cost penalties; and so, there would seem to be a basis for real hope of drastically reducing emissions through combinations of voluntary restraints and international agreements, of which the Montreal Protocol limiting the production of CFCs is an example (granting that the impetus for it was *not* concern about global warming but rather the prospect of destruction of stratospheric ozone).[6]

There are three major and fundamental problems in trying to "do something" about the GHG problem, each of which alone would be enough to discourage a Dr. Pangloss: the uncertainty as to the magnitude and seriousness of climate change, the "commons" problem, and the time scales of concern.

The Impact of Uncertainty

Although at some point warming would surely be, on balance, disadvantageous for the world as a whole, there is presently *no solid basis* for believing that a *modest* degree of warming would be so.[7] Moreover, from the earlier commentary on modeling, both of the climatic effects of changes in GHG loading and of growth in energy consumption, it should be clear that it will be at least some years before we can have even modest confidence about whether, and when, the threat might become serious; about the details, e.g., whether, in a given area, precipitation will change, and if so by how much; and about who will be winners and who will be losers.

The fact of enormous uncertainty will, of course, be used by those skeptical about the GHG/global warming thesis to argue against mitigation initiatives that might be costly or socially disruptive. They could be right to the extent that one might compensate for delay by a combination of adaptation and more vigorous mitigation efforts that could be effected beginning at a later date. But proponents of early action can be expected to argue that, in the face of uncertainty, one must act on the basis of worst-case analysis: that if there is a significant possibility of climatic change that would be so severe that no combination of delayed adaptive and mitigative measures could be effectively ameliorative, mitigative measures should be undertaken promptly, the uncertainties not withstanding. They would be right to the extent that such measures were cost-free. But it will turn out that truly effective measures are likely to be costly to at least some people, interest groups, or nations, if not to the world as a whole; and if this is true, one cannot escape having to weigh benefits that are very uncertain (the avoidance of possible catastrophe, the very nature of which may be unforeseeable) against costs that seem certain (although in this case, perhaps not predictable with much precision). The problem is not unlike hedging against some other catastrophes. If one lives in California, one might want to buy insurance against earthquakes or make structural changes in one's home if possible damage might be catastrophic, *provided* the costs were not too high; but if they seemed excessive, or if one felt that he or she could cope with what he or she judged to be the worst plausible case, then he or she would forgo such investment (perhaps until the state of earthquake prediction and/or that of structural response to earthquakes had been refined to the point where better estimates could be made of expected damage).

The fact of uncertainty is likely, then, to greatly reduce the impetus to early and costly mitigation initiatives and tip the argument strongly in favor of adaptation as compared with mitigation. There is surely a case for research to reduce some of the uncertainties in climate modeling and societal responses, and since much can be done at *relatively* modest cost, greater emphasis on this is an obvious meeting ground for those committed to early mitigative action and those favoring delay.

The "Commons" Problem

In the classic version of the "commons" problem, the presumption is that maintenance of the "commons" is in everyone's interest, but in the case of global warming there will almost certainly be some who will benefit from warming, or believe that they are likely to benefit, and so will not have an interest in climate stabilization. Thus, and even putting aside the complicating fact of great uncertainty, getting agreement on some instrumentality to insure that everyone—or at least a significant number—makes an appropriate contribution to a group effort to achieve the benefits of a well-maintained commons will be more difficult than in the usual case.

The global warming problem will differ somewhat from the classic commons problem in another respect. In the latter, it is assumed that no single agent will benefit enough from his own actions to justify a solo effort. In the global warming case, at least some unilateral actions can probably be justified on cost-benefit grounds. Of agents, nations are almost certainly of greatest interest, and of these, the largest merit particular attention, primarily because they are the greatest contributors to the greenhouse problem. To the extent that loss from adverse climatic change might scale with size, they would also have the most to gain from mitigation.

Because it is the largest GHG contributor, the first candidate for unilateral mitigative action would likely be the United States. Moreover, since its GNP is about one-fourth of the world total, one might also argue that it could perhaps capture one-fourth of the total benefits of any unilateral mitigation effort it might undertake. If so, such an effort would be rational on economic grounds if the benefit-to-cost (B/C) ratio for the world as a whole were to exceed four. If one assumes the benefit from mitigating climate change to be proportional to population rather than GNP, the prime candidate for unilateral action would, of course, be China, and with almost a quarter of the world's population, one again arrives at a critical B/C ratio of four. Considering the dubious nature of the underlying assumptions—and that adaptation to change will generally be relatively easier for large nations than for smaller ones, *ceteris paribus,* these ratios should certainly not be taken very seriously. In fact, it is quite plausible that the United States, China, or both might not even be "losers." The fact remains, however, that the United States, China, and maybe the Soviet Union, India, and Japan are so large that unilateral mitigation efforts by one or more of them *might* make good sense. This would hold also for the European Community (EC), assuming a degree of unity that would permit concerted action, and, *a fortiori* for, say, the OECD. To an extent, then, the GHG climate problem may differ somewhat from the usual one of the commons.

But even if it could be demonstrated that substantial unilateral mitigative action by one of these entities would make sense, such action would be of exceedingly limited utility, unless there were extensive emulation by others. This is because it must be expected that the benefit-to-cost ratio will drop dramatically with increasing effort. While the United States might, as a result of policy decisions, quite plausibly reduce its GHG emissions by, say, 5 percent below the levels that would otherwise obtain, thereby effecting a delay in the realization of a doubling of GHG loading by perhaps nine months, to "buy" an additional nine months' time would likely be much more costly. If the United States were to *eliminate* its emissions, the cost would be astronomically great and the delay in GHG doubling would only be about twenty years. In fact, of course, elimination of emissions will be politically, if not physically, totally unrealistic, at least for the foreseeable future.

For practical purposes, then, the GHG problem has to be seen essentially as a commons problem, notwithstanding the fact that *at the margin,* the largest actors might logically find some unilateral mitigation initiatives attractive. Some steps already taken, albeit for other reasons, e.g., constraining CFC emissions, may be exemplary,[8] but to effect really major reductions, concerted action by at least most of the major GHG producers will be required.[9]

While many political leaders have expressed concern about global warming, getting concurrence on *broadly based actions* that might result in mitigation is, then, the problem. The degree of motivation and the negotiating leverage available to the interested parties will vary enormously. It may be instructive to speculate on exemplary cases.

The most predictable adverse effect of global warming is probably rising sea level (although there is doubt even about this). This suggests that nations with large populations and/or valuable land at risk from flooding—the United States, the Netherlands, Egypt, Bangladesh, the Maldive Islands—would have especially great interests in the mitigation of GHG emissions. For the United States, the costs of such flooding could well be more or less offset by the costs and/or by possible benefits of global warming. But for the others, rising sea level would almost certainly be, on balance, highly undesirable. None of the others would, however, have much bargaining power in a negotiation focused narrowly on the global warming problem since none are significant contributors to it. But their situations would be rather different. With adaptation probably a realistic option for the Netherlands, mitigation would be presumably less important to it; yet it would be in a stronger position to influence the outcome of negotiations because linkages to other issues could be drawn on to elicit support for its views from the European Community as a whole, which would have great bargaining power, and from the other members. And Egypt would be in a stronger bargaining position than Bangladesh because of its key role in the volatile Middle East and because of world concern about stability there. (That U.S. aid to Egypt is about five times as large as that to Bangladesh, notwithstanding the latter's having twice the population and only 35 percent of the per capita GNP of the former, is one measure of the relative willingness of Americans to commit resources to the well-being of the peoples of these two countries.)

Consider Austria, Poland, and East Germany. There is no reason at this time to believe that any would suffer especially from global warming, and in particular no reason to believe that the effects would be significantly worse (or better) for one than for another. Yet their interests in the implementation of a global convention on limiting CO_2 emissions would differ. At the one extreme, East Germany produces a great deal of coal, about a third as much (if lignite is included) as the United States (and about five times as much per capita), and so would presumably be very heavily impacted by a carbon tax or other agreement to constrain the production or consumption of coal. Poland would also be hard hit. At the other extreme, Austria would be virtually unaffected. Because of its enormous economic problems and debt, Poland would be particularly vulnerable to pressure from the advanced industrial countries to accede to any international agreement, whereas Austria would not be. With the likelihood of union with West Germany, East German interests would likely be subsumed in those of a larger Germany, and to an extent in the EC, and policy regarding the mining and use of coal and lignite would likely be far more influenced by concern about regional acid rain than by concern about global warming.

Then there are the cases of the Soviet Union and China, special because they are such large contributors to the GHG problem (together, their contribution is now about 25 percent of the world total) and because, in the absence of severe constraints on the use of fossil fuels, their contributions will grow disproportionately (to perhaps a third of the world total within the next century). It is not clear that either will see moderate global warming as particularly disadvantageous to it, and both are likely to see restrictions on the use of fossil fuels as costly. This is particularly true of China, which is now more than 50 percent dependent on coal for primary energy (compared with 33 percent and 20 percent for the United States and the Soviet Union, respectively) and which has the world's largest coal reserves by far, and the most expansive plans for its increased use. With other serious demands on resources, and with its population still growing at about 1.5 percent per year, it is hard to see how China might be induced to enter into an international agreement to limit GHG growth if the near-term costs were perceived to be large. Similar arguments would apply to India, which is also a very large producer and consumer of coal.[10]

One concludes that negotiating an effective international agreement to limit global warming by imposing constraints or taxes on the burning of carbonaceous fuels is likely to be exceedingly difficult—*far* more difficult than the Montreal Protocol. Some of the largest contributors to the problems would likely judge the direct benefits, if any, not commensurate with the costs to them, and most of those likely to reach the opposite conclusion on the cost-benefit issue would have little leverage to induce accession by the major actors.

The Problems of Time Delay and Discounting

Attempting to limit global warming through government intervention (or initiatives by individuals or other entities) is made especially difficult because of the delay in climatic response to interventionary activities. This is in significant measure a consequence of the upper layers of the oceans acting, as has been mentioned, as a great heat sink. This alone can account for a delay in response of a decade or two. More important is the fact that the effects of GHG buildup will be cumula-

tive over a time scale measured in centuries. This follows because at issue is not just the exchange of CO_2 between the
atmosphere and the upper layers of the ocean, but also exchange involving the ocean depths and because, with the exception of methane and ozone, the other important greenhouse gases have lives in the range of 50 to 175 years.
Accordingly, assuming there are benefits in mitigation of GHG
emissions, they may be important over time periods of many
generations. The costs of mitigation may also be significant
over very long periods—really, until such time as energy (and
agricultural and industrial) needs can be met more cheaply
through non-GHG emitting processes than through those that
produce GHGs. This is also a matter of at least generations, if
it can ever be done.

One is confronted, then, with the problem of comparing
costs and benefits, with the interval between the imposition of
some of the costs and the realization of some of the benefits
being measured in many generations.

The usual approach to such problems involves, of course,
calculating whether an investment makes sense, depending on
whether the discounted value of the benefits exceeds the discounted costs. Determining what discount rate may be appropriate is straightforward in some cases—for industry, it will be
the cost of raising money through some combination of borrowing and sale of stock, adjusted to take account of taxes, and
perhaps risk—but for public policy decisions, what is appropriate may be more contentious, even aside from the question of
how risk factors should be dealt with. What is at issue is how
society should allocate resources between current consumption and investment in the future. Those supporting high social discount rates generally contend that past history and the
prospect of technological progress suggest that future generations will be so much better off than our own that we need not
worry particularly about investment on their behalf. Proponents of low rates, on the other hand, argue that however individuals may feel about saving versus consumption, government has a special responsibility to invest in the future.[11] Some
argue, additionally, that while in the past living standards have

improved over time, this may not be true as we look to the future, and that the major argument for high discount rates may accordingly no longer be valid. How significant all this is and how sensitive it is to the particular choice of social discount rate is reflected in the fact that at a rate of 3 percent, the benefits of better climate, say, a hundred years hence, get discounted 19-fold but that at a discount rate of 10 percent, more than 13,000-fold. Even over a period as short as twenty-five years, the differences are very significant: twofold discounting at 3 percent versus more than tenfold at 10 percent. Although most economists would presumably settle on a figure of between 3 and 10 percent, in constant dollars, i.e., before making an upward adjustment for inflation, there is no consensus on a preferred value, notwithstanding decades of debate among interested parties.

Perhaps not surprisingly, many argue, with the realization of the implications of such accounting, that discounting at a non-zero rate is simply inappropriate in consideration of protecting the environment.[12] But the fact remains that most, though by no means all, individuals—and governments acting as their surrogates—do heavily discount the future when it comes to laying cash on the line, as distinct from expressing pious concern about, say, the preservation of rare species or the welfare of generations more than, say, two removed (or for that matter, about distant populations now living). Moreover, such interest as there has been in the welfare of others seems to be falling off, at least in the United States. Note that our contributions to foreign aid, our per capita rates of savings, and our investment in social infrastructure are small compared to those of other advanced countries and compared to our behavior in the not-distant past. And, however much low investment in the future may be justified in the case of most countries outside the OECD on the grounds of poverty and immediate domestic needs, their records are even worse.

One is forced to the conclusion that when the benefits of an investment are remote in time or space, or particularly both, most individuals and most governments are not likely to be willing to make great sacrifices. We are not likely to see substantial efforts to mitigate global warming by limiting GHG emissions if the costs are perceived to be large and if the adverse consequences of such warming are not likely to be severe for at least another generation. Reluctance to make such efforts is especially likely when adaptation to change would seem to be quite feasible for posterity and, on a discounted cost basis, cheap. Certainly on the record of the last decade, one must be particularly pessimistic about American leadership in respect to these matters.

Conclusion about Direct Mitigative Action

When account is taken of all this, it is hard to escape the conclusion that attempts to slow the rate of global warming and the consequent climatic changes by trying to change patterns of energy use are likely to fail *to the extent that the rationale is mitigation of such change.* This is likely to be the case whether the concern is with just some of the worst "culprits" or about developing a broad international agreement on mitigation. Generally, the hope of reducing GHG emissions, and affecting any other factors that might bear on world climate, probably must lie primarily in "selling" measures—political, institutional, and technical—that are likely to have mitigating effects on climate change, not explicitly on those grounds but on *others,* e.g., on the grounds that they make sense in terms of reducing a nation's dependence on others for energy, that they are attractive because they may have rather immediately palpable environmental benefits, such as reducing smog or acid rain, or that they are likely to benefit powerful special interests.

Is there any reason to believe in—or hope for—more effective action of this kind than would occur in the absence of the possibility of climatic change? Almost certainly there is. While they are surely not a majority, at least in "Western" cultures, there are many people who are not likely to view climatic change simply from the utilitarian or economic self-interest perspective that has underlain most of the preceding discussion: people who, as noted earlier, attach very special—even spiritual or religious—value to the preservation of biological species, variegated cultures, and the kind of physical environment they have known. It can reasonably be expected that many holding these views will work with greater zeal to implement measures affecting energy use, *which might be perceived to be beneficial on other grounds,* than they otherwise would if they also believe that those measures would be useful in mitigating climatic change that could be destructive of those special values to which they attach such weight.

The Linkage Between Global Climatic Change, Energy Conservation, and Local and Regional Environmental Problems

Some energy options raise questions of conflicts between the objectives at issue in this section, economics even aside. Thus increased reliance on coal generally would contribute to energy independence for the United States (and China and India), and its use as feed stock for the production of methanol could lead to reductions in noxious automobile emissions, but all uses of coal would, of course, exacerbate the GHG problem.

Fortunately, though, most measures that might be taken in the interest of realizing any one of the objectives of interest here will have beneficial effects, or no effects at all, in respect to the others. And fortunately, from the perspective of mitigating climatic change, very strong cases can be made for undertaking actions that will conserve energy and/or reduce noxious emissions that are locally or regionally harmful, and which will *also* make global warming less likely.

Very importantly, the three main impediments to action on the climatic change problem either do not apply in respect of these other objectives or are much attenuated.

There can hardly be any qualitative argument about desirability of energy conservation. It is important because we live in a world of finite resources and because the profligate use of them raises the prospect of future shortages and of conflict over them. And the dispersal of nitric and sulfur oxides is clearly—and, to an extent, calculably—undesirable because of the palpably adverse effects on human health and that of other biological species and, less importantly but nevertheless measurably, on structures. While there may be arguments as to the magnitude of effects and the costs of mitigation, there can be no serious claims—in contrast to the situation as regards global warming—that there will be "winners" in the event of failure to realize these other objectives, and no serious argument to the effect that profligate use of energy and the production of noxious gases from combustion can be dismissed as nonproblems.

The commons issue does arise in trying to deal with these other objectives, but difficult as it may be, it is far more tractable than in the global warming case, in large measure because the problems tend to be regional. Consequently, there are generally more effective instruments for dealing with them than in the global commons case: local governments in many instances, the United States government in disputes between our states, the possibility of the use of EC offices in the case of transfrontier pollution in Europe, and of bilateral negotiations in the case of the United States and its two immediate neighbors. Here the problems of time delay will be much less severe than in the global warming case. The public felt the effects of the oil shocks of the 1970s almost immediately in increased fuel prices and in shortages, and the adverse consequences on human health of noxious gases are felt almost immediately in the event of atmospheric inversions in many cities, and in some areas of Eastern Europe, almost continuously.

All of which is to say that the prospects of doing something to conserve energy and to reduce the emissions of undesirable by-products of its generation are *comparatively* good. Fortunately, there are many options for meeting energy demands and for reducing them in acceptable ways that are attractive on cost effectiveness grounds—some, probably so, even putting externalities aside. It may be appropriate here to do no more than note some that coincidentally offer great promise in reducing GHG emissions.

Foremost on any list must be conservation through greater energy efficiency. While great price-induced improvements have been realized, especially within the OECD countries, as a response to the oil shocks of the 1970s, the intensity of energy use continues to be uneconomically high in many countries, notably in the United States, Canada, the Soviet Union, Eastern Europe, and many developing countries. The problems are not primarily technical but rather structural: deliberate subsidization of energy use, especially in developing countries; pricing that is unrealistically low—just another form of subsidization—common throughout Eastern Europe and the Soviet Union; and lack of knowledge, incentives, and access to capital at low rates, common everywhere, that might induce consumers and builders of housing to make capital investments that would be demonstrably beneficial in total life cycle costs.

Developments in solar generation of electricity and its possible application to the generation of hydrogen could substitute effectively and beneficially for hydrocarbon fuels. While great progress has been made in reducing the costs of solar-generated electricity, largely through the development of amorphous silicon technology, the point has not yet been reached where these possibilities are likely to have a significant impact on either the greenhouse problem or others of environmental concern.

Nuclear power has had an impact—CO_2 emissions are now less than they would have been without it—and its continued exploitation offers prospects second, in the near term, only to energy efficiency for further reduction in such emissions, but the prospects for its further growth remain decidedly clouded. There is now little doubt that reactors can be built that are "inherently safe," i.e., that are so configured that their ability to dissipate waste heat in the event of an accident or unscheduled shutdown will be sufficient to preclude a "meltdown" and the widespread dispersal of radioactive materials; but the memories of Three Mile Island and Chernobyl, the appalling mismanagement of military nuclear wastes, continuing concerns about the disposal of wastes from power reactors, and worry about the possible spread of materials usable for the manufacture of nuclear weapons cannot be lightly dismissed. While the nuclear option will no doubt continue to be pursued in some countries, the choice will be difficult for most, even where the option appears to be economically competitive with fossil fuel generation of electricity.

Summary—A Basis for Planning

It is now all but certain that anthropogenic activities will lead to global warming that will be noticeable sometime in the next century. It is also, however, probable that the magnitude and details of the effects on climate and on human welfare will remain highly uncertain until sometime in that century.

Because of the uncertainty, the very long lag-times involved, and the fact that effective mitigative action is likely to require something approaching a global consensus, the prospects for near-term action *directed at reducing global warming* must be seen to be poor. These factors, and particularly the synergism between them, tend to make mitigation a less likely response to the "threat" than delay and eventual adaptation. Public policy would be well advised to face this reality.

This does not mean, however, that it will be either reasonable or desirable to base policy on simple projections of past trends in the emission of GHGs. Actions have been taken, and more are likely—and they should be encouraged—that will mean that such projections are likely to be unrealistically high. The CFC problem is on the way to being solved, mainly because of concern about ozone destruction and because solution seems not likely to be very costly; and desires for energy efficiency and concern about local and regional adverse effects of the combustion of fossil fuels will result in other GHG emissions being less than would be expected in a "business-as-usual" world.

It is clearly desirable that there be a better understanding of the nature and seriousness of the global warming problem, and so further research efforts merit strong support. Perhaps with the results of such research in hand, it will be possible to mobilize support for directed mitigative action, but pending that, betting on measures that can be effectively rationalized on other grounds, and planning on adaptation, will be important and probably more realistic.

Notes

[1] Actually the process is a bit more complex. The earth dissipates heat not only by radiating it away, but also by evaporation of water and convection to the atmosphere. Were it not for these last processes, the earth would be considerably warmer than it is.

[2] It is widely believed that changes in the earth's orbital parameters may have been important, if not the dominant, causal factors. Changes in solar luminosity and volcanic activity may also have been contributing factors.

[3] It is likely that the rates of change will be at least as great as those that occurred at the end of the medieval warm period and the beginning of the little ice age, and an order of magnitude greater than those that occurred at the end of the last great ice age, approximately 15,000 years ago.

[4] This is not to say that many individuals and their families would not suffer. Many did during the exodus from the dust bowl of the 1930s when Nebraska, Kansas, and Oklahoma lost 3.6 percent of their population while the rest of the country grew by 7.8 percent.

[5] One cannot help but feel that some analysts, obviously concerned about global warming, "reach" a bit as they argue that beneficial effects of warming may be offset by adverse effects. One analyst, for example, after noting that warming would likely have beneficial first-order effects on agricultural productivity in Japan and Finland, suggests that this could actually be unfortunate because the prices of rice in the former and of agricultural products in general in the latter are maintained at artificially high levels, as matters of governmental policy. The implication is that subsidization would continue in the event of warming to the net disbenefit of Japanese and Finnish taxpayers. Interestingly, in noting that warming might reduce production of American wheat, he does *not* comment on the benefits to American taxpayers of reduced costs of subsidization.

[6] The fact that significant progress has been made and that solutions to the CFC problem appear to be relatively simple ought not to be cause for complacency. CFC emissions have been increasing much more rapidly than in the case of other GHG gases, and molecule for molecule, the CFCs are much more troublesome—even aside from the additional problem of their catalysis of ozone destruction. Much remains to be done. It should be noted that some of the possible "solutions" to the ozone problem may not be benign from a GHG perspective. Use of HCFC-134a as an alternative to CFC 12 might be attractive inasmuch as it contains no chlorine, and hence does not catalyze the depletion of ozone, but it has troublesome GHG properties.

[7] One should be cautious, however, about taking comfort in the possibility that such warming might be tolerable for either the world as a whole or for

particular regions. One of the most worrisome aspects of the greenhouse problem arises because of the likelihood—virtual certainty, in the absence of strong mitigative actions—that a realized "modest degree of warming" will foreshadow substantial additional warming because of the aforementioned phenomena of a decade or more's lag-time in the equilibration of atmospheric and upper ocean level temperatures.

[8]As noted earlier, acceptable alternatives to CFCs are likely to be available at relatively low-cost penalties; conceivably even at no penalty at all. Thus the imposition of severe constraints on use by any of the largest countries could well have made sense, even aside from the question of ozone damage and actions by other nations, assuming, of course, that the country in question believed it might be seriously damaged by GHG-induced warming.

[9]These points can be perhaps usefully illustrated using some estimates due to W.D. Nordhaus, which he emphasizes are very approximate and preliminary, (discussion paper for MIT workshop on energy and environmental modeling, 1989). He calculates damage from GHG-induced warming to the U.S. by 2050 to be 0.25 ± 2 percent of national income, in the absence of mitigation efforts. If one assumes the central value, i.e., 0.25 percent, one can calculate, using other estimates from his paper, that it would make sense for the United States, acting alone, to reduce its CO_2 emissions by about 5 percent. (Were we to try to go further, on our own, the costs to us would exceed the benefits of additional mitigation.) If, on the other hand, all nations could be induced to reduce their CO_2 emissions proportionally, the optimal reduction would be about 10 percent. If one assumes damage at the upper bound of Nordhaus's estimate, 2.25 percent, it makes sense to go further with CO_2 mitigation. His lower bound, -1.75 percent, implies, of course, that the U.S. would benefit from GHG-induced warming.

[10]In the case of both China and India, the production of coal has been quite heavily subsidized, so there might be some hope that consumption could be reduced in these cases—or at least be expanded less rapidly than is planned—at little, if any, cost.

[11]This argument goes back at least to Pigou (1932).

[12]While this has been a matter of strong convictions and much argument, there ought to be no conceptual difficulty in accepting non-zero discounting if it is recognized that the fundamental problem lies really in valuing the benefits at issue. What those who would decry discounting perhaps really means is that they attach such a high value to some aspects of environmental protection—say, the preservation of biological diversity—that for them, the benefits of preservation would exceed the costs of prevention of destruction—in our case, the costs of mitigation of climatic change that might lead to such destruction—at *any* discount rate. That discounting should be used in consideration of (at least some of) the implications of climatic change will be apparent if one thinks about the need for water for agricultural purposes. It is usual when contemplating the construction of a dam for irrigation purposes to discount the value of the irrigation water that it might provide. Surely it would be bizarre to discount such benefits from irrigation but then to argue that the benefits from future rainfall that might be realized by an investment in the avoidance of climate alteration should not be discounted.

6

Managing the Transition: The Potential Role for Economic Policies

TOM H. TIETENBERG

Introduction

The well-known story of a thoroughly disoriented tourist is deeply entrenched in Maine folklore. Enticed by unusually brilliant fall foliage, a tourist forsook the security of the well-marked main highways for some less traveled country roads. After an hour of driving, he was no longer sure he was even headed in the right direction. Seeing a Maine native mending a fence, he pulled over to the side of the road to seek

TOM H. TIETENBERG is the author of four books, including *Environmental and Natural Resource Economics,* and nearly forty articles and essays on environmental and natural resource economics. He was elected president of the Association of Environmental and Natural Resource Economists for 1987–88, and he has served as the director of the Macroeconomic Impact Division in the Federal Energy Administration and as consultant on environmental policy to both domestic and foreign corporations and governments. Dr. Tietenberg is currently a professor of economics at Colby College, Waterville, Maine.

assistance. After hearing the tourist's destination, the native sadly shook his head and in his best Maine accent responded, "If I was goin' they-uh, I sure wouldn't start from he-uh!"

The underlying message is both timely and relevant. Had we known long ago that human activities could seriously impact environmental life support systems and could deny future generations the quality of life to which our generation has become accustomed, we might have chosen a different, more sustainable, path for improving human welfare. The fact that we did not have that knowledge and therefore did not make that choice years ago means that current generations are faced with making more difficult choices with fewer options. These choices will test the creativity of our solutions and the resilience of our social institutions.

Background

How can we facilitate the transition to a sustainable global economic system? The question is much easier to ask than to answer because the task is so formidable. As Jim MacNeill, the former director of the World Commission on Environment and Development, stated recently, "If current forms of development were employed, a five to tenfold increase in economic activity would be required over the next fifty years to meet the needs and aspirations of a population twice the size of today's 5.2 billion, as well as to begin to reduce mass poverty." Whether increases of this magnitude can be accomplished while still respecting the atmospheric and ecological systems on which all economic activity ultimately depends is not at all obvious. Most observers seem to believe that to meet the challenge we need to take an activist stance by controlling population and forcing a transition to new forms of development.

The task of managing the transition to sustainable development is made all the more difficult by the fact that some entrenched development paths are not only themselves unsustainable, but they have so dominated sustainable strategies that switching from one to the other has become very difficult. Southern California represents a case in point. In the Los Angeles air basin the ambient air quality standards, designed to protect human health, are currently violated on the order of 180 out of the 365 days a year. How can air quality be restored to legally acceptable levels?

Due to the way the city has developed, regulators in Los Angeles now face a very difficult problem. As a prime example of an automobile city, population growth in Los Angeles has spawned land use patterns that accommodate the automobile and are, in turn, accommodated by the automobile. Responding to a massive program of highway construction and low gasoline prices, the city has become very spread out with highly dispersed residential and employment locations. Since the efficient use of mass transit requires the existence of high-density travel corridors, an effective public transit alternative is now difficult to implement, though it could have been quite possible before the highly dispersed land use patterns became so firmly entrenched. The options left open to these regulators have steadily diminished over time. The entire fabric of life in the Los Angeles area is so interwoven with automobile access that the problem cannot be solved without envisioning fairly radical changes in lifestyle.

Overview

Despite the difficulty of the task, the essential message of this chapter is that solutions are possible. To meet the challenges of the next century it will be necessary to foster and to support institutional change by being somewhat more creative in the way that we deal with environmental policy. One key to exploiting these opportunities involves harnessing the power of the marketplace and focusing that power on the reduction, or hopefully even eradication, of poverty in an environmentally sound manner. In this chapter I shall briefly review some of the challenges that need to be faced in order to produce these changes, as well as some of the opportunities that are created by the new international political landscape. The various kinds of economic policies that can be used to refocus the power of the global market by restructuring the incentives to which it responds will be discussed, as well as some of the advantages and disadvantages of each approach. The chapter will close by exploring the potential role for some innovative regulatory strategies to facilitate cooperative international approaches to international environmental problems.

Challenges and Opportunities

Barriers to International Cooperation

As the scale of economic activity has proceeded steadily upward, the scope of environmental problems triggered by that activity has transcended both geographic and generational boundaries. Whereas the nation-state used to be a sufficient form of political organization for resolving environmental problems, that may no longer be the case. Whereas each generation of humans used to have the luxury of being able to satisfy its own needs without worrying about the needs of those generations to come, that is no longer the case either.

Solving problems such as poverty, global warming, ozone depletion, and the loss of biodiversity requires international cooperation. Ideally, the search for solutions would also involve intergenerational cooperation, but, of course, that is not possible. Future generations cannot speak for themselves; we must speak for them. Our policies must incorporate our obligation to future generations, however difficult or imperfect that incorporation might prove to be.

International cooperation is by no means a foregone conclusion. Global environment problems can trigger very different effects on the countries that will be represented around the negotiating table. While low-lying countries could be completely submerged by the sea level rise predicted by some global warming models, or arid nations could see their marginal agricultural lands succumb to desertification, other nations in traditionally intemperate climates may see agricultural productivity rise as warmer climates support longer growing seasons.

Countries that unilaterally set out to improve the global environmental situation run the risk of making their businesses vulnerable to competition from less conscientious nations. Industrialized countries that undertake stringent environmental policies may not suffer greatly at the national level (due to offsetting employment and income increases in the industries producing pollution control equipment), but some individual industries facing the stringent regulations will face higher costs than their competitors, and can be expected to suffer accordingly. Declining market share and employment in industries confronted by especially stringent regulations are powerful political weapons that can be used to derail efforts to implement an aggressive environmental policy. The search for solutions must accommodate these concerns.

Forging new international agreements is not enough. To produce the desired effect, the agreements must be enforceable. Enforceability will be a difficult criterion to satisfy as long as the agreements infringe upon significant segments of society with legitimate claims to an alternative future. The most legitimate such claim is perhaps advanced by those in abject poverty.

Poverty is both a cause and an effect of many of the environmental problems to be confronted. Survival strategies may necessarily sacrifice long-term goals simply to ward off starvation or death. Trees needed to provide moisture and nourishment for the soil over the long run may be cut down to provide immediate income or warmth. Highly erodible land may be brought into necessarily temporary cultivation simply because the only realistic alternative is starvation. It will be virtually impossible to solve global environmental problems without simultaneously solving the problem of global poverty.

Many individuals and institutions currently have a large stake in maintaining the status quo. Fishers harvesting their catch from an overexploited fishery are loathe to undertake any reduction in harvests, even if the reduction is necessary to conserve the stock and to return the population to a healthy level. Farmers who have come to depend on fertilizer and pesticide subsidies will be reluctant to give them up. The principle of inertia applies to politics as fully as to physical bodies; a body at rest will tend to stay at rest unless a significant outside force is introduced. Changing economic incentives can provide that force.

Opportunities

While this list of barriers to international cooperation is certainly imposing, the new global environmental problems also offer new opportunities for cooperation, opportunities that in some ways are unprecedented. Although the degree to which various nations are affected by these problems differs, a point made above, it is also true that some potential common ground exists.

One important foundation for this common ground is the inefficiency of many current economic activities. In many cases these inefficiencies are very large indeed; resources are being wasted. Whenever resources are wasted, much more environ-. mental improvement could be obtained for current expenditures, or the same improvement could be realized with a much smaller commitment of resources. By definition, moving from an inefficient policy to an efficient one creates gains to be shared. Agreements on how these gains should be shared among the cooperating parties can be used to build coalitions. Although later in this chapter I will give specific, concrete examples of how this can be done, let me at this point at least sow the seed of the idea.

A creative use of policy instruments could, for example, institutionalize and regularize a system for sharing the costs of meeting global pollution control goals. As the Eastern European countries take hesitant steps toward market economies and Third World countries seek to provide a higher standard of living for their people, most observers believe that the ability of these nations to pay for substantial improvements in environmental control is questionable. Some sort of cost sharing arrangements between the industrialized nations and the less industrialized nations is seen as one possible resolution of this conflict.

The level and form of any such cost sharing arrangements,

however, are usually not clearly specified. By the appropriate choice of policy instruments, much of this cost sharing could be handled by normal market forces. Market-based economic incentive strategies would offer industrialized nations the opportunity to receive more environmental improvement per dollar spent, and would offer the less industrialized nations the opportunity to receive financial help in their efforts to reduce pollution. Both would share in the resulting improvement in the global environment.

The natural reluctance of nations to impose increasingly stringent environmental policies within their borders can be diminished by assuring that the policies imposed are cost effective. We live in an age when the call for tighter environmental controls intensifies with each new discovery of yet another injury modern society is inflicting on the planet. But resistance to additional controls is also growing with the recognition that the cost of compliance is increasing as all the easy techniques are used up. By choosing cost effective and flexible policy instruments, the potential for backlash can be reduced.

Policy instrument choice can also affect enforceability. In developing countries local communities typically have the greatest accessibility to and knowledge about local biological resources. As these countries have undergone a centralization of political power, including the power to control these resources, some of the local commitment to them has been lost. Policy instruments that reestablish this commitment by offering these local communities a stake in the preservation of the resource can enhance enforceability. Subsequent sections present some specific examples of how this can be accomplished.

By being creative in the design of policy instruments, the incentives of local and global communities can become compatible. In some cases being creative requires the use of conventional economic instruments in unconventional ways, but in others it requires the use of unconventional instruments in unconventional ways.

Unconventional approaches are not pipe dreams. Most of them have been successfully employed in one form or another in local communities around the globe. The experience with these instruments in their current setting provides a model for their use on an international level. How well this model fits remains an open question, but it is better to sit down for a dinner with a full menu offering some novel, but interesting, choices rather than for one offering only a limited selection of familiar, unappetizing fare.

The Menu of Economic Policy Instruments

The menu of available policy instruments is large and varied. The items on that menu range from conventional policy instruments, which have focused almost exclusively on traditional economic targets (such as stabilizing the economy or improving the trade deficit), to quite unconventional instruments such as emission trading and emission charges, which have focused more directly on environmental targets. Some of the traditional policy instruments can have very strong unintended effects on the environment. Fiscal and monetary policies provide a case in point.

Fiscal and Monetary Policies

One of the admonitions traditionally associated with thinking globally is to take the long view. Policy makers and businesses are urged to consider the long-term consequences of their actions and not to give in to myopic strategies, but that is easier said than done. The frequency of reelection campaigns and highly competitive global markets exert significant pressures toward demonstrable achievements in rather short periods of time. Certain fiscal and monetary policies can intensify these pressures, making myopic strategies distressingly common.

Long-range planning in both private and public sectors typically relies on one of two mathematically equivalent means of comparing the consequences of proposed actions: the present value criterion and the internal rate of return. For both of these techniques the implicit project rate of return has to exceed a target rate of return, typically called the hurdle rate, to justify using the funds in this manner. Under this system of budgeting, the higher the hurdle rate, the less important in the decision are any financial consequences (regardless of whether they are revenues or costs) that occur in the future.

As a practical matter many business firms and public agencies tend to use the rate of interest as the basis for the hurdle rate. When monetary and fiscal policy conspire to yield high interest rates, as was the case in the United States in the mid- to late 1980s, business and public planning necessarily become more myopic. High real interest rates are an unintended and largely unrecognized, but nonetheless significant, barrier to managing the transition to a more sustainable economy.

The tendency toward myopic planning resulting from high interest rates is exacerbated by current practices that deviate from the correct use of the present value or internal rate of return planning techniques. Although the correct use of these procedures combines the *real* interest rate with constant-price projections of the costs and benefits, current practice frequently uses the much higher *nominal* interest rate. (The real interest rate is the nominal interest rate minus the expected rate of inflation.) Since higher interest rates automatically reduce the impact of future consequences in this type of planning, the use of the higher nominal interest rates in place of real interest rates reduces the likelihood of taking the long view.

Transitions to new forms of economic activity (investing in a new energy efficient manufacturing facility, for example) frequently involve an early transition period with meager, possibly negative, economic returns followed by a period with positive economic return. In periods of high real interest rates, the dominance of returns in the earlier periods over those in later periods in the present value or internal rate of return calculation would make both businesses and planners using those criteria more reluctant to make the transition. In subsequent sections some ways in which the public sector can facilitate these transitions are discussed.

The magnitude of the real interest rate is not the only channel of influence for monetary and fiscal policy. Another is the means used to raise revenue. One aspect of fiscal policy that is receiving increasing attention in Europe is the potential for shifting the burden of taxation from taxes on labor and capital to taxes on emissions or on the extraction of natural resources. By raising the cost of acquiring capital and supplying labor, traditional taxes have an unintended discouraging effect on these particular activities. Since the transition to new economic activities will require considerable investment and the active cooperation of the labor force, discouraging investment or labor supply may well be counterproductive. These taxes could be reduced without reducing revenue by introducing compensating increases in taxes on commodities that affect the environment. Common candidates include taxes on materials that enter the waste stream or on resources that have been underpriced because their environmental costs have been successfully transferred from the polluters to the victims. Packaging taxes, severance taxes on minerals, production taxes on toxic substances, effluent or emission taxes on pollutants injected into the air or water, and taxes on fossil fuels are a few of the examples that have been discussed.

By offering the possibility of meeting budgetary goals while encouraging the transition to more sustainable forms of economic activity, these nontraditional taxes serve a dual purpose. Not only do they raise revenue, but they send market signals to all users of these resources that their true cost is higher than previously recognized. Whereas the damage caused by pollution, for example, is normally borne by those affected by it, and therefore is not recognized as a true cost of doing business by the polluter, the judicious use of these kinds of taxes would change the market signals and make clear the real cost of the activity to both producers and consumers.

Environmental taxes also have one main drawback. They may not provide as reliable a revenue source as more traditional tax bases. To the extent that they succeed in reducing the activity being taxed, environmental taxes undermine the tax base. This has been the experience in Japan, for example, with air pollution charges. Declining emission rates have forced rather large increases in the tax rates to keep revenue from declining; the higher tax rates precipitate even larger declines in emission rates and a politically explosive downward spiral results.

Another increasingly important aspect of monetary and fiscal policies, particularly in resource-dependent economies, involves the structure of the national income accounts. By providing feedback on how the economy is doing, the accounts enable policy makers not only to judge how successful past actions have been, but also to assess the likelihood of success for proposed future actions.

The signals policy makers are receiving from these accounts provide misleading information. In particular the accounts fail to distinguish between economic growth resulting from a true increase in income and economic growth resulting from a depreciation in what economists have come to call "natural capital," the stock of environmentally provided assets such as the soil, the atmosphere, the forests, wildlife, and water.

The traditional definition of income was articulated by Sir John Hicks (*Value and Capital,* 1946):

The purpose of income calculations in practical affairs is to give people an indication of the amount they can consume without impoverishing themselves. Following out this idea, it would seem that we ought to define a man's income as the maximum value which he can consume during a week, and still expect to be as well off at the end of the week as he was at the beginning.

While human-made capital (such as buildings, bridges, etc.) is treated in a manner consistent with this definition, natural capital is not. As human-made capital wears out, the accounts set aside an amount called depreciation to compensate for the decline in value. No increase in economic activity is recorded as an increase in income until depreciation has been subtracted from gross returns. That portion of the gains that merely serves to replace worn out capital is not appropriately considered income.

No such adjustment is made for natural capital. Depreciation of the stock of natural capital is currently counted by the national income accounts as income. Development strategies that "cash in" the endowment of natural resources are in these accounts indistinguishable from development strategies that do not depreciate the natural capital stock; the returns from both are treated as income.

Consider an analogy. Many high-quality private educational institutions in the United States have large financial endowments. In considering their budgets for the year, these institutions take the revenue from tuition and other fees and add in some proportion of the interest and capital gains earned from the endowment. Standard financial practice, however, does not allow the institution to attack the principal, that is, to draw down the endowment and to treat this increase in financial resources as income. Yet that is precisely what the national accounts allow us to do in terms of natural resources. We can deplete our soils, cut down our forests, and spill oil over ocean coves, and the resulting economic activity is treated as income, not as a decline in the endowment of natural capital. Because the Hicksian definition is violated for natural capital, policy makers are misled. By relying upon misleading information, policy makers are more likely to undertake unsustainable development strategies.

Adjusting the national income accounts to apply the Hicksian definition uniformly to human-made and natural capital could, in resource-dependent countries, make quite a difference. For example, Robert Repetto of the World Resources Institute studied the growth rates of gross national product (GNP) in Indonesia using both conventional unadjusted figures and figures adjusted to account for the depreciation of natural capital. His study found that while the unadjusted gross national product increased at an average annual rate of 7.1 percent from 1971 to 1984, the adjusted estimates rose by only 4 percent per year.

Motivated by a recognition of these serious flaws in the current system of accounts, a number of industrial countries have now proposed (or in a few cases have already set up) systems of adjusted accounts (including Norway, France, Canada, Japan, the Netherlands, Germany, and the United States). Significant differences of opinion on such issues as to whether the changes should be incorporated in a complementary system of accounts or in a complete revision of the standard accounts remain to be resolved.

Trade Policies

Trade policies have also had a major role in distorting economic activity away from sustainable development. Agricultural trade flows, for example, not only demonstrate how price distortions can be translated into unsustainable development, but they also show how poverty, itself a significant factor in promoting unsustainable economic activity, can be exacerbated.

In general, price distortions and artificially supported exchange rates have resulted in a pattern of trade that involves excessive agricultural production in the developed world and too little in the developing world. Agriculture in the developed world is supported by a number of different subsidies. In the western United States, for example, irrigation water is priced substantially below its true cost. Energy, a prime component of agricultural production in industrialized nations, does not reflect its full cost (the most obvious omission being its contribution to global warming). A variety of direct government subsidies to farmers further lowers the private, but not the social, cost of this agriculture. With apparent costs lower than actual costs, both the level of agricultural activity and the form of that activity have been affected. Underpriced inputs lower production costs and promote overproduction.

In the developing world the bias operates to promote underproduction rather than overproduction. Overvalued exchange rates increase the attractiveness of importing food and decrease the attractiveness of exporting food. Domestic price controls frequently further reduce the incentives facing domestic producers, and highly skewed patterns of land ownership force the poor to cultivate lands poorly suited for sustainable agriculture.

Though the law of comparative advantage makes it clear

that national self-sufficiency in food would not be an appropriate goal for many developing countries, the effect of this system of price and exchange rate distortion is to produce an excessive dependence on food production in the industrialized world. By discouraging small-scale agriculture in developing countries, an activity that would provide income to a segment of the population faced with the most severe forms of poverty, biased trade flows exacerbate the poverty problem. Furthermore, since income increases targeted on this particular group typically lead to slower population growth, even some of the population pressures on the environment could ultimately be related to biases in current trade patterns.

Another pernicious effect of trade policies on the environment occurs when political forces in the developed countries conspire to eliminate or substantially reduce natural markets for the developing countries. These policies not only exacerbate poverty in the developing nations, but they have a direct degrading effect on the environment.

The Multi-Fiber Arrangement, originally implemented in 1974, is a case in point. Its effect has been to severely reduce developing country exports of textiles and other products made from fibers. In developing countries fiber products are produced by labor-intensive techniques, causing the employment impact to be high. For local sustainable agriculture, the opportunity to provide the fiber raw materials is another source of employment. By artificially reducing the markets for these products in the industrialized countries, the agreement has forced some developing nations to substitute resource-intensive economic activities, such as timber exports, for the more environmentally congenial fiber-based manufacturing in order to earn foreign exchange.

Eliminating the current distortions in trade patterns, the most obvious strategy, is not the only way trade patterns can be used to manage the transition to a more sustainable economy. Another is to use trade restrictions to discourage unsustainable activities. At a meeting in October 1989, for example, members of the 106-nation Convention on International Trade in Endangered Species of Wild Flora and Fauna

(CITES) voted to add ivory to a long list of goods banned in international trade. By approving a total ban on all trade in products derived from elephants, the CITES agreement has attempted to reduce the pressure on the elephant population by reducing the economic returns to poaching.

The threat posed to the elephant population has become serious. In eight years Africa's elephant population has been cut in half. It has been estimated, for example, that Kenya's elephant population has fallen from about 140,000 a decade ago to roughly 20,000 today. Both Tanzania and Zambia have experienced similar drastic declines in their elephant herds.

Similar trade restrictions have been targeted at imports of timber harvested from rain forests. While many types of forests can support sustainable harvests through appropriate silvaculture techniques, foresters have not yet discovered how to regenerate rainforests sufficiently rapidly to replace anywhere near the current level of harvests. The rainforests are being depleted.

Though a potential step forward, these trade policies are necessarily an incomplete approach because they do not eliminate black markets. Indeed, one side effect of prohibiting legal trade is to increase the price in the black market. Prohibiting trade does not eliminate the demand. As long as the black market demand remains high, depleting the stocks of endangered species remains a viable economic activity for poachers. Ultimately the only permanent long-run solution is to give local communities a stake in preserving the resource. Once the gains to local communities from preservation exceed the gains from poaching, progress in saving these species can be made. The concluding section of this chapter provides an example of how that can be done.

Another use of trade policy attempts to prevent those nations that choose not to sign an international agreement from exploiting their unrestricted status in such a way as to undermine the success of the agreement. An example of this approach is provided by the Montreal Protocol to protect the ozone layer. In addition to calling for a freeze on the production and use of selected substances at 1986 levels, with subsequent reductions of 20 percent and 50 percent expected in the early 1990s, the signatory countries also agreed not only to cease gradually all controlled substance imports from nonsignatory nations, but also to prohibit all imports of products manufactured with controlled substances. These provisions make it difficult for any nonsignatory country to exploit the opportunity to ship computer chips cleaned with controlled substances or foam products made with controlled substances to the signatory nations. The Montreal Protocol also banned exports of controlled substances from the signatory nations, and it was agreed that exports of technology for producing controlled substances would be "discouraged." Trade restrictions provide at least some measure of protection for the domestic markets of businesses in the signatory nations.

Debt Reduction Strategies

Many Third World countries have staggering levels of debt service. In periods of high real interest rates, servicing these debts puts a significant drain on foreign exchange earnings. Using these foreign exchange earnings to service the debt eliminates the possibility of using them to finance imports for sustainable activities to alleviate poverty.

The large debts owed by many developing countries also encourage these countries to overexploit their resource endowments to raise the necessary foreign exchange. Timber exports represent a case in point. As Gus Speth, the president of the World Resources Institute, points out, "By an accident of history and geography, half of the Third World external debt and over two-thirds of global deforestation occur in the same fourteen developing countries."

The loss of biodiversity precipitated by deforestation is perhaps most deeply felt by the industrialized world, not the countries that control the forests. Currently, the technologies to exploit the gene pool this diversity represents are in widest use in the industrialized countries; it is therefore not surprising that the most vociferous opposition to the loss of biodiversity is mounted in the industrialized nations.

Private banks hold most of the debt, and they are not typically motivated by a desire to protect biodiversity. Nonetheless it is possible to find some common ground for negotiation of strategies to reduce the debt. Banks realize that complete repayment of the loans is probably not possible. Rather than completely writing off the loans, an action that not only causes harm to the income statement, but also creates adverse incentives for repayment of future loans, they are willing to consider alternative strategies.

One of the more innovative policies that explores common ground in international arrangements has become known as the debt-nature swap. It is innovative in two senses: (1) the uniqueness of the policy instrument, and (2) the direct involvement of nongovernmental organizations (NGOs) in implementing the policy. A debt-nature swap involves the purchase (at a discounted value in the secondary debt market) of a developing country debt, usually by a nongovernmental environmental organization. The new holder of the debt, the NGO, offers to cancel the debt in return for an environmentally related action on the part of the debtor nation. In July 1987, for example, an American environmental organization purchased $650,000 worth of Bolivia's foreign debt from a private bank at a discounted price of $100,000. It then swapped the face value of the debt with the government of Bolivia in return for an agreement to put together a public-private partnership. This partnership has developed a program that combines ecosystem conservation and regional development planning in 3.7 million acres of designated tropical forestland. The agreement also includes a $250,000 fund in local currency for establishing and administering a system for protecting the forest reserve.

Other arrangements involving different governments and different environmental organizations have since followed this lead. The main advantage of these arrangements to the debtor nation is that it can essentially pay off a significant foreign exchange obligation with domestic currency. Debt-nature swaps offer the realistic possibility to turn what has been a major force for unsustainable economic activity (the debt crisis) into a force for resource conservation.

Though it does represent one small, useful piece of a much larger patchwork quilt of policy, it would clearly be naive to believe that the debt-nature swap would serve as a sufficient vehicle for ending tropical deforestation. The magnitude of the debts and their importance in intensifying environmental degradation call for holder measures to reduce the debt pressure and to enhance the status of environmental protection in developing countries. It is difficult to escape the conclusion that increased financial transfers from the industrialized nations to the developing nations must be part of any package that affords adequate protection for biodiversity.

Judicial Policies

Not all environmental risks can be effectively handled by regulation. Regulations are by their very nature *ex ante;* they prescribe or prohibit specific activities before they occur. Some environmental incidents, such as oil spills or toxic contamination, may persist in spite of the existence of a rigorous regulatory system. Regulations tend to reduce the likelihood of an incident, but typically not to zero, particularly when discretionary human behavior is an important ingredient.

Is it possible to design a system of incentives so that responsible parties could normally be expected to discover the magnitude of the risks, investigate the menu of risk-reducing strategies, make a socially acceptable choice, and act accordingly? Increasingly, court remedies are being relied upon to provide exactly this kind of system of incentives. In cases such as oil spills and contamination of water supplies by toxic substances leaching from disposal facilities, the courts have forced responsible parties not only to pay for cleaning up the contaminated sites, but also to compensate those who suffered damage in one form or another from the contamination. Legislative action to expand the use of criminal penalties in environmental law, including jail sentences for gross negligence by key officers, has further raised the cost of causing environmental injury. Criminal penalties are especially significant as a deterrent since, in contrast to civil penalties, they cannot be covered by insurance.

By establishing legal precedents that make it clear that future incidents will trigger similar financial responsibilities, these decisions provide powerful incentives for potentially responsible parties to take all possible cost-justified precautions. It is by no means a coincidence that several U.S. corporations hit by rather large environmental lawsuits have immediately created high-level environmental departments within the corporate structure to prevent recurrence. Apparently, once judicial remedies become a part of the policy apparatus, an ounce of prevention really is worth a pound of cure.

While judicial remedies offer the potential to force all of those (both producers and consumers) dealing with environmental risks to consider the social consequences of those risks, in practice the current system does not fully live up to this potential. U.S. legislation dealing with oil spills, for example, sets a liability cap on the amount of damage payments to be paid by the responsible party. In most, if not all, major oil spills this cap has served to limit the payments actually made. By allowing the payments to be less, and in some cases substantially less, than the damage, the liability cap sends a false signal to responsible parties. By understating the liability, it undervalues precautionary behavior. While the uncompensated costs are part of the true social cost of producing, transporting, and selling these commodities, they are not paid by the consumers of those commodities. Rather they are paid by the victim. As a result, typically too much of this activity is undertaken and too little precaution is exercised. Inappropriate incentives trigger inappropriate behavior.

Emission Taxes

One rather unconventional economic policy, an emissions tax, is now being used quite extensively in Europe and Japan, but in only a minor way in the United States. (The U.S. currently imposes a tax on chlorofluorocarbons (CFCs) as a part of its policy to fulfill the mandates of the Montreal Protocol, but this tax is designed to eliminate windfall profits rather than to reduce emissions.) Emission tax approaches involve charging a per unit fee on each unit of pollutant emitted into the environment. One of the most attractive features of this particular approach is that it offers the potential for using market forces to produce a cost effective (and possibly even an efficient) allocation of the pollution control responsibility, a feature not even remotely possible under the traditional command-and-control style of regulation.

Why emission charges offer the possibility for cost effective allocation of the control responsibility, but standard command-and-control does not, is not difficult to understand. One of the most important theorems of environmental economics demonstrates that a cost effective allocation of the emission reduction responsibility is achieved when the marginal cost of control (the cost of achieving the last unit of emission reduction) is the same for all sources of that specific pollutant. This theorem is valid for all global pollutants having the characteristic that the damages caused by a unit of emissions does not vary by region; both global warming and ozone depletion gases appear to exhibit that characteristic.

To demonstrate the validity of the theorem, suppose the marginal costs were not equalized. It would always be possible to reduce costs further by giving a little more control responsibility to the lower marginal cost source, and a little less to the higher marginal cost source, resulting in the same total level of control, but lower total control cost. The only case when it is not possible to lower costs by reallocating the responsibility is when the marginal costs are equalized.

A second important theorem in environmental economics demonstrates that polluters faced with emission taxes will minimize their cost by controlling until the marginal cost of control is equal to the per unit tax. More control than that would raise costs unnecessarily because the cost of the additional control would exceed the cost of the alternative, simply paying the tax. Less control would also result in an unnecessarily high cost, because the additional tax paid on the uncontrolled emissions would exceed the cost of simply eliminating those emissions. By eliminating the emissions, the source could avoid the associated tax, a cheaper alternative.

Taken together, these theorems imply that forcing all polluters to face the same per unit tax on emissions results in an allocation of the control responsibility that is cost effective; the marginal costs would be equalized by polluters acting to minimize their own costs. Since uniform tax rates may well be perceived as being more just than differentiated taxes (and therefore administratively easier to implement on a global basis), the finding that uniform taxes are a cost effective means of reducing emissions is rather significant.

One additional virtue of an emission tax is that it can stimulate the development of new, environmentally benign technologies and it can stimulate the *reduction* of waste, not merely the *control* of the waste. Under a traditional command-and-control regulatory system based on emission of effluent standards, once the source has met the legal standard, further effort to reduce emissions is neither necessary nor in its economic interest. With an emission tax, on the other hand, *all* uncontrolled emissions trigger an additional financial burden. Adopting a new control technology that would permit additional emission reduction at reasonable cost would be an attractive strategy for a source facing emission taxes, but not for a source currently meeting emission standards. By encouraging new markets for more environmentally benign technologies, an important component of the transition to sustainable development, emission taxes could be expected to stimulate more research and development in both controlling and reducing emissions.

Emission taxes also produce revenue. In Europe, where emission taxes are quite common, most of the revenue has been earmarked for environmental improvement projects related to the taxed emissions. For example, revenue from taxes on water pollutants has been used to subsidize waste treatment plants.

Emission taxes also have a significant disadvantage. Sources confronted by emission taxes face an additional financial burden that serves to diminish their enthusiasm for the approach.

Under traditional command-and-control regulation, sources pay only for the required pollution control equipment. With emission taxes, however, not only do they have to pay for the control equipment, but they also have to pay the taxes on uncontrolled emissions. A number of studies have made it clear that the additional financial burden associated with the taxes can be substantial.

While some tactics to reduce the financial burden of emissions taxes exist (tax rebates or taxing only emissions above a certain level), these tactics have not been very successful in deflecting political opposition. In recognition of and response to this burden, industries in the United States have been reluctant to accept an emission tax approach, fearing that the resulting rise in pollution control costs would make them competitively vulnerable in world markets. In Europe, concern over the financial burden has not been sufficient to prevent emission taxes from being instituted, but it has served to keep the tax rates lower than economists believe they should be.

One positive role for emission taxes on a global scale would be in terms of the coalition-building opportunities created by the revenue they would raise. One approach to exploiting this opportunity would commit the revenue to a global trust fund. By making access to the funds conditional on signing the agreement, incentives to participate could be created. For example, if only signatory nations would be eligible to apply for trust funds to undertake projects related to sustainability, the benefits of signing would be enhanced.

Transferable Permits or Quotas

In the United States the economic incentives approach to pollution control has taken a rather different form. Instead of putting a price on pollution (the concept behind emission taxes), the emissions trading approach sets transferable quantity limits on emissions. Emissions trading begins with traditional command-and-control regulation in which each discharge point is assigned an emissions limit. Sources that voluntarily wish to reduce pollution more than required by this limit are allowed to have the excess reduction certified as an "emission reduction credit." Compliance with the law is achieved at a particular discharge point by combining sufficient emission reductions and emission reduction credits to meet the legal standard.

One way in which this particular approach was used rather creatively and successfully is called the "offset" policy. In the mid-1970s several geographic regions in the United States found themselves in violation of the ambient air quality standards that had been designed to protect human health. The law provided that new industries would not be allowed to move into those areas if they added any more of the pollutant responsible for the standard being violated. Since even those potential entrants adopting the most stringent control techniques would typically add some of the pollutant, in effect that policy prohibited those new firms from locating in nonattainment areas. This was a serious political blow to mayors eager to expand their employment and tax base. How could they allow economic growth while assuring that the air quality would steadily improve to the level dictated by the ambient standard?

To respond positively to this conflict of goals, regulators adopted the offset policy. Under this policy any new firm wanting to move into an area currently in violation of the ambient air quality standard would be required to acquire 1.2 emission reduction credits for each 1.0 unit of emissions added by the new plant. Since the resulting reduction from sources already located in the area would necessarily exceed the amount being added by the new source, air quality would improve every time a new firm moved into the area. With this policy the confrontation between economic growth and environmental protection was diffused. New firms were not only allowed to move into polluted cities, but they became one of the main vehicles for improving the quality of the air. With the offset policy, economic growth facilitated, rather than blocked, air quality improvement.

Emissions trading shared with emission taxes the characteristic that it promotes both cost effectiveness and technology development. Cost effectiveness is promoted because those sources that can reduce their emissions most cheaply choose to do so, selling the resulting emission reduction credits to others. The proceeds can then be used by the selling source to finance the additional control. In these transfers the price of the emission reduction credits plays the same role in stimulating the cost effectiveness as does the tax rate in the emission charge system; it encourages a reallocation of control responsibility until the marginal control costs are equalized. Similarly, technological progress is stimulated by emissions trading because additional control creates emission reduction credits that can be sold.

One of the most potentially significant characteristics of the emissions trading approach is the opportunity it offers for cost sharing. It is not at all uncommon for some emission sources to be underregulated due to their financial vulnerability. When firms are on the brink of going out of business, regulators are reluctant to subject them to stringent regulations that might push them off the financial brink. Yet in many cases the costs of securing additional emission reductions from these sources would be substantially lower than the cost of securing further reductions from already controlled sources.

Under traditional command-and-control regulations, the emissions from financially vulnerable sources would remain uncontrolled while remaining sources would necessarily be controlled to a proportionally higher degree. With emissions trading, however, financially vulnerable sources could voluntarily create emission reduction credits, using the revenue from the sale of those credits to finance the additional cost of control. Meanwhile the sources purchasing the emission reduction credits would find acquiring the credits a far cheaper alternative than controlling their own emissions to a correspondingly higher degree. While ultimate air quality would be the same in either case, the fact that trading reduces compliance costs usually means that the mandated improvements are achieved more quickly with trading and with less litigation. This capacity of emissions trading to facilitate cost sharing could potentially be very important on a global scale, a point discussed further in the concluding section of this chapter.

Although emissions trading was initiated to deal with pollution problems occurring within U.S. borders, it has now been extended to cover the gases associated with stratospheric ozone depletion. As part of its strategy to fulfill the requirements of the Montreal Protocol, the United States has adopted a system of transferable production and consumption allowances for the controlled substances named by the agreement. To produce or consume these substances it is necessary to possess the required number of production or consumption allowances. The allowances were allocated to current producers and consumers on the basis of 1986 production and consumption levels. The amount of production or consumption permitted by the allowances declines over time in accordance with the reductions mandated by the protocol. By making these production and consumption allowances fully transferable, the government sought to stimulate technological progress in the area and to facilitate the flow of these allowances from those who can most easily find substitutes to those who cannot. As market forces change, the transferability of these allowances assures that the allocation of the control responsibility can adjust to the changes, while also assuring continued compliance with the terms of the agreement.

Should other nations adopt transferable production and consumption allowances as their means of meeting the dictates of the Montreal Protocol, these allowances could flow across national borders. Not only would an international flow of these allowances facilitate a more cost effective allocation among nations, but it would leave the valuation of these transfers to what is now a global marketplace. Since all transfers would be voluntary, allowances would not be transferred unless it was in the interest of both participants.

One key problem in establishing international markets in these allowances would be seeking agreement on the initial allocation of the allowances. Since any production or consumption above that permitted by the allowances requires the purchase of additional allowances from others willing to give them up, the initial distribution becomes very important. Nations that receive too few allowances in proportion to their perceived need will have to acquire the additional allowances on the open market, presumably at a substantial cost.

Different schemes for defining the trading baseline have very different consequences. Awarding allowances on the basis of current production or consumption levels, the approach embodied in the Montreal Protocol, favors those who currently have the requisite technology. A much more favorable outcome for the populous developing nations would be to allocate the allowances on the basis of population. Should this initial allocation rule prevail, the industrialized nations would find themselves having to purchase significant amounts of the allowances simply to justify the status quo. Reaching an international agreement on the initial distribution of these allowances prior to allowing trade would probably be one of the most difficult hurdles to overcome in developing a transferable allowance approach to ozone depletion gases.

Transferable quotas have been applied in a very different way to protect overexploited, renewable resources. Due to their desirability and the traditional open access to the fishery, the populations of several species of fish off the coast of New Zealand were being depleted. While the need to reduce the amount of pressure being put on the population was rather obvious, how to accomplish that reduction was not at all obvious. Although it was relatively easy to prevent new fishers from entering the fisheries, it was harder to figure out how to reduce the pressure from those who had been fishing in the area for years or even decades. Because fishing is characterized by economies of scale, simply reducing everyone's catch proportionately would not make much sense. Proportional reductions would only force all fishers to face higher costs and waste a great deal of fishing capacity as all boats sat around idle for a significant proportion of time. A better solution would clearly be to have fewer boats harvesting the stock. That way each boat could be used closer to its full capacity without depleting the population. Which fishers should be asked to give up their livelihood and leave their industry, however, was not an easy question to answer.

The economic incentive approach addressed this problem by imposing transferable catch quotas on all fish harvested from the fishery. Revenues derived from the annual fee charged for renewing these quotas were used to buy out fishers who were willing to retire their quotas and to forgo any future fishing for the relevant species. Essentially each fisher stated the lowest price that he or she would accept for leaving the industry; the regulators selected those who could be induced to leave at the lowest price, paid the stipulated amount from the fund financed by the annual fees, and retired their catch quotas for the affected species. It was not long before a sufficient number of licenses had been retired, the harvest was reduced to levels that would allow the population to be replenished, and the fishery was protected. Because the program was voluntary, those who left the industry only did so when they felt they had been adequately compensated. A difficult and potentially dangerous pressure on a valuable natural resource was avoided by the creative use of an approach that changed the economic incentives of the participants.

Possibilities for the Future

It now remains only to show how these variable policies would be woven together in a manner that facilitates international cooperation in the resolution of international environmental problems. Four principles provide the foundation for this approach.

The Full Cost Principle

Gaining acceptance for the full cost principle would be an important first step in achieving international cooperation in the resolution of global environmental problems. According to the full cost principle, all users of environmental resources should pay their full cost. Those using the environment as a waste repository, for example, would be presumed responsible not only for controlling pollution to the full extent required by the law, but also for restoring environmental resources damaged beyond some *de minimus* amount and for compensating for damage caused.

This principle is based upon the presumption that humanity has a right to a reasonably safe and healthy environment. Since this right has been held in common for the stratosphere and the international sections of the oceans, no administrative body has either the responsibility or the authority for protecting that right. As a result it has been involuntarily surrendered on a first come, first served basis without compensation.

The principle that some rights may necessarily be involuntarily transferred is recognized by the American legal system. Automobile accidents are a classic example: the right to safe passage is involuntarily surrendered at the moment of impact. But the legal system also recognizes that when involuntary transfers take place, compensation is to be awarded. Requiring compensation serves the twin purpose of attempting to restore victims to their preaccident position, insofar as possible, and to provide incentives for all drivers to take the cost-justified level of precautions.

Although global warming and ozone depletion impose an environmental cost, currently that cost is not being borne, or even recognized, by those who ultimately control the magnitude of the problem. Furthermore, those choosing unilaterally to reduce their emissions expose themselves to the higher costs associated with mitigating strategies. Applying the full cost principle would send a strong signal to all users of the environment that the atmosphere is a scarce, precious resource and should be treated accordingly. Products produced by manufacturing processes that are environmentally destructive would become relatively more expensive; those produced by environmentally benign production processes would become relatively cheaper. Implementing the full cost principle would end the implicit subsidy that all polluting activities have received since the beginning of time. When the level of economic activity was low, the corresponding subsidy was small and therefore probably not worthy of political attention. Since the scale of economic activity has grown, however, the subsidy has become very large indeed; ignoring it leads to significant resource distortion.

The full cost principle is similar to, but not the same as, the "polluter pays" principle being applied in the Organization for Economic Cooperation and Development (OECD) nations. While the polluter pays principle requires polluters to bear the cost of installing the pollution control equipment, the full cost principle requires them to bear the cost of any environmental damage above some *de minimus* threshold caused by uncontrolled emissions as well. Furthermore, the polluter pays principle usually is applied only to industries; the full cost principle is applied to all emitters, including homeowners and automobile owners.

What policy implications would flow from the acceptance of the full cost principle? A first implication is that emissions of harmful substances should bear an emission charge. For the global warming problem, this could take the form of a tax on all greenhouse gases emitted into the atmosphere. The "carbon tax," which is currently being widely discussed in Europe and the United States, could be one component of this package. Since carbon dioxide is only one of the greenhouse gases, however, taxes would necessarily be imposed on other gases as well. The appropriate level of this tax for each gas would depend upon its per unit contribution to the global warming problem; gases posing a larger per unit risk would bear higher tax rates.

Taxes on fossil fuels are not a radical concept. Gasoline taxes have routinely been levied for years. Though gasoline taxes are imposed on an input to combustion rate, rather than an emission rate, the administrative ease with which they can be implemented and the close relationship between the composition of the fuel and the composition of the emissions make them a popular candidate for use as one component in a package of corrective measures to reduce global warming.

Since gasoline taxes have already been implemented by nations for their own purposes, examining the degree to which these taxes deviate from the full cost principle provides some indication of how complex the international negotiations to reform gasoline taxes so they would conform to the principle would be. To the extent that the current system of taxes approximates the ideal, conditions would appear favorable to negotiating a transition. In fact, the gasoline taxes now in use around the world fail to fulfill the requirements of the full cost principle in two main respects: the use of the revenue and the uniformity of the tax rates.

Whereas the full cost principle requires that the tax rates reflect the damage caused by emissions, thereby fostering a reduction in emissions, current gasoline tax rates are commonly determined by the revenue needed to build more roads; added roadway capacity ultimately translates into more emissions, not fewer emissions. Because they are driven by the need to finance capacity expansion rather than to account for the environmental effects of combustion, gasoline taxes are currently not in conformance with the full cost principle.

Although applying the full cost principle for global warming also requires that the tax rates be uniformly applied, that condition is a far cry from actual experience. According to the Energy Information Administration publication *International Energy Prices 1980–84,* in 1984 gasoline taxes (expressed in U.S. cents per gallon) ranged from $0.21 in the United States to over $1.00 in the majority of European countries. When the tax rates differ by a factor of five or more, the allocation of control responsibility for reducing gasoline-related emissions does not fulfill the uniformity requirement.

Substances contributing to ozone depletion would also be taxed according to the fuel cost principle. Since the ozone depletion tax and the global warming tax would be separately assessed, substances such as chlorofluorocarbons that contribute to both global warming and ozone depletion would bear both taxes.

The transition to a more sustainable economic system will depend upon the development of new technologies, and upon much greater levels of energy efficiency than are currently being achieved. Those transitions will not occur unless the prevailing economic incentives support and encourage them. Once the greenhouse gas and ozone depletion taxes were in effect, the incentives would be changed; greater energy efficiency and the development of new technologies would become top priority objectives.

Since environmental taxes would generate revenue, a common goal fund could be established to receive and dispense that revenue. Controlled by representatives of the signatory nations, this fund could conceivably dispense funds for projects as diverse as reforestation or the promotion of solar powered projects to provide income and subsistence to poor areas of the world. A fund financed by environmental taxes would help to reduce the twin causes of environmental problems: distorted market signals and poverty.

One interesting precedent for this approach is the World Heritage Convention, which established a World Heritage Fund. This fund is used to protect environments of "outstanding universal value." Each signatory is required to give at least one percent of its contribution to the regular budget of the United Nations Educational, Scientific and Cultural Organization (UNESCO) to this fund every two years. In practice this means that the fund is financed almost entirely by the industrial nations, but smaller nations can tap its resources. Some ninety nations have signed this agreement, suggesting that the fund arrangements have successfully exploited some common interests. Since subscribing to the agreement apparently confers benefits on the signatories, it is essentially self-enforcing.

Determining the appropriate rate for any per unit environmental tax would not be a trivial matter. Although to apply the full cost principle correctly the rate should be equal to the marginal social damage caused by a unit of emission, current valuation techniques would not identify that level with any reasonable degree of confidence. The high degree of scientific uncertainty associated with the magnitude of the global warming threat makes precise valuation impossible. But that may not be a fatal flaw since zero, the current rate, is not correct either. Even establishing a low tax rate would be a step in the right direction; as more information is gained, the rate could be adjusted.

Implications for the legal system would flow from the full cost principle as well. For example, international laws should permit full recovery for damage caused by oil spills or other environmental incidents. Not only should the contaminated site be restored insofar as possible, but those suffering demonstrable losses should be fully compensated.

Making explicit environmental costs that have been hidden is only one side of the coin; the other is eliminating inappropriate subsidies. Subsidies that are incompatible with the full cost principles should be eliminated. Implicit subsidies should be targeted as well as explicit subsidies. For example, when the pricing of environmental resources is subject to government regulation (such as water in the American Southwest), prices should not simply be determined by historic average cost; they should reflect the scarcity of the resource.

Incremental block pricing provides a practical means of implementing this recommendation without jeopardizing the traditional legal constraint that water distribution utilities can earn no more than a fair rate of return. With incremental block pricing the price of additional water consumed rises with the amount consumed per unit time. While the first units consumed per month up to some predetermined threshold would be relatively cheap, units consumed beyond the threshold would face a much higher price that truly reflects the scarcity of the resource. By assuring that the marginal units consumed were priced at full cost, adequate incentives to conserve would be introduced.

The transition to full cost could proceed gradually, beginning in certain sectors, moving to others as greater familiarity with the approach was gained. A complete, immediate transition is not an essential ingredient of a rational approach. Current electric utility practices in New York State demonstrate the point. A competitive market has been established in which independent power producers bid against each other for contracts to supply the host utility with power. Suppliers relying upon fossil fuels are required to add one cent per kilowatt/hour to their bids to account for air pollution effects and an additional half cent per kilowatt/hour to account for other environmental consequences. Incorporating the full cost of the fossil fuel power sources affords renewable sources and energy conservation the opportunity to compete on a level playing field with fossil fuel power.

The Cost Effectiveness Principle

A second principle suggests that the policy package should be cost effective insofar as possible. A policy is cost effective if it achieves the policy objective at the lowest possible cost. Cost effectiveness is an important characteristic because it can reduce the amount of political backlash by limiting wasteful expenditures.

Complete acceptance and appropriate implementation of the full cost principle would automatically produce cost effectiveness as a side benefit. Should acceptance of the full cost principle falter, however, cost effectiveness could be elevated to a primary policy goal, worthy in its own right. It provides a desirable, if less than perfect, fallback position.

Political acceptance of the full cost principle is by no means a foregone conclusion. While taxes on greenhouse and ozone depletion gases can go a long way toward rectifying some of the current distortions in resource pricing, they will do little to reassure those whose vision of the future is defined in terms of specific limits on emissions, not correcting price distortions. It would be very difficult to establish a set of tax rates that could guarantee a specific emissions target.

Establishing a limit on emissions and allocating the proposed reductions among the nations of the world would be one of the most difficult aspects of any international agreement on global warming or ozone depletion faced by this alternative approach. Fairness will no doubt be one critical aspect of the negotiations, and it is likely that some form of cost sharing will result. How are the costs to be shared?

Emissions trading becomes a reasonable approach for implementing the cost effectiveness principle, either as a complement to or a substitute for the taxes discussed above. When used as a complement, the process of establishing emissions trading in greenhouse or ozone depletion gases would be initiated by setting transferable limits on the amounts each nation could emit on an annual basis. Nations achieving reductions greater than required by the agreement could receive transferable emission reduction credits that could be sold to other nations. By purchasing these credits, the acquiring nation could increase its quota by the amount covered by the emission reduction credits. All emissions authorized by the quotas could still be subject to an environmental tax. If emissions trading were used as a substitute for environmental taxes, transferable quotas would be established, but no taxes would be levied on authorized emissions. In either case the total emission limit negotiated by the agreement would be binding; no trade leading to a net increase in aggregate would be approved.

As long as the sum of emissions was equal to the total permitted annual emissions, cost effectiveness could be achieved regardless of how these emission allowances were initially allocated across countries. An international market in emission reduction credits would facilitate the movement of credits from those countries with the capacity to create them most cheaply to those countries faced by very high costs of additional control. The capacity to achieve cost effectiveness regardless of how the initial emission allowances are allocated is a significant attribute of an emissions trading approach that can be exploited for developing a market approach to cost sharing.

With emission trading as the strategy of choice, those forging new international agreements have a very large latitude in attempting to establish emission limitations that are fair and politically feasible without jeopardizing cost effectiveness. It would be quite possible, for example, to allocate production allowances to nations on the basis of their population in some past year, say 1986, rather than on current energy use. This particular choice, of course, would lead to many more allowances being granted to populous Third World countries and many fewer allowances being granted to the Western industrialized world. A middle ground might reserve a significant growth increment (50 percent of their current use, for example) for the developing countries, reducing the share going to the industrialized countries sufficiently to produce the desired target. Because of the very different current emission levels, a

50 percent growth increment for developing countries would necessitate a much smaller than 50 percent compensating reduction in the developing countries. As the Western nations acquired by purchase the necessary production allowances at market prices from those nations selling them, significant financial transfers would take place. The size of these transfers would be dictated by market forces, not by negotiation.

A precondition for the successful operation of this market is the assurance to all participants that the created production allowances or emission reduction credits are permanent, surplus, quantifiable, and enforceable. This assurance can only be given if some trusted international agency is granted the power to certify these transfers on a case by case basis. While the potential trading partners would establish the price of the transfer between themselves, no transfer could take place until the international agency was satisfied that the offsetting reductions satisfied the four criteria.

A system of possible offsets for emissions trading in carbon dioxide gases would also be possible. Suppose, for example, that international negotiations produced an agreement to hold aggregate carbon dioxide emissions at current levels. Under this scheme all future increases in carbon dioxide emissions would require the acquisition of offsetting reductions; these reductions could be secured from any country in the world. Undertaking any approved carbon dioxide reducing strategy resulting in reductions greater than required by the agreement would create an equivalent number of offsetting production allowances, which could be sold on an international market to those seeking offsets. These transfers would necessarily be subject to the certification process described above.

It is not difficult to imagine a similar kind of scheme operating on a regional basis for acid rain. In Europe, for example, many of the Western European nations are at the point where further control of their own emissions is very expensive. A disproportionate share of the remaining emissions affecting Western European nations is coming from Eastern Europe. However, since most of the Eastern European nations have troubled economies that can ill afford the shock of major new expenditures, they are not likely to engage in major pollution control reductions in the near future. One solution to this problem is to seek agreement that all nations would implement some minimum level of control for all sources within their borders, allowing the Western industrialized nations to buy reductions above and beyond this minimum control level from the Eastern European nations. In most Western countries, that would represent the cheapest means of reducing acid rain, much cheaper than controlling their own emissions to an even higher level. The Eastern European nations would then use the revenue from the sale of acid rain reduction credits to finance the installation of control equipment. In many cases this equipment would probably be produced and sold by the Western nations, an additional inducement to participate in cost sharing.

The Sustainability Principle

A third step in resolving future environmental problems involves acceptance of the sustainability principle. According to this principle, all resources should be used in a manner that respects the needs of future generations. For biological resources this implies that the harvest rates should not allow extinction; harvest rates and regeneration rates need to be synchronized. For finite resources the sustainability principle implies an obligation to maintain reasonable substitute options for succeeding generations.

Adjusting the national income accounts would be an immediate implication of the sustainability principle. The income accounts must conform with the Hicksian definition of income. All of the costs, including the depreciation of natural capital, should be subtracted from the gross receipts in producing a national income figure. Failure to do this, as is the current practice, provides very misleading signals to the public sector. These misleading signals provide powerful incentives for public figures to engage in economic activities that violate the sustainability principle.

Adopting the sustainability principle would also have consequences for the conduct of trade policy. Trade in commodities produced in violation of the principle would be prohibited or subject to trade sanctions.

The process to implement this change in policy is already in place. Under the General Agreement on Tariffs and Trade (GATT), current trade practices are scrutinized to ferret out those that are unfair. Dumping, defined as selling abroad at a price below the home market, is one trading practice that currently receives that scrutiny. Under U.S. antidumping statutes, when dumping is proved, the U.S. Department of Commerce applies an antidumping duty as an offset and adds on a penalty. Nonsustainability could become another of the practices receiving such scrutiny without altering the current process by which the GATT agreement is enforced.

Less targeted trade sanctions could also be used to make both signing an agreement and fulfilling its terms more attractive to reluctant signatories. The Packwood-Magnuson Amendment to the U.S. Fishery Conservation and Management Act (1976) requires the U.S. to retaliate whenever foreign nationals undermine the effectiveness of the International Whaling Convention. Specifically, an offending nation automatically loses half of its allocation of fish products derived from U.S. waters. Continued disregard of the convention by the foreign national leads to revocation of the right to fish in U.S. waters.

Though the economic literature on sustainability is still in its infancy, it has begun to yield a number of useful insights on the application of the sustainability principle. Perhaps one of the most important implications is that the solutions to global environmental problems prescribed by cost-benefit analysis do not necessarily satisfy the sustainability principle. Under some circumstances the recommendations from cost-benefit analysis would normally be sufficient to produce sustainable levels of economic activity. But they are not always sufficient.

The use of depletable resources by the current generation is one area where stronger measures may be necessary to preserve the interests of future generations. Fossil fuels used today are unavailable for the use of future generations. While the concept of sustainability does not automatically foreclose the option of the current generation to use depletable resources, it does suggest that part of the proceeds from using those resources should be set aside in ways that will compensate future generations for the loss of this particular option by creating other options. Such a strategy might envision, for example, setting aside through taxation a certain proportion of all proceeds from depletable resources to fund research on substitutes likely to be used by future generations. In the case of fossil fuels, for example, one might subsidize research into fusion power or solar energy so that as fossil fuels are depleted, future generations would have the ability to switch to alternative sources easily without diminishing living standards in the process.

Global climate change is another area where cost-benefit analysis may not be a sufficient guide to rational public policy. Since the present value component of cost-benefit analysis emphasizes short-term over long-term consequences, the application of cost-benefit analysis will weigh the current costs of controlling emissions more heavily than the distant future damages caused by global warming. Though this approach is not inherently biased against future generations, their interests will only be adequately protected if they would be willing to accept monetary compensation for a modified climate, and if current generations were willing to set aside sufficient proceeds to provide this compensation. Since it is not obvious that either condition would be satisfied, the long lead times associated with this particular problem place in jeopardy the interests of future generations in maintaining a stable climate.

The Property Rights Principle

The fourth step in the sustainability program would be to gain acceptance for the "property rights principle." According to the property rights principle, local communities should have a property right over flora and fauna within their border. This property right would entitle the community to share in any benefits created by preserving the species. Assuring that local property rights over genetic resources are defined and respected would give local communities a much larger stake in some of the global benefits to be derived from the use of those resources and would enhance the prospects for effective enforcement.

Consider the problem of stemming the decline in the elephant population as an example. Insofar as permitted by the migratory nature of the herd, the property rights principle would confer the right to harvest a fixed number of elephants on the indigenous peoples who live in the elephant's native habitat. The amount of harvest permitted would be low enough to assure conservation of the population. Should the elephant population grow, the harvesting rights would grow as well, giving local communities an incentive to increase, not merely to maintain the population. Indigenous people could also be hired as enforcers and given jobs in the tourist industry associated with the elephants. Ownership of harvesting rights and the possibility of continued employment as long as the herd was preserved would assure an income to the local community, giving them a stake in preserving the herd. Preventing poaching would become easier because poachers would become a threat to the local community, not merely a threat to a distant national government that inspires little allegiance.

A somewhat related application of the property rights principle could provide an additional means of resolving the diminishing supply of biologically rich tropical rainforests. One of the arguments for preserving biodiversity is that it offers a valuable gene pool for the development of future products such as medicines or food crops. Typically, however, the nations that govern the forestland containing this biologically rich gene pool have not shared in the wealth created by the products derived from it. One solution to this problem is to establish the principle that the nations that contain these biologically rich resources within their borders would be entitled to a stipulated royalty on any and all products developed from the genes obtained from these preserves.

Currently, nations cutting down their tropical forests have

little incentive to protect the gene pool harbored within those forests, because they are unlikely to reap any of the rewards that will ultimately result. Exploitation of the gene pool and the economic rewards that result from it typically accrue only to those nations and to those companies that can afford the extensive research. By establishing the principle stipulating that royalty payments would accrue to the nation from which the original genes were extracted, local incentives would become more compatible with global incentives.

Implementing this recommendation would not be trivial. Though it is not hard to envision licenses being required of all those conducting research or collecting specimens of local flora or fauna, it is more difficult to imagine a process that would guarantee royalty payments on every new derivative genetic discovery. For Third World countries to be aware of new discoveries would be difficult enough, but the need to enforce the terms of the license on a company that is physically located in another country could prove inordinately time consuming and expensive.

In conclusion, the search for solutions must recognize that market forces are extremely powerful. Attempts to negotiate international agreements that seek to block those forces or to meet them head on are probably doomed to failure. Nevertheless, it is possible to negotiate agreements that harness those forces and channel them in directions that enhance the possibilities of international cooperation. To take these steps will require thinking and acting in somewhat unconventional ways. Whether the world community is equal to the task remains to be seen.

7

The World Economic Climate

RICHARD N. COOPER

T his chapter addresses the dominant trends in the world economy over the next quarter century. Such a horizon is appropriate when the principal concern is with greenhouse gases, since the evidence for their importance will mount only slowly. A somewhat shorter horizon may be appropriate for negotiations among countries on what might be done about greenhouse gas emissions; something will be said about that issue at the end of the chapter.

RICHARD N. COOPER has been the Maurits B. Boas Professor of International Economics at Harvard University since 1981. He previously served as under secretary for economic affairs in the State Department during the Carter administration, deputy assistant secretary of state for international monetary affairs from 1965–66, and senior staff economist for President Kennedy's Council on Economic Advisors. Currently Dr. Cooper chairs the Federal Reserve Bank of Boston, the Advisory Committee of the Institute for International Economics, the Executive Panel to Chief of Naval Operations, and the Advisory Committee of the Committee for Economic Development. He is a member of the Trilateral Commission and the Council on Foreign Relations. He has published over 300 articles and books.

Population Growth

Three features of the international economic environment will be especially important over the next twenty-five years. The first is rapid population growth. Between 1965 and 1986 the world's population grew by 1600 million persons, or about 1.9 percent a year. It is true that there was some slowdown in population growth toward the end of this period, especially in China and in a number of middle-income countries, such as South Korea, as well as in the industrialized countries. But China was the exception among low-income countries. Population growth normally accelerates at first after a country begins to see increases in per capita income, as longevity increases and infant mortality rates fall with better nutrition and medical care. A slowdown in population growth usually occurs only after per capita income reaches around $1,000, when modes of production change, parents realize that the probability of survival of their children has risen, and parents become better informed about family planning techniques. There are still over 3 billion persons living in countries with average per capita incomes below $1,000 (in 1986), mostly in Africa and Asia. Even if global population growth slows by a substantial 0.3 percentage points, to 1.6 percent a year, the world population would still reach 7.7 billion by the year 2015, an increase of 2.8 billion from the mid-1980s. More people mean more demand for energy—for warmth, food preparation, illumination, motive power, and production processes. It would take extraordinary efforts of a nature and magnitude not generally contemplated to alter this projection consequentially, although more modest efforts now could have consequential effects beyond our twenty-five year horizon.

Rising Incomes

The second dominant feature of the world economy is the all-but-universal aspiration for higher standards of living in all but the richest parts of the world. In this respect the world has been westernized; it has absorbed the notion and the expectation of material progress. So in future there will not only be more people, but more people wanting higher standards of living. And we now know how to achieve higher standards of living: install a stable social system with incentives for effort and risk taking. Most of the world does not need to generate new technology or even savings to grow—they can be borrowed from the rest of the world.

Historically, economic growth is associated with an enormous growth in demand for commercial primary energy. In the two strong decades following 1950, the demand for primary energy in the industrialized countries more than doubled; in the two decades following 1960, the demand for primary energy in the centrally planned economies increased by a factor of nearly 2.5; and in the two decades following 1965, the demand for primary energy in the developing countries trebled. If gross world product grows by a plausible 4 percent over the next quarter century (1.6 percent in population and 2.4 percent in per capita income), the demand for primary energy on historical relationships between energy and growth would increase by a factor of 2.6 over present energy consumption. Put another way, improvements in the efficiency with which the world economy uses energy must exceed 4 percent a year if we are to avoid increased demand for energy over current levels.

An increase in demand for commercial energy does not translate one-for-one into increased greenhouse gas emissions, since some of this demand is substituting, in poor countries, for traditional local sources of energy, mainly wood. But the bulk of it entails a net increase in energy use, hence in emissions unless nonemitting forms of energy generation are installed in great volume in the coming two decades.

Two qualifications to the above projections need to be mentioned. First, since 1975 there has been a sharp drop in the growth of energy demand traditionally associated with economic growth. This reflected a widespread response to the oil shocks of 1974 and 1979–80, and especially to the sharp increases in energy prices associated with those shocks. We do not know yet whether this lower ratio between energy consumption and growth represents a new trend, or whether it represented a transitional period of conservation that, when exhausted, will lead to restoration of the traditional relationship. But the experience of the years since 1975 has clearly shown that a given level of gross national product (GNP) can be sustained with lower levels of energy consumption, country by country, and there is no reason to think that with further incentives to conserve energy, that process could not continue beyond what has already been achieved. The marked improvement in economy-wide energy efficiency that has been achieved in industrial countries was due in part, but only in relatively small part, to increased imports of energy from developing countries in indirect forms such as steel.

The second qualification is that growth of developing countries as a group (excluding China) slowed enormously in the 1980s, suggesting that a 4 percent growth in gross world product over the next twenty-five years may be too high. But there are no signs that the aspirations for higher living standards have been diminished. The 1980s are thought of as a period of temporary setback that must be overcome. A best guess would be that the economic growth of developing countries will accelerate from the low levels of the 1980s. (Appendix A provides some data on growth in population, output, and energy consumption after 1965.)

During the late 1980s and into the 1990s many developing countries are burdened by heavy external debt, acquired during the more buoyant 1970s and in the early 1980s, following the second major increase in oil prices. Difficulties in servicing this debt have led private lenders around the world to hesitate to lend to many of these countries, especially those in Latin America and in Africa. As a consequence, the net flow of resources into developing countries as a group has diminished substantially from levels of a decade ago, and some individual countries are even transferring resources to the creditor nations insofar as their actual interest payments exceed new inflows of capital. Over the course of the next twenty-five years, however, this problem is likely to be solved, so that from the perspective of 2015, the "debt problem" will be seen as a historical event of the 1980s and the early 1990s. For some countries, especially those in Latin America, the solution will lie largely in outgrowing the debt, thus reducing debt-to-gross domestic product (GDP) and debt service ratios, to the point at which these countries will again become creditworthy and attractive places to invest. For others, mainly the very poor countries of Africa, the problem will be solved largely by effective write-offs of consequential portions of the debt. In any case, while the heavy debt currently influences significantly the relation of heavily indebted countries to the international community, that influence is likely to diminish over time, and as noted, economic growth will accelerate from the low levels of the 1980s.

Increased International Mobility

The third important feature of the world economy is its increased integration, in the specific sense here that business enterprises increasingly take, and are driven by competition to take, a more-than-regional or national perspective in framing their business decisions. This is true not only of markets and sources of supply, which have been internationalized for some time, and of sources of capital, which have been internationalized over the past two decades, but increasingly also of the location of production and the related issue of labor force. With the secular decline in transportation costs, especially in the past two decades of air freight and bulk carriage, transportation costs are no longer a decisive factor for determining the location of production of many goods. Not only Persian Gulf oil but also South African coal and Liberian iron ore can be moved long distances to processors. Under these circumstances many industries in principle become footloose, able to locate at a variety of convenient places. They seek an inexpensive labor force able to meet the required skill qualifications, social stability, and a tax and regulatory environment favorable to low production costs. These developments imply that a country far out of line in one dimension that is not adequately compensated in some other dimension will lose those economic activities that do not require close proximity to markets. The influence of higher mobility should not be exaggerated. The management of many enterprises still has strong ties of loyalty to its home society and culture, as well as useful but specialized knowledge about how best to operate in a known political environment, and it is subject to the inertial forces that affect most human beings. But the trend is clear: competitive pressures are eroding these factors, and more and more firms are moving some of their activities away from their historical bases.

What are the implications of this third feature for the environment? Individual countries cannot impose stiff environmental regulations and expect to retain the economic activities that are especially hard hit, unless for one reason or another the activities are immobile, or unless the firms in question see some direct benefit flowing from the regulations. Over time, the activity will shift to lower-cost locations. With increasingly mobile production, there will be increasing conflict between each nation's exercise of its sovereign right of regulation and its ability to retain the regulated activity.

It is still possible to regulate products in the face of mobility of firms, since a country can impose requirements on products and prohibit imports as well as local production of nonconforming products, for example with respect to safety features or materials of fabrication (e.g., ivory). Even here, however, when the product is used in further production, as most traded goods are, regulations on products will raise costs to local producers who use the product, relative to their offshore competitors.

High mobility of business enterprise reduces the effectiveness of traditional nation-based regulation and taxation. But of course governments are not oblivious to this trend. They attempt to cope with the increased mobility in a variety of ways: import prohibitions, extraterritorial reach, deregulation. But they also increasingly recognize the need to cooperate with other likeminded governments, and even sometimes those that are not so like minded. Cooperation is especially evident in the area of financial regulation, where principally domestic agencies, such as the Securities and Exchange Commission and the Federal Reserve, increasingly collaborate with their counterparts to preserve the effectiveness of their (now collective) actions. So increased mobility of enterprises will also lead to new cooperation among national authorities, at least at the technical level. By 2015 these practices may have become habitual.

Negotiating Environment

Rapid population growth, continued aspiration for and some success in achieving higher material standards of living, and increased international mobility of business enterprise are three dominant features of the world economy over the next quarter century. What about the international negotiating environment in the near future, over the next five years? There is increased consciousness among leaders and intellectual elites in developing as well as in developed countries of environmental degradation as a result of human activity—not least because some of the large urban areas in developing countries have become so unattractive from an environmental point of view. But while there is increased consciousness of environmental degradation compared with ten to twenty years ago, other issues command much more attention. Leaders in developing countries must deal with the fact that (in general) the 1980s have not been a good decade in terms of economic development. Large external debts continue to weigh heavily on many countries. A number of governments are politically shaky, in part (but only in part) for economic reasons, and some are even embroiled in civil war. These are much more pressing issues than the environment, even than the possibility of dramatic climate change in the next century. Governments in developing countries are not likely to constrain their economic growth, hence their demand for energy, for the sake of environmental improvement. Furthermore, they will argue with some plausibility that apart from local air and water pollution, global environmental degradation is due overwhelmingly to economic activity and consumption in the rich countries, with some consequential help from the centrally planned economies. Despite lower population, these countries use much more energy and generate much more waste. This position is largely correct with respect to present and past conditions, and the fact that the relative contributions can change markedly with successful economic development is a matter that they are likely to be willing to take seriously into consideration only after that development has occurred.

The bottom line is that many developing countries will cooperate with developed countries in reducing the emission of greenhouse gases into the atmosphere so long as it does not require great commitment on their part (e.g., in terms of domestic political conflict), and so long as the developed countries incur the extra costs associated with that cooperation.

Indeed, developing countries individually or as a group may attempt to extract a price for cooperation on environmental matters beyond the incremental costs of changing their behavior, to the extent that they detect that the environment has become a priority issue for the developed countries. Developing countries have long felt frustrated over lack of adequate "bargaining leverage" with respect to the rich countries, many of which were former colonial powers. This helps to explain the apparently perverse applause by many oil-importing developing countries in 1974 when the Organization of Petroleum Exporting Countries (OPEC) raised sharply the price of oil, as giving developing countries as a group important bargaining leverage. That price increase certainly caught the attention of the publics as well as the leaders of the developed countries in a way that no previous issue (except wars for independence) had done, although in the end it proved to be a weak bargaining weapon, in large part because there was no way to wield it effectively.

Even when the governments of developing countries agree on the desirability of improving the environment, or restraining its deterioration, their priorities will be elsewhere, and it would not be surprising to find them trying to extract some quid pro quo for their environmental cooperation in some other area in which developed countries can be helpful to them. One such area will concern intellectual property rights, already a source of contention between developed and some developing countries, especially insofar as it bears directly on the reduction of harmful emissions and improvements in efficiency in the use of energy. We know from the diverse experience of different countries that the large amounts of energy used now, e.g., by Poland and the German Democratic Republic, are not necessary to sustain present levels of output even with their current industrial structures. Some developing countries also use energy very inefficiently. Here is an obvious area of potential cooperation between environmentally oriented developed countries and growth oriented developing countries.

Appendix

Some Important Growth Rates[a]			
	1965–1980	1980–1986	1986–2000[b]
Population			
Low-income countries[c]	2.3	2.3	1.9
Middle-income countries	2.4	2.3	2.1
Industrial Market economies	0.8	0.6	0.4
Centrally-planned economies	1.0	1.0	0.8
Gross domestic production			
Low-income countries[c]	4.8	7.5	
Middle-income countries	6.6	2.3	
Industrial Market economies	3.6	2.5	
Commercial energy consumption			
Low-income countries[c]	8.2	5.6	
Middle-income countries	6.6	2.8	
Industrial Market economies	3.0	0.4	
Centrally-planned economies	4.4	2.9	

[a]Annual averages
[b]projection
[c]Includes China

Source: World Bank, *World Development Report 1988,* Tables 2, 10, and 27.

8

International Cooperation: The Environmental Experience

PETER H. SAND

There are two reasons why our generation will bear a heavier responsibility for the future of planet earth than any generation before it. First, we *know* better—having gained access to an unprecedented wealth of new scientific information and a vastly improved capacity for analysis and prediction. Second, we can *do* better—having accumulated enough experience, technological and institutional, to take the necessary international action.

PETER H. SAND is senior environmental affairs officer with the United Nations Economic Commission for Europe in Geneva. A German citizen and international lawyer, he has served as chief of the environmental law unit at the United Nations Environment Programme in Nairobi and as assistant director general of the International Union for Conservation of Nature and Natural Resources. Before joining the UN system in 1970, he was associate professor of law at McGill University. Dr. Sand is author of "Marine Environment Law in the United Nations Environment Programme" and of numerous articles on international law and environmental policy. Views and opinions expressed in this chapter are those of the author and do not necessarily reflect those of the UN/ECE.

The first point needs no elaboration. It is well illustrated by recent examples, such as the ongoing research project by a team of French and Russian paleoglaciologists, which have offered persuasive proof for the link between global warming and greenhouse gases in our atmosphere. The analysis was carried out on a 2000-meter-deep ice core "excavated" by the Soviet Antarctic Expeditions in Vostok, East Antarctica. The beauty of this material is that it consists of successive layers of ice deposited year after year in completely undisturbed conditions over the past 160,000 years. Each layer of ice contains myriad air bubbles that had remained trapped and hermetically sealed for thousands of years, and that have now been "opened" by scientists in Grenoble and Saclay (France). Their exact chemical composition has been identified by gas chromatography and their age determined by calculating the rate of ice sedimentation.

The net outcome of this analysis, which involved technology and computer calculations more sophisticated than any used even a few years ago, is a continuous historical record not only of the earth's atmospheric conditions, but also of the corresponding temperature changes on the surface of the Antarctic continent. The obvious next step was to compare this priceless new data base with other available information, including similar ice cores from Siple Station in Western Antarctica and from Greenland, maritime data from the Indian Ocean region, and more recent global monitoring data on atmospheric chemistry—for example, the continuous carbon dioxide (CO_2) measurements from the Mauna Loa station in Hawaii, which began in 1958. These comparisons show a perfect match between the most recent ice core data for carbon dioxide in Antarctic air and contemporary Mauna Loa measurements of atmospheric CO_2—both agree on a clear and steep upward trend. They also show a consistent correlation between the rise and fall in carbon dioxide, methane (the second major greenhouse gas), and global temperature.

Perhaps the most significant message here is not only that the greenhouse effect is a reality, an established fact; even more striking is the degree of international scientific coopera-

tion by which this fact has been established. Let us recapitulate
the sequence of events: the Vostok ice core was drilled and
extracted by Soviet Antarctic expeditions as part of the scientific programs authorized under the Antarctic Treaty; under a
French-Russian bilateral agreement, the whole sample was
analyzed in laboratories in France; the data were then compared with other ice core data obtained by Swiss glaciologists
at an Australian Antarctic station, and with atmospheric chemistry data from an American monitoring station in Hawaii; and
the results were eventually reviewed and published in a British
science magazine.

Nor does the sequence end there: the new Antarctic evidence is now before the Intergovernmental Panel on Climate
Change (IPCC) set up in 1988 jointly by the World Meteorological Organization (WMO) and the United Nations Environment Programme (UNEP). The IPCC will use the data for its
report to the second World Climate Conference, which in turn
will formulate specific recommendations for action by governments.

In terms of international machinery for environmental assessment, therefore, we seem to be doing rather well these
days. Worldwide scientific cooperation in this field is well established and functional; it includes formal bilateral and multilateral channels as well as informal transnational mechanisms
for information sharing and "peer review." While global demand for environmental knowledge remains enormous, there
are indeed many examples of successful assessment programs
at hand—from the ongoing International Geosphere-Bio-
sphere Programme of the International Council of Scientific
Unions (ICSU) to the 1987 report of the World Commission
on Environment and Development (Brundtland Commission).
The question is: how well established and how functional are
institutions and mechanisms that can now translate these assessments into collective action?

When it comes to international environmental management—or governance, as Harlan Cleveland (*The Future of International Governance,* 1986) and others have called it—the focus
of current performance evaluations is on the structure established by and after the 1972 Stockholm Conference on the

Human Environment, i.e., primarily the United Nations Environment Programme and global and regional institutions formed after UNEP. Yet the history of international environmental cooperation did not begin at Stockholm. Conventions for marine pollution control were already drafted twenty years earlier by the International Maritime Organization (IMO). The constitutional mandate of the UN Food and Agriculture Organization (FAO) for the "conservation of natural resources" was formulated in 1945. Standards to protect workers against occupational hazards in the working environment were adopted by the International Labour Organization (ILO) as early as the 1920s. Transboundary agreements for the protection of migratory birds and for the management of shared water resources date to well before World War I, as do international arrangements for the sharing of atmospheric data by nineteenth century precursors of the World Meteorological Organization. The first serious, if unsuccessful, attempt at global environmental management was probably Theodore Roosevelt's initiative in 1909 to convene at The Hague a world conference for natural resource conservation.

All this goes to say that we would have difficulties pleading innocence or lack of experience in this field today, considering the amount of international know-how already available. The purpose of the present survey is to take stock of this experience and to highlight innovative mechanisms for environmental standard-setting and implementation directly related to some of the decision making ahead. In political science terms, these mechanisms may be defined as *regimes*, i.e., norms, rules, and procedures agreed to in order to regulate an issue-area. I prefer to describe these regimes as *transnational* rather than international, considering that they are not confined to intergovernmental relations between nation-states, and frequently are hybrids—partaking of the international and domestic legal order, of the public and private law sector. In fact, one of the most significant features of transnational environmental regimes seems to be their ability to switch channels, to change and adapt techniques when needed in the light of experience—in short, a propensity for innovation.

Innovations in Standard-Setting

The traditional institution for international standard-setting is the ad hoc diplomatic conference to negotiate and adopt a treaty, which then has to undergo national (i.e., usually parliamentary) ratification to become legally binding. International environmental lawmaking is no exception to these rules; typically, therefore, most recent proposals for international action on global warming envisage a convention on climate change or on a "law of the atmosphere," along the lines of the United Nations' 1982 Montego Bay Convention on the Law of the Sea.

As distinct from national environmental legislation, however, treaty standards laid down by conventional diplomatic "ad-hocracy" (borrowing a term by Alvin Toffler, *Future Shock,* 1970) have two fundamental drawbacks:

- *First,* they are based on consensus or unanimity of all participants, since no sovereign state is under an obligation to sign or ratify a text that it does not want to accept. Unlike decisions by a national legislature, which normally result in a median standard determined by majority vote that also binds the outvoted minority, internationally agreed standards tend to reflect the lowest common denominator, the bottom line.

- *Second,* the formal requirement of parliamentary ratification creates a built-in time lag, deliberately delaying the effectiveness of international agreements. Unlike national laws— which can fix their own dates of application, including immediate applicability or amendment if necessary— multilateral treaties can only be brought into force, or amended, after ratification by a specified number of signatories. The purpose, of course, is to ensure a measure of reciprocity and to avoid situations where initial compliance by a few diligent parties would create disproportionate benefits to the "free-riders" remaining outside the treaty. Setting a threshold number, however, also delays implementation to the speed of the slowest boat in the convoy.

It has often been pointed out how antiquated and cumbersome this conventional process is. Diplomatic treaty making may be a useful way to formulate principles of behavior and a framework for intergovernmental relations. It may be doubted, however, whether traditional treaty techniques are suitable for effective environmental governance at the global or regional scale once international action must pass from declarations to operations. Environmental problems typically involve unforeseeable change of circumstances, often under crisis conditions, in the face of continuous scientific-technological progress. What is crucial for successful international management, therefore, is the capacity of a normative system to respond to frequent and rapid change. If the classical treaty, that "sadly overworked instrument" (Lord McNair, *The Law of Treaties*, 1961), lacks this capacity, it is high time to explore alternative methods.

While it is difficult to see how the traditional treaty process can be avoided altogether, there are ways to deal with some of its shortcomings, or as Mancur Olson put it (*International Organization*, 1971), "politically feasible ways to increase the incentives for collectively rational behavior." A few of these are sketched here in the light of practical experience with transnational environmental standards.

Asymmetrical Standards:
How to Beat the Bottom-line Rule

Multilateral agreements based on the lowest common denominator are well documented. In international fishery regimes, for example, a "law of the least ambitious program" has been diagnosed by Arild Underdal (*The Politics of International Fisheries Management*, 1980):

Where international management can be established only through agreement among all significant parties involved, and where such a regulation is considered only on its own merits, collective action will be limited to those measures acceptable to the least enthusiastic party.

Significantly, though, the author goes on to note that a reluctant party can often be persuaded to modify its position through "arguments, side-payments, or various kinds of political pressure."

So there are ways out of the dilemma, and Underdal's cata-

logue of exceptions to the rule of the least ambitious program
is far from exhaustive. As negotiating experience in the wider
field of international environmental agreements shows, there
are several options to make ambitious programs or better-
than-minimum standards attractive to parties, including a variety of selective incentives, differential obligations, recourse to
regional solidarity, and promotion of overachievement by lead
countries.

Selective Incentives. The concept of "selective incentives" is
well established in economic group theory as one of the motives for collective action: certain fringe benefits may persuade
a party to participate in a program or standard that it would
otherwise find unacceptable. The familiar parliamentary practice of coalition building and majority building by judicious
distribution of special favors has obvious parallels in the negotiation of multilateral treaties.

A case in point is the 1987 Montreal Protocol on Substances
That Deplete the Ozone Layer: under Article 2(5), production
increases by way of "transfers" were authorized between
small-scale producers; by virtue of Article 2(6), the USSR was
granted "grandfather rights" for factories under construction
until the end of 1990; in Article 2(8), the member states of the
European Community were authorized to aggregate their national consumption limits; in Article 5, developing countries
were allowed to postpone compliance by ten years; and so on.

It is easy to criticize the outcome as a compromise full of
loopholes that were built in to accommodate special interests.
But without these "rider" clauses, the agreement would either
have lost some important signatories or might have jelled at a
lower level of collective commitment. Paradoxically, therefore,
loopholes can serve to upgrade the overall standard of obligations in an agreement—above the predictable common denominator, that is.

The selective incentives commonly used in environmental
treaty bargaining are access to funding, access to resources,
access to markets, and access to technology.

Access to funding as an incentive for adherence to international conservation standards is perhaps best illustrated by the 1972 Paris Convention for the Protection of the World Cultural and Natural Heritage that, with 111 member states, is the most widely accepted environmental treaty today. Under Articles 13 and 19 of the convention, parties are eligible for financial assistance from the World Heritage Fund to support conservation measures for national sites included in a "world heritage list," in return for maintaining these sites at agreed standards of protection. The fund—administered by the United Nations Educational, Scientific and Cultural Organization (UNESCO)—now has an annual working budget of $2.2 million, financed by a combination of mandatory and voluntary contributions, and split about evenly between projects for cultural and natural heritage sites.

Access to the sustainable use of natural resources is an economic incentive for participation in many international regimes attempting to reconcile rational exploitation and conservation. Examples range from the annual catch quota established under numerous regional agreements for marine fishing and seal hunting, and worldwide under the 1946 International Convention for the Regulation of Whaling (until the entry into force of the moratorium in 1986), to the 1980 Canberra Convention on the Conservation of Antarctic Marine Living Resources. The acceptance of environmental restrictions in return for the prospect of sharing in the utilization of mineral resources is as much part of the UN Law of the Sea Convention as of the 1988 Wellington Convention on the Regulation of Antarctic Mineral Resource Activities.

Similarly, access to the world market for wildlife and wildlife products in return for observance of agreed conservation standards has been recognized as an economic incentive for countries to join the 1973 Washington Convention on International Trade in Endangered Species of Wild Fauna and Flora (CITES), which led to specific quota schemes for marketing of "controlled" crocodile hides and (until 1989) ivory.

A more recent addition to the catalogue of selective incentives in international regimes is access to technology, first and most prominently used as an incentive for participation in the

1968 Treaty on the Nonproliferation of Nuclear Weapons. While early environmental agreements (such as the UNEP-sponsored regional seas conventions and protocols since 1976) contain only generic recommendations on the subject of technical assistance to developing countries, specific provisions to facilitate technology transfer have made their appearance in recent treaties, from the 1985 Vienna Convention for the Protection of the Ozone Layer to the 1989 Basel Convention on the Control of Transboundary Movements of Hazardous Wastes and Their Disposal. In this context, the 1990 review of the Montreal Protocol considered the establishment of an international trust fund for transfer of technology and financial assistance to developing countries.

Clauses for the preferential acquisition of new environmental technology have thus become a major bargaining issue, not only in North-South negotiations but also in the context of East-West relations. For instance, a provision on "procedures to create more favorable conditions for the exchange of technology to reduce emissions of nitrogen oxides" was considered by East European countries faced with Western export restrictions on strategic high technology, as one of the prerequisites for accepting the 1988 Sofia Protocol to the Convention on Long-range Transboundary Air Pollution. An intergovernmental task force on exchange of technology has since been set up for this purpose under the auspices of the Executive Body for the Convention.

Differential Obligations. Since selective incentives by definition lead to special treatment for selected parties, they skew an otherwise symmetrical system of reciprocal rights and obligations. Such manifest discrimination, particularly in the case of "add-on" selective incentives resulting from last minute negotiations, can seriously undermine the credibility of a multilateral agreement. A more straightforward alternative, therefore, is to start out with an asymmetrical regime that does not even pretend to treat states equally, and instead differentiates treaty obligations according to the special circumstances of each party.

As an example, the European Community's 1988 Directive on the Limitation of Emissions of Certain Pollutants into the Air from Large Combustion Plants (88/609/EEC) lays down a country-by-country time plan, taking into account the particular economic and technological situation in each of the twelve member states: while Belgium, France, the Netherlands, and the Federal Republic of Germany are to reduce their sulphur dioxide emissions 70 percent by the year 2003, the target for Denmark was set at 67 percent, for Italy at 63 percent, for Luxembourg and the United Kingdom at 60 percent; at the same time, Greece, Ireland, and Portugal were authorized to increase emissions temporarily.

Skewed as these obligations may seem, they are not unlike the differential assessment scales that have been developed for multilateral funding of a number of environmental agreements. Under the 1976 Bonn Convention for the Protection of the Rhine Against Pollution by Chlorides, for example, the four riparian countries—the Netherlands, the Federal Republic of Germany, France, and Switzerland—agreed to share abatement costs (currently estimated at about $136 million) in percentages of 34:30:30:6, respectively.

The various UN trust funds set up since 1977 to finance joint programs under the Mediterranean Convention (annual budget $3.8 million), the Endangered Species Convention ($1.6 million), the Transboundary Air Pollution Convention ($1 million), and the Ozone Layer Convention ($1 million with the Montreal Protocol) all use a weighted key of contributions based on the global assessment scale laid down by the UN General Assembly, which rates countries according to a combination of economic, geographic, and demographic criteria. (The only political limit to this prorated scheme is a 25 percent ceiling for individual contributions, introduced in 1972 at U.S. insistence that no single party should be assessed at more than one quarter of the total budget.)

Differential scales are thus a well-established way of enabling even the smallest countries to participate on an equal footing without destabilizing a treaty's budget—with Singapore, at an annual fee of $1500, exercising the same member-

ship rights as the United States at $300,000 under the Vienna/
Montreal ozone layer agreements.

Skew is carried one step further by the "critical loads" approach now being developed in the context of the Transboundary Air Pollution Convention. As defined in the 1988
Sofia Protocol Concerning the Control of Emissions of Nitrogen Oxides or Their Transboundary Fluxes, critical load
means

a quantitative estimate of the exposure to one or more pollutants
below which significant harmful effects on specified sensitive elements of the environment do not occur according to present knowledge.

When this approach is translated into national abatement
targets, it is bound to lead to differential obligations (equitable
rather than equal) for each party. The basic idea of the critical
loads approach is quite similar to the concept of "safe minimum standards" in natural resources management, which also
aims at the equitable allocation of a common property resource without jeopardizing its long-term conservation for all
users. Yet the transition from "egalitarian" flat rates to highly
individualized allocations also introduces a new level of complexity in multilateral treaty making, typically reflected in the
amount of computer time now being spent on the subject.

Regionalization. Custom-built asymmetrical regimes are, of
course, more easily achieved within existing groups of countries where enough trade-offs (to compensate for the asymmetries) are available as a result of close regional integration and
solidarity. Furthermore, if broadening the scope of an international regime means lowering its common denominator (with
universal membership at the absolute bottom line), then the
reverse should also be true: restricting membership should
raise the standard, particularly where such restriction adds an
element of geographic or other affinity between members.

Again, international experience in environmental governance would seem to bear out this observation. The degree of
institutional cooperation accomplished under regional agree-

ments for marine environment protection—such as the 1974 Helsinki and Paris Conventions for the Baltic and the North Sea, and the UNEP regional seas agreements starting with the 1976 Barcelona Convention for the Protection of the Mediterranean Sea Against Pollution—has consistently been higher than under comparable global regimes, except possibly for ship-based pollution regulation by the International Maritime Organization. At a time when the UN Law of the Sea Convention (with its Chapter XII on global protection and preservation of the marine environment) has still not entered into force, more than fifty states are already legally bound by conventions and protocols concluded under UN environment programs for the Mediterranean, the Caribbean, the west-central African coast, the Red Sea, the Gulf, and the Southeast Pacific. While UNEP's own global guidelines on offshore mining (1981) and on land-based marine pollution (1985) generated little more than lip service from governments, a number of countries did accept specific regional commitments and emission standards under the UNEP-sponsored Athens (1980) and Quito (1983) Protocols on pollution from land-based sources, and under the 1989 Kuwait Protocol on pollution from offshore mining.

But if regionalization can raise the quality of standard-setting, it can also introduce further asymmetries or reinforce existing ones. Far from offering a panacea for all transnational environmental problems, regional regulation may be manifestly unsuitable for some. For instance, when the Organization for Economic Cooperation and Development (OECD) in 1984 initiated a regional draft convention for transboundary shipments of hazardous waste, it was able to draw on a higher level of solidarity and consensus among its membership (limited to Western industrialized states) than would have been conceivable under a worldwide treaty. On the other hand, it soon became clear that the very prospect of tightened waste controls in the OECD region had an undesired spillover effect, reorienting trade flows to countries outside the region that were unlikely to abide by OECD-imposed regulation. The OECD member states eventually had to abandon their project in favor of a less ambitious but globally applicable regime under UNEP auspices, the 1989 Basel Convention. However, with the Organization of African Unity (OAU) now drafting a separate regional agreement on the topic, the waste trade issue will continue to provide trial-and-error lessons in transnational regime building.

Promoting Overachievement. To be sure, under Article 11 of the Basel Convention countries remain free to enter into additional arrangements, as long as such arrangements are not less environmentally sound than the agreed global standards. The European Community (EC) has already announced its intention to implement the convention by tighter requirements, as it previously did with regard to other treaties, e.g., the Council of Europe's 1968 Agreement on the Restriction of the Use of Certain Detergents in Washing and Cleaning Products, which required synthetic detergents to be at least 80 percent biodegradable, was upstaged by a 1973 European Economic Community (EEC) Detergents Directive requiring at least 90 percent biodegradability.

A number of environmental agreements expressly confirm the right of parties to take more stringent measures individually or collectively. Examples are the 1973 Endangered Species Convention, the 1985 Ozone Layer Convention, and its 1987 Montreal Protocol. Under "framework" conventions, this right is frequently exercised in optional additional protocols concluded between some of the parties only. Within the 1979 Geneva Convention on Long-range Transboundary Air Pollution, a ten-member "club" of countries first moved ahead in 1984 with a joint voluntary commitment to a 30 percent reduction of sulphur emissions, though at that time not all of the thirty-one parties to the convention were prepared to go along. When the 30 percent commitment was formally adopted as a protocol to the convention at Helsinki in 1985, twenty-one states signed it. During the negotiation of a further protocol on nitrogen oxides in 1987, a club of five "likeminded" states again pressed for a 30 percent reduction target; even though the target did not become part of the protocol that was finally signed at Sofia in 1988, twelve of the twenty-five signatories eventually agreed to commit themselves to an additional voluntary 30 percent reduction.

In each of these cases, the progressive "club within the club" played a pilot role in overall target setting. It also had a "bandwagon effect," with other parties climbing aboard as it gathered political momentum.

The 1985 Helsinki Protocol, in calling for sulphur emission reductions "by at least 30 percent" had actually introduced what may be described as an upwardly mobile target. Since national reduction achievements and pledges are recorded annually, internationally compared, and widely publicized, any overachievement is rewarded by public attention and recognition. As of 1988, twelve of the parties to the Helsinki Protocol reported that they had already reached the 30 percent target ahead of schedule, and ten parties went on to announce that they would reduce emissions by more than 50 percent.

A similar trend can be documented for the Montreal Protocol on ozone-depleting substances. While the 1987 meeting after much bargaining had settled for chlorofluorocarbon (CFC) reductions by a modest 50 percent until 1999, the London Conference pledge by the twelve-member European Community in March 1989 for 85 percent "as soon as possible" and 100 percent by the end of the century eventually led to the Helsinki Declaration by eighty-two countries in May 1989 calling for a complete phase-out by the year 2000. This upward revision of the original bottom line was partly motivated by new scientific evidence of the "ozone hole," but it was largely influenced by media coverage and the worldwide publicity given to individual or collective pledges of overachievement.

There is ample legal room for stricter national rules "going it alone" on bona fide environmental grounds—provided they are nondiscriminatory—under Article XX of the General Agreement on Tariffs and Trade (GATT), and Article 2.2 of the 1979 Tokyo Round Agreement on Technical Barriers to Trade. Article 601 of the 1988 U.S.-Canadian Free Trade Agreement similarly recognizes them as "legitimate domestic objectives."

Difficulties may arise, however, in the context of closer regional integration regimes, and have already arisen in the European Community, e.g., over stricter national standards regarding fuel quality and engine emissions, or conversely in the case of national subsidies for "clean cars." Although Article 130T of the EC Treaty as revised by the 1986 Single European Act expressly authorizes more stringent national measures for environmental protection "compatible with this treaty," and Article 100A(4) enables member states to derogate for environmental reasons from agreed harmonization measures, unilateral derogations are now subject to prior notification to the EC Commission (which may object in case of noncompatibility) in order to avoid arbitrary restraints of trade. In the end, it is the trade regime that determines, if not the bottom line, at least the margin of tolerable asymmetries in the EC's environmental regime.

Fast Tracks: How to Beat the Slowest Boat Rule

Possibly the most serious drawback of the treaty method is the time lag between the drafting, adoption, and entry into force of standards. Besides the period of negotiation—which in the case of the Law of the Sea took fourteen years, and in the case of the Ozone Layer Convention more than three years—a treaty, once signed, must undergo a lengthy process of national ratification by the required minimum number of countries before it can become effective.

A 1971 study by the United Nations Institute for Training and Research (UNITAR) showed that there are definite patterns of drag in treaty acceptance that tend to postpone the date of effectiveness to somewhere between two and twelve years after formal agreement has been reached; and that the average "tempo of acceptance" for multilateral treaties according to UNITAR is about five years. While some—like the Law of the Sea Convention (minimum number of ratifications required: sixty)—have still not entered into force seven years after signature, most environmental treaties seem to be doing rather better. The Mediterranean Convention and the Ozone

Layer Convention, for instance, took less than two years.

Considering the need for rapid action that is characteristic of most environmental problems, even two years may be too long. The CFC reduction rates agreed under the Montreal Protocol in September 1987 were already obsolete by the time the protocol entered into force, and had to be revised by recourse to an improvised "fast-track" procedure not foreseen in the treaty—the Helsinki Declaration on the Protection of the Ozone Layer, adopted on May 2, 1989.

The traditional ratification process and its notorious delays can however be by-passed in a number of ways. Among the devices used for this purpose in international environmental practice are provisional treaty application, various "soft-law" options, and delegated lawmaking.

Provisional Treaty Application. Pending the formal entry into force of an international agreement, states may agree to bring it into operation on an interim basis. Provisional application is a recognized procedure under the Vienna Convention on the Law of Treaties (Article 25); a classic example is the 1947 General Agreement on Tariffs and Trade, which never legally came into force but has operated for more than forty years now on the basis of a Protocol of Provisional Application.

In the environmental field, the signatories to the 1979 Geneva Convention on Long-range Transboundary Air Pollution also decided, by separate resolution, to "initiate, as soon as possible and on an interim basis, the provisional implementation of the convention," and to "carry out the obligations arising from the convention to the maximum extent possible pending its entry into force." As a result, the Executive Body established by the convention took up its functions initially as "Interim Executive Body," holding regular annual meetings, creating subsidiary working groups, and so on, well before the convention came into force in 1983.

When adopting the first protocol under the convention in 1984, on long-term financing of the European Monitoring and Evaluation Programme (EMEP), the signatories again decided by resolution, pending the entry into force of the protocol, "to contribute to the financing of EMEP on a voluntary basis, in an amount equal to the mandatory contributions expected from them under the provisions of the protocol if all signatories had become parties." Even though not all signatories complied, voluntary interim funding along these lines generated over $3.4 million dollars, enabling the EMEP program to operate effectively until 1988, when the protocol entered into force and contributions became mandatory.

The final act of the 1989 Basel Convention on the Control of Transboundary Movements of Hazardous Wastes took a similar, albeit more timid, approach with its resolution that "until such time as the convention comes into force and appropriate criteria are determined, all states refrain from activities which are inconsistent with the objectives and purposes of the convention," and with other resolutions to establish preparatory technical working groups and an interim secretariat with voluntary funding. This, too, may be considered provisional application, born of the signatories' concern to avoid a potential "anarchic hiatus" created by ratification delays.

Soft-law Options. Alternatively, states may decide to forgo the treaty method altogether and to recommend, by joint declaration, common rules of conduct—usually referred to as "soft law" to distinguish them from the "hard law" of formal legal agreements. Environmental diplomacy has come up with a wide variety of such declaratory instruments. Their recognized practical advantage is that they are not subject to national ratification, and hence can take instant effect. Their inherent risk, however, is precisely that lack of formality that makes them attractive as a shortcut. To illustrate the quandary, no sooner had the 1988 Sofia Declaration on the 30% Reduction of Nitrogen Oxide Emissions been signed on behalf of the Federal Republic of Germany by its minister for the environment, than the secretary of state for economic affairs publicly questioned the legal force of the declaration.

One of the most prolific soft-law makers has been the Governing Council of the UN Environment Programme itself, with a whole series of "environmental law guidelines and principles" proclaimed since 1978 and invariably addressed to states in typical treaty language, except for copious use of the verb "should" instead of "shall." After initial adoption by ad hoc groups of experts nominated by governments, these provisions are normally approved by the UNEP Governing Council for submission to the UN General Assembly, which either incorporates them in a resolution (as in the case of the 1982 World Charter for Nature) or less solemnly recommends them to states for use in the formulation of international agreements or national legislation (as in the case of the 1982 Conclusions of the Study of Legal Aspects Concerning the Environment Related to Offshore Mining and Drilling Within the Limits of National Jurisdiction). In a number of cases, promulgation remained at the level of UNEP Governing Council decisions (e.g., the 1980 Provisions for Cooperation between States on Weather Modification).

Soft law may be hardened by later international practice: when the government of Uganda, under gentle World Bank pressure, had to consult other Nile Basin countries on a proposed water use project for Lake Victoria in December 1983, it did so by way of reference, *inter alia*, to the 1978 UNEP Principles of Conduct in the Field of the Environment for the Guidance of States in the Conservation and Harmonious Utilization of Natural Resources Shared by Two or More States. Three months later, the governments of Egypt and Sudan in their replies in turn referred to the guidelines as "jointly honoured principles of cooperation," thereby quietly promoting them to the status of common regional standards.

UNEP soft-law instruments have also served as forerunners of subsequent treaty law (as in the case of the 1985/1987 Cairo Guidelines and Principles for the Environmentally Sound Management of Hazardous Wastes, leading up to the 1989 Basel Convention), or as a mandate for new mechanisms of intergovernmental cooperation (as in the case of the 1984 Provisional Notification Scheme for Banned and Severely Restricted Chemicals). Recommendations by other international organizations in the environmental field have played a similar role, especially those of the Organization for Economic Cooperation and Development.

Even soft-law declarations by nongovernmental expert

groups (such as the International Law Association's 1966 "Helsinki Rules" on the uses of the waters of international rivers) may attain reference status, with or without intergovernmental blessing. One recent example is the set of Proposed Legal Principles for Environmental Protection and Sustainable Development appended to the 1987 Brundtland Report to the UN General Assembly. Others are the guidelines for drinking water quality and air quality published under the auspices of the World Health Organization: though drafted by ad hoc expert groups and never intergovernmentally adopted, they have become a reference source for national standard-setting and a yardstick for comparative evaluation of environmental quality, largely by virtue of the organization's prestige. Similarly, a number of worldwide technical standards for measuring environmental parameters are laid down and updated by the International Organization for Standardization (ISO), which ranks as "nongovernmental" even though more than 70 percent of its members are national public standards authorities, and whose system of voting by correspondence is not subject to any diplomatic clearance or ratification.

Delegated Lawmaking. Another way of by-passing the ratification process is to delegate powers to adopt and regularly amend "technical" standards to a specialized intergovernmental body. This technique was gradually developed and refined among several global and regional organizations that had to cope with frequent technological change: the International Telecommunication Union (ITU), the Universal Postal Union (UPU), and a number of European conventions on rail and road transport each placed their international standards in separate "technical annexes" or "regulations" that are periodically revised in intergovernmental meetings without having to go through ratification.

Among the most advanced and smoothly functioning regulatory regimes so developed are the "international health regulations" of the World Health Organization (WHO); the "standard meteorological practices and procedures" of the World Meteorological Organization; the standards for facilitation of international maritime traffic, enacted by the International Maritime Organization; and the international food standards of the Codex Alimentarius Commission, a joint technical body of WHO and the Food and Agriculture Organization of the United Nations.

The significance of "ecostandards" as a method to expedite international environmental decision making is now widely recognized. Besides a wide range of ongoing global mechanisms for standard-setting in this field, simplified—i.e., unratified—amendments of standards contained in technical annexes (as distinct from formal amendment of the main treaty provisions) are used under several regional agreements, including those for the protection of the Baltic and the Mediterranean marine environment.

Expeditious as it may be, however, leapfrogging the ratification process also raises the question of democratic controls over the delegated standard-setting so established—as Karl Kaiser put it (*International Organization*, 1971): "Transnational relations as a threat to the democratic process?" Different environmental regimes have come up with different answers to this question. One option—which, however, seems practicable only under conditions of close regional integration—is to create a "supranational" parliamentary body for this purpose; this is the case of the independently elected European Parliament, whose Environment Committee has begun to play an important watchdog role in the community's lawmaking process. The alternative is to retain a measure of national endorsement, short of parliamentary ratification, for agreed common standards, either by requiring affirmative acceptance by governments (as in the case of the international food standards of the Codex Alimentarius Commission), or by providing the possibility for dissenting states to "opt out" of an agreed standard or amendment within a specified time period (as stipulated, e.g., in the constitutions of the WHO, the WMO, the UN conventions on narcotic drugs, and in several international fisheries agreements).

An example of the opting out procedure, applied to a problem of global pollution control, is the adoption and amendment of technical annexes under the 1944 Chicago Convention on International Civil Aviation. Pursuant to Articles 37 and 54 of the convention, worldwide standards on aircraft noise and aircraft engine emissions have been laid down since 1981 by the Council of the International Civil Aviation Organization (ICAO). The council is elected every three years by the 161 member states represented in the ICAO Assembly; its thirty-three members must accept full-time residence at the organization's headquarters in Montreal, not unlike elected representatives in a national parliament. Once adopted in the council by a two-thirds majority vote, an annex becomes mandatory, without ratification, for all states who do not within sixty days notify the council of their intention to apply different national rules, and for all air traffic over the high seas. This flexible "tacit consent" procedure, designed with a view to reconciling the divergent requirements of developed and developing countries, facilitates progressive technical adjustment of standards by majority decision without forcing complete uniformity.

The ICAO method of standard-setting may well be the closest we have come to global environmental legislation so far. All the evidence suggests that this regime copes successfully both with the "bottom line" syndrome (by facilitating upward revision) and with the "slowest boat" syndrome (by dispensing with ratification). The net result is, in Derek Bowett's words (*The Law of International Institutions*, 1982):

not that there has occurred any dramatic change in the basic rule of international law that States assume new obligations only with their consent, but rather a pattern of procedures for improving the chances of a decision of the majority (be it simple or two-thirds) of a "legislative" character securing general consent.

Innovations in Implementation

Once international standards have been set, there must be institutions that apply them, by authorizing or prohibiting activities covered by the standards, and by imposing sanctions against noncompliance. The problem with most international, as distinct from national, environmental standards is the absence of international institutions empowered to implement them, whether through licensing (regulatory authority) or sanctioning (judicial authority).

A number of recent initiatives, such as the Declaration of The Hague signed by representatives of twenty-four countries in March 1989, have called for "new institutional authority" not only to set environmental standards but also to implement them. Short of radical reforms in world government, however, transnational regimes in this field still have to cope with a dual handicap:

- *First*, in the absence of a supranational regulatory institution, administrative licensing of authorized activities (including assessment of their environmental impact) can be carried out only by national institutions. To the extent that these institutions apply agreed international standards for this purpose, they may be said to act on behalf of the international community by way of "dédoublement fonctionnel," to use a celebrated term coined by Georges Scelle (*Précis de Droit des Gens*, 1932). Yet their relationship with each other is strictly nonhierarchic, requiring far more complex procedures of reciprocity than when applying national standards.
- *Second*, there is currently no compulsory jurisdiction for the settlement of disputes regarding most multilateral environmental regimes. The dispute settlement clauses contained in the majority of global agreements concluded since the 1970s invariably give each party a veto against reference to arbitration or to the International Court of Justice in The Hague, usually by stipulating that third-party adjudication requires common agreement.

Initially, these veto clauses were inserted at the insistence of the USSR and other East European countries that refused to accept compulsory third-party adjudication as an infringement on sovereignty. More recently, the United States became the champion of the jurisdiction veto, in the wake of its rather painful court experience in the Nicaragua case. In a bout of

"Hague phobia," starting with the 1983 Cartagena Convention for the Protection and Development of the Marine Environment of the Wider Caribbean Region, the U.S. State Department introduced a new variety of dispute settlement clauses in all UNEP conventions, which reserve each party's right to block third-party adjudication while leaving an option to waive the veto right upon signature of the treaty. This U.S.-inspired veto clause was also introduced—against strong resistance from sixteen other (mostly Western) countries favoring more stringent third-party adjudication—in the 1985 Vienna Convention for the Protection of the Ozone Layer and in the 1989 Basel Convention on the Control of Transboundary Movements of Hazardous Wastes and Their Disposal.

It should be remembered that Canada's reservation in 1970 with regard to the Arctic Waters Pollution Prevention Act had already dealt a first blow to the World Court's potential as a forum for environmental dispute settlement, later reassurances by judges and friends of the court notwithstanding. Under present circumstances, most multilateral environmental agreements are not enforceable by supranational judicial institutions. The imposition of sanctions for noncompliance thus requires different (i.e., nonhierarchic) approaches, again involving reciprocity, further complicated by the fact that mutual obligations under multilateral agreements are more difficult to individualize than in bilateral dispute situations.

In spite of these complications, transnational environmental regimes have learned to use alternative methods and institutions to ensure implementation of agreed standards. I shall single out a few examples, with the emphasis on innovative features that may be suitable for wider application and further development.

Alternatives to Supranational Regulation

The conspicuous absence of international regulatory institutions for environmental governance in no way prevented the proliferation of transnational regimes using a variety of regulatory mechanisms: environmental permits, environmental impact statements, environmental labels, and so on. Experience has shown that rather than building yet another bureaucratic superstructure at the international level, regulatory functions can very well be left to existing national bureaucracies, provided there is a workable measure of compatibility and mutual recognition of procedures, supported in practice by what political scientists describe as "epistemic" cooperation between specialists across national boundaries.

Mutual Recognition. Rather than conferring licensing powers on an international body, many environmental agreements provide for the reciprocal recognition of licenses and permits by competent national authorities, provided these are properly authenticated, and that certain agreed-upon standards for the granting of such permits are observed. Uniform sanitary and vaccination certificates have thus been issued over the past forty years by national medical and veterinary services under the WHO International Health Regulations, as are phytosanitary certificates for exports and re-exports under the 1951 International Plant Protection Convention. National maritime and inland water authorities issue international oil pollution prevention certificates for ships pursuant to the 1973 Convention for the Prevention of Pollution from Ships (MARPOL); they also issue waste disposal permits for substances listed on the "gray lists" of at least ten global and regional agreements for the prevention of marine and inland water pollution, starting with the 1972 London Convention on the Prevention of Marine Pollution by Dumping of Waste and Other Matter. The waste export notifications and authorizations pursuant to the 1989 Basel Convention on the Control of Transboundary Movements of Hazardous Wastes and Their Disposal will also be issued exclusively by national authorities.

Much of the international trade in chemical products depends on reciprocal recognition schemes. For example, under the World Health Organization's Certification Scheme on the Quality of Pharmaceutical Products Moving in International Commerce, introduced in 1975 and now applied by more than one hundred countries, the health authority of an exporting

country is required to certify upon request whether the manu-
facturer has been found on inspection to comply with defined
standards of practice in the manufacture and quality control of
drugs. Some countries have gone further toward multilateral
harmonization of reference procedures, such as the chemical
test guidelines and principles of good laboratory practice laid
down by the Organization for Economic Cooperation and Development; the 1970 Convention for the Mutual Recognition
of Inspections in Respect of the Manufacture of Pharmaceutical Products, adopted within the framework of the European
Free Trade Association (EFTA) in Geneva but also followed
by a number of non-EFTA countries; or the 1979 "sixth
amendment" to the European Community's Directive on the
Approximation of Laws, Regulations and Administrative Provisions Relating to Classification, Packaging and Labelling of
Dangerous Substances, also followed by a number of countries
outside the EC. The basis of these regimes invariably remains
one of reciprocal acceptance of national certification.

Similarly, the 1973 Washington Convention on International Trade in Endangered Species of Wild Fauna and Flora
has established worldwide trade controls based on mandatory
permits and certificates covering the export, import, and re-
export of plant and animal species or products listed in the
appendices to the convention. Yet none of these permits is
issued by an international institution; the entire CITES regime
relies on mutual recognition and verification of national permits issued by designated authorities in each of the 106 member states. The international secretariat merely provides coordination and "switchboard" services.

This approach has, of course, numerous historical anteced-
ents in international relations, from seaworthiness and airwor-
thiness certificates for ships and aircraft to the classification
and labeling of dangerous substances. The incentive for governments to participate in any such regime (and the primary
sanction of the regime) is its reciprocity, and the practical economic advantages this offers to the participating state, e.g.,
where compliance facilitates international communications or
the export of certain products.

A pertinent example is environmental licensing of imported cars in Europe, under the 1958 Geneva Agreement concerning the Adoption of Uniform Conditions of Approval and Reciprocal Recognition of Approval for Motor Vehicle Equipment and Parts. Under this regime, authorizations for marketing of new cars are based on type-approval of vehicle models, including certification of compliance with uniform technical criteria for engine emissions. Even though these emission standards are harmonized and periodically updated by the Inland Transport Committee of the UN Economic Commission for Europe (ECE)—again, under a simplified procedure of delegated lawmaking without ratification, requiring approval by only two of the twenty-two member states to bring a technical regulation or its amendment into force—the actual licensing of vehicles is never done by an international body but by designated national agencies. A license issued by one agency is given official recognition in all other participating countries, which makes the system particularly attractive to car manufacturers as a shortcut to foreign markets (to wit, the Japanese government maintains permanent observer status in the ECE Working Party concerned). At the same time, the ECE regional standards so applied are increasingly becoming models for national licensing in other countries outside the European region, de facto expanding the geographical scope of the regime.

Model Diffusion. Harmonization may also occur informally through voluntary adoption of foreign regulatory models. Many developing countries today admit imported chemical products without national evaluation if the product was duly licensed in its country of origin, thereby relying on the presumed effectiveness of foreign controls. On the other hand, several European countries, in an effort to go beyond current ECE standards on automobile emissions, unabashedly "borrow" U.S. federal or California state standards for their new national legislation.

The international transfer of innovative norms and institutions (a transcultural process described as "mimesis" by Arnold J. Toynbee, *A Study of History: Reconsiderations,* 1961) follows patterns of geographical diffusion quite similar to the spread of technological innovations. Some social geographers have even drawn parallels with the spread of contagious diseases, vindicating a metaphor already used by Goethe (*Faust* I, Scene IV):

> All rights and laws are still transmitted
> like an eternal sickness of the race,
> from generation unto generation fitted
> and shifted round from place to place.

A case in point is the Environmental Impact Assessment (EIA) procedure first introduced by the 1969 U.S. National Environmental Policy Act. While attempts at internationalizing the procedure by way of a treaty, advocated by U.S. Senator Claiborne Pell since 1978, were manifestly unsuccessful and never progressed beyond a "soft-law" declaration in the UN Environment Programme, the underlying concept of the legislation rapidly and quite informally became a model for at least thirty countries worldwide. EIA now is a household legal term not only in anglophonic countries from Australia to Zambia, but also as *declaración de efecto ambiental* in the 1974 Colombian Code of Renewable Natural Resources and Environment Protection; as *étude d'impact sur l'environnement* in the 1976 French Nature Conservation Act (followed by legislation in other francophonic countries, such as Article 130 of the 1983 Algerian Act on Environment Protection); and as *Umweltverträglichkeitsprüfung* in the 1990 West German EIA Act (based on a 1985 EEC Directive on the Assessment of the Effects of Certain Public and Private Projects on the Environment), as well as in 1988 East German legislation. Here again, parallels may be drawn with transnational diffusion of other institutional models, such as the "TVA syndrome" in river basin management and its imitation or "pseudo-imitation" abroad, diagnosed by Albert O. Hirschman (*Development Projects Observed,* 1967).

Another widely diffused model of this kind is the concept of a financial charge prorated to the volume of pollutant emissions. Originally developed as "effluent fees" for regional pollution control by water management associations in the Ruhr River Basin as early as 1904, emission charges have since been introduced in many other regions and countries, and applied to a wide range of other environmental issues. The basic idea is to levy a charge or "pollution tax" on specified economic activities, depending on their degree of environmental harmfulness, with the proceeds from the charge earmarked for specific countermeasures. Effluent charges for water pollution are now part of national legislation in both Germanies and elsewhere in Western Europe (the Netherlands, France, Italy) and Eastern Europe (Czechoslovakia, Hungary, Poland), and have been proposed for adoption in the U.S. and the USSR. Landing charges for aircraft noise, prorated according to engine type or aircraft weight, are levied in Japan and at several West European airports. Since March 1989, all domestic air traffic in Sweden is subject to a prorated charge on aircraft engine emissions of nitrogen oxides and hydrocarbons.

Surprisingly, emission charges seem to function both in market economies and in centrally planned economies: it was the (East) German Democratic Republic that first introduced a "dust and gaseous emissions fee" on industrial enterprises emitting air pollutants in excess of specified levels, starting on an experimental basis in two of the most polluted districts (Halle and Bitterfeld) in 1969, and extending the system countrywide by legislation in 1973. Hungary and Poland followed; and in July 1985, France enacted a "parafiscal air pollution tax" on all large fossil fuel combustion sources emitting more than 2,500 metric tons of sulphur dioxide per year (i.e., some 480 plants representing about two-thirds of total sulphur emissions in the country), taxed at 130 francs per metric ton SO_2 (i.e., about two cents per kilogram), with the proceeds going to antipollution investments in the industry sectors concerned. From 1990 onwards, the tax will be raised to 150 francs per ton and extended to industrial emissions of nitrogen oxides (NOx), later to be followed by volatile organic compounds (VOCs). Finland enacted a whole package of "environmental taxes" on fossil fuels as part of its 1990 budget legislation; and similar measures, including a new charge on carbon dioxide emissions at the rate of 25 ore (about four cents) per kilogram CO_2, are now under discussion in Sweden. It should be pointed out, though, that none of the existing emission charges today is considered to be severe enough to achieve the full "polluter pays" effect postulated in welfare economics, i.e., to internalize all social costs generated by a pollution source; their function rather is to raise parafiscal revenue through environmentally rational penalties.

A more recent example of transnational diffusion is the "environmental label" for consumer products, first introduced in the Federal Republic of Germany in 1978. There, an expert jury under the auspices of the Federal Environment Ministry awards to consumer products an official environmental quality label, popularly known as "blue angel" (based on the international logo of the United Nations Environment Programme). Against payment of a license fee to the nongovernmental National Institute for Quality Assurance and Certification (RAL), the label may then be used in commercial advertising and packaging on products ranging from low-emission oil combustion units to "environmentally benign" (recycled) toilet paper. The scheme turned out to be highly popular and successful, some lawsuits by disgruntled competitors notwithstanding, and there currently are some 3,500 products on the market bearing the blue angel mark. Similar systems of product labeling and licensing, partly based on the West German experience, were introduced in 1989 both in Canada (EcoLogo) and in Japan (EcoMark). In November 1989 the Nordic Council of Ministers adopted a joint environmental label for consumer products (miljömärkt) to be used in all Scandinavian countries, based on national certification following common guidelines. (See Appendix A.)

Each of these schemes includes participation by the private sector through representatives of nongovernmental industrial, environmental, and consumer protection associations. Licensing functions may actually be conferred directly on nongovernmental institutions. In the Federal Republic of Germany, most antipollution equipment for motor vehicles and stationary emission sources is certified by regional engineering societies known as TÜV (Technischer Ueberwachungs-Verein, i.e., technical inspection association). France now plans to introduce a similar system on an experimental basis. In Norway, technical certification of offshore mining platforms is carried out by a private company (Det Norske Veritas), following the century-old practice of classification for seaworthy ships initiated by insurance companies such as Lloyd's, and plans are now underway to extend the system to other areas of environmental licensing. The Geneva-based Société Générale de Surveillance (SGS), through its various subsidiaries and affiliates in 140 countries, also provides services for environmental quality certification under commercial contracts.

To be sure, wider diffusion of these institutional models is bound to raise transnational problems. Already more than 10 percent of the current environmental product labels in the Federal Republic of Germany are held by foreign firms (including fourteen from the Netherlands, eleven from Austria, and thirty-three from ten other West European countries, as well as some Japanese car manufacturers and American chemical companies), and the trend is rising in anticipation of the free trade regime of the 1992 European Common Market. Conversely, exported West German products carrying the "blue angel" are now reported to be gaining new market shares in the United Kingdom and in other environmentally conscious consumer countries. To avoid unfair trade practices, arrangements for mutual recognition of national labels will become necessary, possibly including harmonized standards and procedures of product selection and identification. For instance, since the West German jury procedure already provides for participation by the state (Länder) authorities of an applicant's principal place of business, there is no reason why the procedure could not be opened to competent foreign authorities where applicable.

Alert Diffusion. Transnational diffusion of regulatory experience is particularly important in environmental risk management. There are approximately 70,000 chemicals in common use today, with some 500 to 1,000 new compounds added every year. While there is still very little known on the toxicity of about two-thirds of these, information is available on national regulatory action concerning certain chemicals considered environmentally harmful or hazardous. Based on a 1982 General Assembly resolution, the UN secretariat regularly publishes a consolidated list of products whose consumption or sale has been banned, withdrawn, severely restricted, or not approved by governments. The fourth (1990) edition lists some 400 chemicals and 300 pharmaceuticals in these categories.

Following regional initiatives by the Organization for Economic Cooperation and Development, and inspired in part by earlier U.S. federal legislation, the Governing Council of the UN Environment Programme in 1984 adopted a "provisional notification scheme" for banned or severely restricted chemicals, requiring countries to exchange standard warnings when exporting any of these categories. Further elaborated by the 1987 London Guidelines for the Exchange of Information on Chemicals in International Trade, the scheme is administered by UNEP's Geneva-based International Register of Potentially Toxic Chemicals. It is implemented by seventy-five countries and by a 1988 EC Regulation Concerning Export From and Import Into the Community of Certain Dangerous Chemicals. Related provisions are found in the International Code of Conduct on the Distribution and Use of Pesticides, adopted by the UN Food and Agriculture Organization in 1985. (Both the UNEP and the FAO procedures were amended in 1989 to include the requirement of "prior informed consent," under which participating importing countries will have to give their express approval prior to import.)

Information diffusion of this kind serves as a danger signal to importing countries, especially with regard to those fifty to one hundred "red flag" chemicals currently banned by more than ten states. While this may seem tantamount to blacklisting, there is actually no international regulatory action involved, since both the UN consolidated list and the UNEP/OECD schemes are based entirely on national regulatory decisions in the countries concerned.

A similar notification procedure debuted under Article 5 of the CITES treaty. Besides the convention's international "black" and "gray" lists of endangered species in Appendices I and II, each party has an option to list on a separate third appendix any species or *taxa* whose export it wishes to ban or control for national reasons. Unlike the listing of species in Appendices I and II, which requires international agreement by a two-thirds majority vote, Appendix III listings are made by simple unilateral notification to the CITES secretariat (Article 16), which in turn communicates it to all other parties with a request to adjust their trade controls accordingly. Though originally not viewed as significant, recourse to Appendix III by CITES member states has increased over the years, to more than 240 *taxa* listed in 1989.

In addition, as a matter of practice gradually developed in the course of treaty administration, the CITES secretariat has begun to send notifications to all parties whenever a member state announces a national ban on exports or imports over and above the controls required by the treaty, in order to solicit international enforcement assistance. While such calls are issued on a voluntary basis—and are not always viewed kindly by other parties, in view of the extra administrative burden involved—they rarely go unheeded, and are duly included in the enforcement instructions given by most governments to their trade control authorities. Precautionary diffusion of foreign restrictions thus tends to produce the desired alert effect, even though it is not strictly mandatory.

Epistemic Networks. A crucial factor for the success of environmental agreements is direct permanent contact between the national agencies, groups, and individuals entrusted with implementation. Reference is often made to the role of "technical elites" or "epistemic communities" to explain consensus building in the negotiation of international agreements. Experience with environmental regimes suggests that epistemes may be even more important at the implementation stage.

A common feature of mutual recognition schemes is their reliance on a permanent network of national focal points, designated as the official channel for transnational communications and authentications. CITES established a network of "management authorities" and "scientific authorities," mostly consisting of wildlife management officers and wildlife biologists. The WHO, UNEP, and OECD schemes to control trade in chemicals (as well as the future Basel Convention network for hazardous wastes) rely on designated public health officials and government chemists. The ECE motor vehicle certification system works through a list of licensing agencies usually staffed by automotive engineers. Monitoring under the Transboundary Air Pollution Convention is carried out by the EMEP network of stations and laboratories, most of which are part of national meteorological services. The transnational expert communities so established often include nongovernmental sectors—industry, research institutions, and competent environmental groups. In each case, the common professional background of participants tends to foster a distinct "epistemic" solidarity across frontiers—the old boys' network.

As a rule, authority for licensing or monitoring decisions of the kind described here (whether they concern imported chemicals, cars, wildlife products, or meteorological data) is delegated to officials at an intermediate technical level. For reasons of administrative efficiency, their communication links with each other and with the international secretariats concerned are usually direct, thereby short-circuiting national departmental hierarchies and virtually by-passing diplomatic channels. As transnational contacts enhance the professional status of participants, they also create strong incentives for the continuity and expansion of international agreements. In the same way that mutual confidence and "cognitive convergence" among specialists develop in the preparation and negotiation of a treaty, technocratic solidarity in monitoring and compliance control feeds back into the national evaluation and further development of environmental regimes. It also makes cheating in treaty implementation more difficult and can prevent or at least defuse disputes.

Alternatives to Intergovernmental Litigation

When evaluating the implementation and effectiveness of international agreements, lawyers tend to focus on judicial or quasi-judicial enforcement, in particular through the principle of state responsibility (now being codified by the UN International Law Commission). There is a growing literature on state responsibility for environmental harm, usually starting from the 1941 U.S.-Canadian Trail Smelter arbitration. Closer analysis of existing international environmental law and practice reveals, however, that intergovernmental litigation of the Trail Smelter type is a rare exception and plays little or no role in the implementation of multilateral treaties and standards; the 1979 Geneva Convention on Long-range Transboundary Air Pollution even expressly excludes the question of state liability for damage.

For a number of reasons, intergovernmental liability suits do not seem to be a promising way of enforcing multilateral environmental agreements. One reason is that, unlike the bilateral Trail Smelter case, which concerned a single point source in Canada causing instant harm to identified victims nearby in the United States, today's multilateral regimes increasingly deal with long-range (up to several thousand miles) and long-term effects (up to several generations) of multiple pollutants from a variety of sources that are difficult to pin down. Another caveat is the time-cost of the Trail Smelter case, which from the first claims in 1926 to the final arbitral award in 1941 took a solid fifteen years—far longer than most environmental problems today can wait.

In spite of these limitations, international lawyers continue to extrapolate principles from this venerable single precedent, like good generals rehearsing the wars of yesteryear. Yet most transnational environmental regimes have learned to avoid the adversarial state-liability approach, and instead have used or developed different methods of ensuring compliance with treaty obligations. A number of alternative channels and mechanisms are available for this purpose, including some promising innovative approaches.

Local Remedies. In considering the Trail Smelter model, it is worth recalling that the case developed into an international arbitration only because of a historical deadlock between local legal remedies: even though nothing prevented American air pollution victims from bringing a private law suit in Canada, the local Canadian courts in the 1930s would have refused—under an ancient House of Lords rule—to take jurisdiction over suits based on damage to foreign land; on the other hand, Washington state law did not permit the acquisition of smoke easements in Washington land by a foreign corporation. Had these domestic procedural obstacles been removed by more flexible rules concerning foreign parties, the case would probably never have moved to arbitration at an intergovernmental level.

More recent environmental case law demonstrates that numerous local legal remedies are available to defuse transboundary problems and to resolve conflicts between the divergent legal systems involved. For example, in the 1957 case of *Poro v. Lorraine Basin Coalmines,* which involved air pollution from a power plant in France causing damage to residents across the border in West Germany, a German appeal court chose to determine damages "in accordance with the law most favorable to the plaintiff" (in this instance, the French Civil Code). Significantly, the bulk of disputes over transboundary pollution damage along the Rhine River since 1975 was resolved by local remedies, either through national courts or by out-of-court settlements and insurance.

It is true that this approach also requires a degree of mutual recognition to be given to foreign decisions—e.g., under the Brussels (1968) and Lugano (1988) Conventions on Jurisdiction and Enforcement of Judgments in Civil and Commercial Matters in Europe—and arrangements to facilitate the participation of foreign parties in local judicial and administrative proceedings, as under the 1974 Nordic Environmental Protection Convention and the Council of Europe's 1980 Outline Convention on Transfrontier Cooperation between Territorial Communities or Authorities. The Recommendations on Equal Right of Access and Nondiscrimination in Relation to

Transfrontier Pollution, adopted in 1976 and 1977 by the Organization for Economic Cooperation and Development, played a pilot role in this field; and a draft "convention on environmental impact assessment in a transboundary context" now under preparation in the UN Economic Commission for Europe aims at harmonizing procedures for environmental planning and decision making in border regions. To the extent that effective dispute resolution is thus available also to foreign parties by recourse to local remedies, it can take a considerable amount of pressure and antagonism off the diplomatic agenda.

Complaints and Custodial Action. As an alternative to legal action against the responsible party, recourse to a nonjudicial international institution may provide a remedy of first instance in case of infringements of environmental agreements. The noncompliance procedure currently being developed under the 1987 Montreal Protocol on Substances That Deplete the Ozone Layer initially foresees the filing of complaints (by one or more parties) with the UNEP secretariat, for further information gathering and eventual submission to a five-party implementation committee. However, even though the procedure so proposed was very cautiously defined as nonjudicial and nonconfrontational, a number of delegations emphasized that "any supranational body to review data would be unacceptable," which does not bode well for the status of such a mechanism.

A much bolder step toward collective compliance control was taken by the 1957 Rome Treaty establishing the European Economic Community. Article 155 designates the EEC Commission as guardian of the treaty's implementation, and Article 169 empowers it to initiate proceedings against any member state in case of infringements, sanctioned if necessary by formal action in the European Court of Justice at Luxembourg. Over the past ten years, this "custodial" procedure has become one of the most important means of enforcing EEC environmental standards.

The EEC infringement proceedings comprise three stages.

As a first step, the commission sends "letters of formal notice" to member states for failure to implement a community directive (i.e., failure to enact or apply the national legislative or administrative measures required, or failure to report on their enactment or application). After giving the member state an opportunity to respond, the commission can next render a "reasoned opinion" confirming the infringement in the light of all factual information gathered. In case of continued noncompliance, it may then refer the matter to the European Court of Justice, with a view to holding the member state in violation of its obligations under the EEC Treaty. During the year 1988, the commission issued a total of ninety-three letters of formal notice, seventy-one reasoned opinions, and eleven references to the court concerning infringements of EEC environmental directives (of which there were more than seventy in force at that time).

What may be the most significant feature of this procedure, however, is mentioned nowhere in the treaty and evolved only gradually in the course of its implementation: more than half of the infringement proceedings initiated against member states were based not on the commission's own monitoring of compliance but on citizen complaints—from private individuals, associations (such as Greenpeace and Friends of the Earth), or entire municipalities. As a result of public information on the complaints procedure and the establishment of a "complaints registry" within the commission secretariat in Brussels, the number of environmental complaints rose dramatically—from 190 in 1988 to 460 in 1989 (the first recorded figure for 1982 was ten). While complaints are usually based on local noncompliance with EEC standards, they may have wider effects; a single complaint by a resident in one of the United Kingdom's two nonattainment areas with regard to the 1980 EEC Directive on Air Quality Limit Values and Guide Values for Sulphur Dioxide and Suspended Particulates triggered an investigation by the commission resulting in infringement proceedings against seven member states.

It should be recalled that the EEC has no powers of physical enforcement comparable to those of a national government.

Although virtually all of the more than thirty judgments rendered by the European Court of Justice in environmental infringement proceedings since 1982 went against the defendant member states and upheld the commission's opinion, not all of them led to compliance, e.g., in the 1988 case of *Commission v. Kingdom of Belgium,* the court noted that Belgium had failed to fulfil its obligations under Article 171 of the treaty by refusing, in defiance of earlier (1982) judgments of the court, to adopt the measures necessary to implement four EEC directives on waste disposal.

Nonetheless, the mere opening of EEC action can have internal political and economic consequences in member states, as in the case of the United Kingdom, where the government's plans for privatization of local water management agencies were stalled in part because of pending EEC infringement proceedings as to water quality standards in the areas concerned. As a result, the custodial action procedure of the EEC Commission—which some already describe as an "environmental ombudsman"—has practically been transformed from a three-stage into a four-stage process, the optional first stage being in the majority of cases a citizen complaint.

Environmental Audits. Besides judicial review at the national or international level, other techniques of compliance control have appeared in the practice of international organizations. Probably the body with the longest experience in this regard is the International Labour Organization (ILO), which has enacted and monitored a long line of multilateral conventions since the 1920s—ranging from bans on white lead paint and other occupational health hazards, to workers' protection against air pollution, radiation, and toxic chemicals in the working environment. All these conventions contain provisions on dispute settlement that would allow states to initiate complaints and ad hoc inquiries against other states for not observing the treaty. However, a detailed study of ILO's enforcement record over more than sixty years shows that this adversarial procedure was rarely used except for occasional political potshots. Instead, ILO member states developed an entirely different procedure that originally had not even been foreseen for this purpose, but which turned out to be far more effective in enforcing compliance: the system of annual or biennial reporting by governments, combined with regular auditing by an independent technical committee of experts to ascertain the degree of compliance in each member state, followed by public debate of these audited reports by the Conference Committee on the Application of Conventions and Recommendations.

Over the years, the ILO "auditing" system—with the active participation of both trade unions and employers' associations—has thus turned into a worldwide public hearing process that clearly induces more compliance by governments than the threat of any intergovernmental legal action would. The UN Commission on Human Rights applies a similar procedure of country reports and public hearings, in which nongovernmental organizations (such as Amnesty International) play an active role.

In the environmental field, the biennial Conference of the Parties to the Convention on International Trade in Endangered Species of Wild Fauna and Flora has become a forum for international review of compliance with the treaty, again with massive nongovernmental organization (NGO) support. Similarly, reviews of treaty implementation by parties and signatories to the Convention on Long-range Transboundary Air Pollution and its protocols are carried out and published at regular intervals by the Executive Body for the convention.

In all these cases, periodic audits (through comparative monitoring and reporting) of compliance with agreed international standards are a well-established routine. Publicity is an essential part of the process, not only in terms of collective review and mutual accountability by all member states, but even more importantly as a means of exposing governmental compliance reports to scrutiny by each country's nongovernmental groups and through them to public opinion at home.

The concept of environmental auditing has also been taken up directly by nongovernmental groups (e.g., by Friends of the Earth in the United Kingdom, with public audits held at the county level) and especially by industry: several major transnational corporations—at least partly perhaps as a result of the Bhopal shock—now carry out regular environmental audits with a view to ensuring that regulatory requirements and long-term environmental liabilities (such as legal waste disposal duties) are accurately reflected in the balance sheets of their subsidiaries. In November 1988, the Executive Board of the International Chamber of Commerce (ICC) adopted a position paper on environmental auditing as guidance for business organizations, reflecting experience in countries and companies where the practice is already well established.

It should be pointed out, however, that there is a fundamental difference between the more limited scope of auditing as an instrument of internal business management and the idea of public review, which emerges as the key element of the international environmental audit procedures presented here. Inherent in this latter concept is public disclosure as a means of ensuring democratic control over the implementation of agreed international standards.

A key factor in favor of environmental audits is that they can make a difference *before* things have gone seriously wrong, unlike traditional judicial review mechanisms based on liability, which can only intervene after the fact. There is a clear need for preventive environmental controls to be scheduled before it is too late to take corrective action. The time may well be ripe to think of a global auditing body that would periodically evaluate the performance of states (and perhaps organizations) in complying with their international obligations—in line with the concept of "mutual accountability" postulated by Seyom Brown and Larry L. Fabian (*International Organization,* 1975).

Maurice Strong has suggested (*International Affairs,* Moscow, 1989) that new functions of this kind should be entrusted to the United Nations Trusteeship Council, an idea far more appealing than prospects of more environmental "action" in the World Court. As in the field of standard-setting and regulation, we need more imaginative approaches to compliance control than those drawn from outdated legal textbooks. An obvious and largely untapped source is the rich institutional and procedural experience of existing transnational regimes for environmental governance.

Outlook: A View from the Anthill

In the current international debate on environmental priorities in the face of global change, a precariously high portion of hopes seem to be pinned on some new utopia of world government. It is most unlikely that problems such as climate modification can be resolved by reorganizing the UN Environment Programme, nor for that matter by yet another epic codification a la Law of the Sea. The most critical need instead, given the urgency of the task, will be to activate and accelerate the entire presently available machinery for international action at all levels.

The obvious disadvantage of having to rely on the existing structure is its sheer complexity. We are dealing with an aggregate, rather than a system, of multiple environmental regimes; and the analogy of the anthill, aptly introduced by Ernst Haas (*World Politics*, 1980), is a euphemism, considering the well-organized hierarchies of social insects. To achieve a workable degree of coherence in environmental standard-setting and implementation under these circumstances will not only require further efforts at coordination within the United Nations family of organizations, but also vis-à-vis the entire range of other global and regional institutions concerned. An impressive start in this direction has already been made by the small Centre for Our Common Future set up in Geneva in 1988 to oversee follow-up to the Brundtland Commission's report.

An advantage of the present structure, and one that hopefully sets it apart from the stereotype of insect societies, is its openness and adaptiveness to change. Any new institutional arrangements in this field should seek to preserve this capacity and actively promote it. Practical devices for this purpose are the built-in review schedules that have made their appearance in a number of recent environmental agreements:

- The 1987 Montreal Protocol on Substances That Deplete the Ozone Layer thus stipulated that "beginning in 1990, and at least every four years thereafter, the Parties shall assess the control measures provided for . . . on the basis of available scientific, environmental, technical and economic information." Four assessment panels, coordinated by an intergovernmental open-ended working group, began to function for this purpose in 1989.
- The 1988 Sofia Protocol to the Convention on Long-range Transboundary Air Pollution provides for regular reviews of the agreement, starting no later than one year after its entry into force, and for negotiations to start no later than six months after entry into force "on further steps . . . taking into account the best available scientific and technological developments." In anticipation of this process, an intergovernmental working group on abatement strategies under the Executive Body for the convention began to function in 1989.
- The 1989 Basel Convention on the Control of Transboundary Movements of Hazardous Wastes and Their Disposal has scheduled an evaluation of the treaty's effectiveness three years after its entry into force and at least every six years thereafter, including the possible "adoption of a complete or partial ban of transboundary movements of hazardous wastes and other wastes in light of the latest scientific, environmental, technical and economic information."

This new generation of radical reviews, which has its equivalent in the overall performance evaluation to be undertaken by the UN Conference on Environment and Development in 1992, clearly is more than a routine inspection and maintenance service. If the mandate of a review is policy reorientation in the light of future knowledge and experience, it will inevitably have to include the option of consequential institutional change. What emerges, then, is indeed close to the new "fluid" model of environmental regimes envisaged by Jessica T. Matthews (*Foreign Affairs*, 1989), "allowing a rolling process of intermediate or self-adjusting agreements that respond quickly to growing scientific understanding." Even though open-ended commitments of this kind are still viewed with apprehension by diplomats, the "feedback loop" seems well on its way to becoming an established instrument of international environmental law in terms of an obligation for governments to take part in a deliberate, preprogramed process of institutional learning.

Appendix A

Environmental Product Labels

"Blue angel"
(West Germany, 1978)

"EcoMark"
(Japan, 1989)

"EcoLogo"
(Canada, 1989)

"Miljömärkt"
(Nordic Council, 1989)

9

Adjustment and Compliance Processes in International Regulatory Regimes

ABRAM CHAYES AND ANTONIA H. CHAYES

I nternational cooperation for the protection of the global environment will take place in large part through a complex network of international institutions and agreements. As the last chapter demonstrates, many of the agreements are already in place. Yet treaties addressing most of the major substantive problems discussed in this volume are still ahead, and the development of an institutional framework for global environmental management remains at a rudimentary stage.

ABRAM CHAYES is the Felix Frankfurter Professor of Law at Harvard University. During the Kennedy administration he was the legal adviser to the State Department. He is the author of many articles and books, including *The Cuban Missile Crisis, International Crisis, and the Role of Law,* and *The International Legal Process* (with T. Ehrlich and A. Lowenfeld).
ANTONIA H. CHAYES is chair of the board of Endispute, Inc. During the Carter administration, she served first as assistant secretary of the Air Force for manpower, reserve affairs, and installations and later as under secretary of the Air Force. Ms. Chayes is the author of numerous articles and papers on U.S. national security issues. She teaches at the Georgetown University School of Law and at Harvard University's John. F. Kennedy School of Government.

Current discussion of future agreements, both in and out of government, is focused primarily on substance—what activities are to be regulated and at what levels. But maintaining an international regulatory regime, once a treaty is concluded, is as difficult and daunting as reaching the initial agreement itself. This chapter addresses the problems of regime maintenance. It identifies and examines two crucial requirements:

First, the ability to adjust the norms and rules in response to the demands of continuous changes in the political, cultural, economic, and technical setting. Both environmental destruction and protection are deeply affected by rapid technological change.

Second, the ability to assure substantial compliance with the norms and rules in the face of powerful centrifugal incentives for free-riding and defection. International environmental regulation seeks to influence not only state action, but the actions of individuals and entities operating inside and across state borders. This both poses difficult problems and suggests new opportunities for regime maintenance.

This chapter describes at some length efforts to provide adaptability and secure compliance in international regulatory regimes in fields such as international trade, arms control, the monetary system, and human rights. Although that experience cannot be carried over directly, it is instructive for the task of international cooperation for the protection of the environment.

Adapting to Changing Circumstances

If an international regulatory agreement is to endure and continue to serve its basic purposes over time, it must be adaptable to inevitable changes in technology; substantive problems; and economic, societal, and political developments. The regulatory treaty is not so much a contract among states as it is a constitutive document. A major function of such a charter—perhaps *the* major function—should be to establish a binding decision process for resolving regulatory issues as they arise and for elaborating, clarifying, and updating the treaty as changes in the economic and technological situation may require.

It is illusory to seek to decide all questions of detailed performance that may arise in the indefinite future. Overall objectives and the main substantive principles can be set out. The level of financial exposure must be fixed. Some matters of specific obligation that have become salient during the negotiating process will have to be settled in the text. The limits of human foresight are quickly reached, however, and even some problems that can be foreseen may be too contentious to resolve in the drafting process. At some point, the drafters must give up striving for more precision and detail and leave questions to be resolved when and as they arise, within the framework of the basic principles laid down in the treaty.

Adapting the treaty to new needs and conditions can occur at two levels. The first may be called the level of legislation or regulation. It involves institutional processes for formulating general rules to meet new needs or changed circumstances, without the requirement of concluding a new treaty or amending the original one.

The second level at which adaptation takes place is less obvious and operates more incrementally. It is the level of enforcing or applying the treaty norms. In a process familiar to common lawyers, interpretation molds the principles and rules to new developments in the course of applying them in particular cases.

The Level of Legislation

First-generation international organizations, like the International Labour Organization (ILO) and International Telecommunications Union (ITU), had no power to make substantive rules and regulations binding on their members. This followed from prevailing conceptions of international law, which held that a state could only undertake international obligations by an agreement expressing its consent—in effect, by the treaty process.

The conventions that established these early organizations contained a statement of the general purposes and principles of the organization. Detailed regulations defining specific requirements for state behavior were to be elaborated in a series of separate treaties. A principal function of the organization was to be the formulation of these treaties.

Thus the ITU Convention contains a general obligation of noninterference with radio transmissions. Periodically, the ITU convenes an Administrative Radio Conference to allocate frequencies to different uses. The conclusions of the conference are not directly binding on any ITU member. They are cast in the form of a treaty (consisting largely of signs and symbols intelligible only to electrical engineers) and submitted to the ITU members for ratification.

In the course of more than a century, the ILO has drafted and promulgated scores of treaties governing terms and conditions of employment, freedom of association, health in the workplace, and the like. The ILO Convention obligates members to ratify these treaties and bring them into operation as a matter of domestic law. In fact, the process of adherence is beset by long delays. Much of the compliance effort of the ILO is devoted to securing ratification of these implementing treaties, as opposed to ensuring that their requirements are observed.

Peter Sand has called attention to the inherent deficiencies of using the traditional lawmaking treaty as the principal legislative instrument in an international environmental regime. Each new treaty must be ratified in accordance with the domestic procedures of the members. At best there is delay. At worst, the political battles that attend the adoption of any important international agreement affecting domestic economic interests may prevent ratification altogether. When (or if) the new treaty ultimately comes into force, it may be with the adherence of less than all the members of the organization or it may contain unfortunate or restrictive reservations.

Despite these drawbacks, discussions of a possible treaty on global climate change seem to envision such a process. A "framework convention" would set out basic principles. Detailed obligations would be contained in a series of "protocols" addressing particular subjects within the broad ambit of the convention. The protocols would be subject to separate ratification by governments. The Vienna Convention on the Protection of the Ozone Layer and its attendant Montreal Protocol seem to be taken as a model. The protocol was approved at what amounted to a diplomatic conference among the parties to the convention. Fortunately, it was ratified by enough countries so that it came into force on schedule on January 1, 1989. The result got a strong assist from the decision of the major producer of chlorofluorocarbons (CFCs), the du Pont Corporation, to phase out production entirely by the end of the century because it found an acceptable substitute.

This approach may reflect a reaction to the experience with the Convention on the Law of the Sea. Environmentalists and others have regarded the decade-long history from 1973 to 1982 as a cautionary tale, a process to be avoided at all costs. Although the final verdict is not yet in, it surely illustrates the difficulties of developing a single comprehensive agreement in a many-faceted area, like the oceans, affecting so many states in so many different ways.

But eagerness to avoid a repetition of the Law of the Sea experience should not erase the memory of the deficiencies of the pre–World War I conception of international lawmaking. The practice of international organizations in recent decades has validated a broad repertoire of ways in which international institutions may be endowed with the capacity to make decisions and regulations binding on members, without reference back to national parliaments for approval. We cite only a few examples:

• In the field of monetary affairs, the executive directors of the International Monetary Fund (IMF) take binding decisions interpreting the Fund Agreement. The key questions— whether drawings against the fund's resources could be made conditional on the economic performance of the drawing state, and the period within which drawings could remain outstanding—were hotly contested at Bretton Woods, but left unresolved. After the Fund Agreement entered into force, both issues were settled by decisions of the executive directors. Article IV of the IMF Articles as amended in 1978 requires the fund to exercise "firm surveillance" of members' exchange rate practices. Decisions of the executive directors define the content of this requirement and the procedures for carrying it out. More recently, the fund used the same mechanism to set up a procedure for "enhanced surveillance" in certain cases of debt rescheduling, for which there seems to be little express warrant in the Articles.

- Peter Sand noted the authority of the Council of the International Civil Aeronautics Organization (ICAO) by a two-thirds vote to make regulations concerning aircraft noise and emissions, without the need of separate ratification. The same authority extends to the whole range of safety and operational requirements for international air transport. Members have a formal right to opt out if they disagree with a regulation, but nobody does, since as a practical matter a country cannot participate in international air transport unless it accepts the rules followed at the major hubs of the system. The International Maritime Organization (IMO) has similar authority. The creation of wholly new obligations (e.g., on aircraft highjacking or marine pollution), as opposed to elaborating and specifying the content of existing ones, may be thought to require a new treaty. But the two categories are separated by a wide gray area, and the distinction between them is not self-evident.
- The ITU itself establishes technical specifications for telecommunications equipment, not by treaty as with frequency allocations, but by adopting recommendations drafted by specially convened industry groups. Again, practical considerations of access to the international service dictate adherence.
- The Organization for Economic Cooperation and Development (OECD) was formed in 1962 among the advanced industrial states to consider common economic problems. Although it is empowered to take binding decisions by unanimous vote of its council, it rarely uses this authority. "Recommendations" seem to suffice most of the time. An especially interesting instance is the adoption by reference

into the 1979 General Agreement on Tariffs and Trade (GATT) Subsidies Code of OECD recommendations on permissible interest charges in official export financing, as revised from time to time.

- The International Coffee Agreement and most other commodity arrangements have given the plenary body of the organization authority to establish and adjust quotas, usually by a special majority vote. In 1965, after a legal panel rendered a unanimous advisory opinion that a "selective quota system" was not permitted by the Coffee Agreement, the Coffee Council, which had final authority to interpret the agreement, decided nevertheless to establish what was in effect a selective quota system.

The key requirement in each of these cases is an international institution or organization created by a treaty that grants it the necessary powers and lays down the processes for action. By ratifying this constitutive treaty, the state accepts the powers and processes specified in it, thus satisfying the international law requirement of consent to the obligations that may be created.

The Level of Application

As in the IMF case, "interpretation" of the agreement is one of the ways by which the organization can bind members without further reference to national legislatures. Interpretation most frequently takes place in the context of a dispute among the parties over the meaning of the treaty. In the decision of the International Coffee Organization cited above, the issue of the legality of selective quotas arose in a dispute between Brazil and the African producers over quota allocation. It can happen as well in the graver setting of national security concerns.

When the Treaty on the Limitation of Anti-Ballistic Missiles (ABM) was negotiated, the United States was concerned that radars used in the highly developed Soviet anti-aircraft defense might be "upgraded" to permit their use in an ABM system. To meet this concern, the treaty provides that non-ABM components may not be "tested in an ABM mode" (Article VI). Despite strenuous efforts, the United States could not achieve a more specific definition of this obligation during the original treaty negotiations. After the treaty went into effect, the United States complained in the Standing Consultative Commission (SCC) established by the treaty that the Soviets were testing air-defense radars in violation of Article VI. In response, the commission has twice worked out "agreed statements" defining what kinds of activities by air-defense radars will be considered "testing in an ABM mode." Not only are these statements unratified; they remain classified and unavailable to the general public. Nevertheless, both the United States and the Soviet Union regard them as binding, and it is said that they embody substantially the U.S. position that the USSR refused to accept in the original negotiations.

In most existing environmental agreements, the dispute settlement provision consists solely of a stipulation for voluntary arbitration or reference to the International Court of Justice. It seems safe to assume that, like the myriad other such compromissory clauses in bilateral and multilateral agreements, these provisions will seldom be invoked. The characteristic distaste of states for judicial settlement is likely to prevail in future international environmental regimes.

On the whole, that may be just as well. Controversies arising under a complex regulatory regime in a fast-changing technical and economic environment are not usefully treated as bilateral disputes between adversaries, with a winner-take-all solution. Although such controversies ordinarily contain a large technical and scientific component, the scientific evidence will rarely be dispositive. As much as one might wish it, there will be no "pure green" environmental agreements. They will embody compromises and trade-offs between environmental, economic, and other interests. Under such an agreement, "dispute settlement" is a management process involving more or less continuous negotiation among the parties, channeled by the framework of principles, norms, and institutions in the agreement.

Despite the reluctance of states to submit to binding third-party decision, dispute settlement under international agreements often involves the use of a neutral element, and this trend is on the increase. Members of the UN Human Rights Commission, panels under the General Agreement on Tariffs and Trade, and the ILO Committee of Experts (all discussed more fully below) are supposed to be neutrals. To protect this status, they serve in their individual capacities rather than as government representatives; they are selected for knowledge of the subject matter; and they are not subject to governmental instructions.

The IMF staff has an enviable reputation for technical and professional competence. So too with the staff of the International Atomic Energy Agency (IAEA), which conducts inspections of nuclear facilities of member states (also discussed below).

The same tendency is reflected in widespread resort by international organizations to a variety of ad hoc committees of experts, study panels, rapporteurs, and the like. The growing role of the UN and regional organizations in monitoring elections and arrangements for the settlement of conflict situations is further evidence of a new acceptability of neutral participation in dispute settlement processes. President Gorbachev has even entertained the possibility of third-party involvement in verification of bilateral arms control agreements. The most far-reaching example of third-party settlement is the elaborate dispute settlement section of the Law of the Sea Convention, establishing compulsory arbitration procedures in the event other methods do not succeed. Although the convention has not yet come into force, Hamburg has offered a site for the International Tribunal for the Law of the Sea and is conducting an architectural competition for its design.

Assuring Compliance

All international regimes face problems with free-riders, holdouts, and defectors. In the environmental field, these difficulties are intensified. Regulation seems to entail large and visible short-term costs to entrenched business interests. It may be seen as discriminating between rich and poor nations. The benefits are widely diffused in space and time, and it is often fairly easy for an actor to extract them without accepting the burdens of compliance.

It is well established, but not always fully accepted by proponents of new areas for regulation, that international law does not deploy a regularized system of coercive sanctions to enforce its prescriptions. Calls for environmental norms "with teeth" or for "coercive measures or regulations necessary to induce cooperative behavior" are unlikely to be satisfied. The structural realities of international life preclude "enforcement" by means of sanctions except in very special circumstances.

Still, although quantitative measures may be hard to find, there is no reason to think that fulfillment by states of their international obligations compares unfavorably to compliance with domestic legal rules—certainly not with those covering the distribution and use of narcotic drugs or even the payment of taxes. As Professor Louis Henkin tells us in *How Nations Behave,* despite some conspicuous departures, *"almost all nations observe almost all principles of international law and almost all of their obligations almost all of the time"* (emphasis in original). Even "realist" students of international relations are beginning to recognize that states tend to comply with the normative requirements of regimes of which they are members—and to try to figure out why.

A point of departure is to recognize that in efforts to induce compliance with international regulation, the prime concern is not to identify and punish "violators." Compliance systems in international regulatory regimes are instruments for maintaining a dynamic equilibrium among strongly backed competing interests, so that the regime continues to be viable in a constantly changing international setting.

The regime will persist if the parties continue to believe that the benefits of membership outweigh the costs. Presumably the ratio was sufficiently favorable to induce the parties to accept the agreement in the first place. Compliance systems help maintain this favorable calculus over the life of the regime by providing a systematic method for ensuring and demonstrating that the conduct of the parties overall warrants continued adherence.

To this end, international regulatory regimes have had to find a substitute for the possibility, in the domestic legal order, of ultimate resort to the imposition of settlement independently of the will of the parties. Most regulatory regimes employ the same basic mechanism for this purpose, although in a variety of forms and combinations. The common feature that substitutes for coercion in international compliance systems is the exploitation of the *accountability* of states by rendering their performance *transparent* to scrutiny by the international community.

This section briefly develops these two ideas, accountability and transparency, and then looks at the dynamics of their interaction in concrete international settings.

Accountability

Despite the persistence of state sovereignty both in law and practice, nations are in fact publicly accountable for their actions, particularly in international regulatory areas of high political visibility. Democratic governments, whose ranks seem to be growing, are of course accountable to domestic political constituencies. States are also called to account by other participants in the international system, either through bilateral diplomacy or in international forums. The international reach and impact of the media also means accountability before a widening international public.

Governments uniformly provide public justification for their public actions and omissions. That in itself is evidence of the importance of the accountability requirement. Much of the daily activity of diplomats and their spokespersons is devoted to this end. If justification is not spontaneously forthcoming, calls from interested parties, foreign and domestic, amplified through the media, usually induce response. Justification ordinarily includes defense of the action in terms of relevant legal principles and norms and other widely held values.

It is true that the justifications states offer for their conduct are not always candid or objective, but at a minimum they provide a basis for questions and clarification by a variety of interlocutors, both in and out of government. A complex structure of public bodies, private groups, and individuals, endowed in different measure with information, concern, energy, and power, subjects the proffered justifications to continuous scrutiny and critique. In every issue area, there are networks of people strategically located in national bureaucracies, political parties, legislative establishments, international institutions, or nongovernmental organizations, well informed and linked by common concern and interest. These individuals and groups interact across international and private boundaries in enforcing accountability of states and other international actors.

Transparency

Accountability is made possible by an environment rich in information about the behavior of parties to an agreement. Rarely is this behavior so visible and unambiguous that its effects can be ascertained without specially developed information. International regulatory regimes employ many different methods for generating the necessary base of information. Once developed, it permits detailed and continuous matching of a party's actions against the applicable treaty norms and the proffered justifications. Pressures for compliance are amplified by the institutional setting created by the treaty and by the issue networks and constituencies to which officials must respond. Indeed, action officers in regulatory areas are often members of these networks and, in a broad sense, share their concerns.

Generating Information. In almost all international regulatory organizations, members are required to report on a regular basis statistical and other information about their activities in the areas of concern to the organization. These reports become the baseline for the regulatory activity of the organization. Country reports may be supplemented by special studies conducted by the staff of the organization, but these too commonly rely on member contributions. In recent years, the contribution of nongovernmental organizations to the flow of available information has become increasingly important. Nevertheless, the primary source of information for the regulatory and compliance activities of the organization is the reports of its members.

The IMF Agreement requires members to supply economic and financial data to the fund. From the beginning, it has published International Financial Statistics, essentially a monthly compilation of member state reports on national accounts. Now, forty years later, the series is invaluable. If not always 100 percent reliable, these figures are the starting point not only for the work of the IMF, but for much private research and analysis on international economics as well. Internationally reported economic statistics carry some assurance of accuracy, since the figures are likely to become the basis for national decision making in the reporting country. It is hard, at least in democratic countries, to keep two sets of books, one for the IMF and a wholly different one for domestic use.

In the arms control arena, the Strategic Arms Limitation Treaty II (SALT II) provided for an "agreed data base" consisting of the names and numbers of the weapons on each side that were to be covered by the treaty. When the Soviet negotiator at Geneva delivered his government's acquiescence in this provision, he said, "We have repealed 900 years of Russian history." The SALT II data base was a brief one-page memorandum listing a handful of weapon types on each side. In the Intermediate Nuclear Forces Treaty (INF), covering fewer types of weapons, the original data base has expanded to nearly one hundred pages, including information not only on weapons, but also on deployment areas, production facilities, training bases, and test locations.

The information included in this protocol is an "agreed" baseline—that is, the parties to the treaty must be satisfied that it accurately represents the state of affairs at the time the treaty is concluded. Annual updates will provide the basis for systematic review of the parties' performance in meeting reductions mandated by the treaty. The notion of an agreed baseline against which compliance with the party's undertakings can be measured has obvious applications in the environmental field.

Obtaining information about party performance—monitoring and verification—has traditionally been the largest obstacle to the conclusion of arms control agreements. Until the mid-1980s, the principal objector was the Soviet Union, which endlessly reiterated that on-site inspection was espionage in disguise. Nevertheless, starting with the Limited Test Ban Treaty in 1963, the parties acknowledged the legitimacy of what could be called a kind of espionage, euphemistically entitled "national technical means of verification" (NTM). Reconnaissance satellites using high-resolution cameras and infrared sensors are perhaps the best known of these means. The phrase also covers observation of any kind from anywhere outside the sovereign territory of the observed state—electronic listening posts on the high seas or on the territory of neighboring states, atmospheric sampling in international air space, oblique angle aerial photography.

All subsequent arms control treaties between the United States and the Soviet Union prohibit concealment and other forms of interference with NTM. SALT II and the Strategic Arms Reduction Treaty (START) contain increasingly stringent provisions to prevent interference with electronic monitoring of weapons tests.

By definition, what is not concealed from the other party to the agreement is also visible to a satellite operated by a nonparty. High-capacity French photographic satellites now orbit over both the Soviet Union and the United States. A proposal for a UN reconnaissance satellite is under consideration. NATO and the Warsaw Pact are currently negotiating a comprehensive open skies agreement that will permit frequent and regular low-level overflight of the territory of all the parties to observe compliance with conventional arms restrictions. Again it is clear that extraterritorial monitoring of performance, especially using an agreed methodology, has important applications for environmental agreements.

In 1987 General Secretary Mikhail Gorbachev withdrew the Soviet objections to on-site inspection. In the INF negotiations, the USSR offered to accept highly intrusive on-site inspections, including "any time anywhere" challenge inspections. At that point, the United States drew back, deciding that there might be something in the espionage point after all. Indeed, a proposal for inspection of privately owned chemical manufacturing facilities under the Chemical Weapons Treaty was thought to raise questions under the Fourth Amendment prohibition against searches without a warrant.

Despite the newly cautious American attitude, the INF Treaty contains the most intrusive array of cooperative inspection measures to date, and the current draft of the START Treaty goes further still. The INF Treaty includes a provision for perimeter monitoring of production facilities that is especially interesting for environmental purposes. Each party stations a team of inspectors with monitoring devices round the clock outside a missile plant of the other to check the output, even though it cannot enter to observe the manufacturing process. A similar concept is actively under consideration for monitoring a low-threshold test ban agreement.

The most elaborate extant inspection arrangement in the arms control field is the safeguards system operated by the IAEA under the Nuclear Non-Proliferation Treaty (NPT). Parties to the treaty that do not possess nuclear weapons are obligated to permit IAEA inspection of all their peaceful nuclear facilities to ensure that they are not diverting nuclear materials useful for weapons production. The far-reaching inspection procedures are set forth in an elaborate protocol drawn up by the IAEA staff and adopted by vote of the governing body. It is refined and updated from time to time by the same procedure.

A special division of the IAEA staff conducts the inspections, periodically visiting each nuclear plant. Inspectors audit the material accounts, check effluents, and test production processes to detect any diversion of nuclear material, deliberate or otherwise. The agency is experimenting with tamper-proof on-line sensing devices to perform many of these functions continuously and report the data in real time. The IAEA director reports the results of the inspection to the Governing Board.

The inspection system has been criticized, especially by some U.S. observers. Although parties are obligated to submit to inspection, each negotiates a separate safeguards agreement with the IAEA, a process that has often been time consuming. The agreements generally give the country some control over the timing of the inspection and the identity of the inspectors. The NPT contains no clear statement of the consequences if the inspection should disclose that nuclear materials are unaccounted for.

These features are obviously unsatisfactory, but it is not clear that they have affected the integrity of the inspection system in practice. In any case, IAEA inspections implicate sensitive national security interests, which would not be the case in the environmental area.

Accountability and Transparency in Combination

Reporting and monitoring. Most international organizations use methods far less intrusive than on-site inspection to generate the information they need to hold parties to account. To start with what might be called a minimalist example, the UN Covenant on Civil and Political Rights establishes a Human Rights Committee of eighteen "experts" serving in a personal capacity. The covenant requires only that parties, when requested by the committee, "submit reports on the measures they have adopted to give effect to the rights recognized . . . [in the covenant] and on the progress made in the enjoyment of these rights." The committee examines the reports and in turn reports to the parties and the UN General Assembly on serious compliance problems. A supplementary procedure established by an Optional Protocol permits the committee to consider complaints of individuals against states that have accepted the protocol.

Starting with this barebones structure, the committee has steadily elaborated and intensified its processes for identifying human rights violations. It promulgated a detailed set of regulations for the content of the reports and the review procedure. Although the committee has no investigative powers, the rules require the reporting state to be present when the committee is considering a report, to respond to questions, and to supply additional information at the request of the committee. Committee members rely on their own expertise and other information in formulating these questions and requests.

In proceedings under the Optional Protocol, the committee submits the individual's complaint to the respondent state for comment. The complainant reviews and may in turn comment on the response. The committee then considers the complaint on the written submissions. Much of the detailed examination of the documentation is done in working groups of not more than five members to permit more intensive scrutiny of the materials. Upon making its decision, the committee forwards its "views" to both the individual and the respondent state. The committee may publicize its findings and in any event summarizes them in its annual reports to the General Assembly. This systematic reporting and evaluation has given rise to increasingly harsh public reaction to the conduct of the violating states.

A sister body, the UN Commission on Human Rights established by the Economic and Social Council (ECOSOC), performs similar monitoring and investigative functions over a broad spectrum of human rights concerns. The Sub-Commission on the Prevention of Discrimination and the Protection of Minorities hears complaints alleging a "consistent pattern of gross violations of human rights." Under the applicable ECOSOC resolutions, it may entertain complaints filed by victims, by persons with "reliable knowledge," and by nongovernmental groups. It has investigative powers and may dispatch an ad hoc committee to observe the situation on the ground, although only with the consent of the country involved, which is not always forthcoming. An important innovation is its practice of appointing a special rapporteur to conduct a global investigation on such subjects as torture, arbitrary executions, and genocide.

Regional human rights organizations benefit from a fairly homogeneous political and legal tradition. Consequently, human rights enforcement, especially under the European Convention on Human Rights, begins to take on the more familiar lineaments of a legal order. A European Court of Human Rights sits at Strasbourg and pronounces judgments binding on states. Nevertheless, the victim cannot apply directly to the court, but must go first to the European Human Rights Commission, which seeks to develop a negotiated solution. If it cannot, the commission decides whether to take the case to the court, and it rather than the victim is the complainant.

The widespread failure of states to live up to their obligations under the human rights covenants and their predecessor, the Universal Declaration of Human Rights, and the "ineffectiveness" of human rights enforcement have been routinely bemoaned. The field of human rights was seen as the paradigm of utopianism in international law. At best, international human rights norms were regarded as aspirational or hortatory. (The victims, it should be noted, did not always share this disparaging view.)

These judgments may have to be revised in the light of current events. Developments since the mid-1980s, first in Latin America and then in the Soviet Union and Eastern Europe, testify to the power and vitality of the norms in the Covenant on Civil and Political Rights. In this field, the relentless interaction of information and accountability ultimately achieved significant results. The work of the official human rights organizations nourished and legitimated a vast array of activities by individual states, nongovernmental organizations, and most important, the victims themselves, that kept these issues insistently at the forefront of international attention. Systematic investigation and reporting of human rights abuses by, for example, the U.S. State Department and congressional committees, Amnesty International, Helsinki Watch and similar organizations, and countless individual journalists and witnesses strengthened the work of the formal enforcement bodies and were in turn enhanced by it. Even during the worst of times, the hopes of dissidents and victims were kept alive and their voices magnified by these processes.

Although the results are less dramatic, the ILO relies basically on a similar system of reporting by member states and intensive review by its Committee of Experts on the Application of Conventions. A special feature is that the convention obligates members to report on their practices in the areas covered by all implementing treaties, even if they have not ratified a particular treaty and are therefore not bound by it. As noted above, almost all regulatory regimes include a reporting requirement, if only to maintain statistics in their area of concern. The statistical series themselves often become a vital information resource supporting the monitoring process.

Target Setting and Surveillance. The negotiation of specific targets with a party, taking account of its particular situation and problems, permits more precise evaluation of and accounting for its performance. This more intensive approach is employed by the IMF in approving drawings and regulating currency practices of its members. Although the problems of international monetary cooperation may seem very different, the fund's procedures are suggestive enough for international environmental regulation to warrant description at some length.

The policies with respect to drawings and stand-bys date from the very early years of the fund and were established almost completely by executive directors' decisions, interpreting what was at best ambiguous language in the agreement. Members can draw against the fund's resources only to meet balance of payments needs. In order to enforce this limitation, the fund requires that the member adopt economic policies to ensure repayment of the drawing within a short time, in the normal case three to five years. To this end, the member executes a "letter of intent" containing specific targets for monetary and fiscal policies, often expressed in precise numerical terms. In periodic performance reviews while the drawing is outstanding, the member must explain any shortfalls and, if necessary, work out new, more stringent measures to ensure that the provisions of the letter of intent are met. If the targets themselves seem to be inappropriate or inadequate, revisions are negotiated.

Obviously the fund is in a strong bargaining position throughout this process. The member is seeking access to the fund's resources, and presumably the fund could deny or terminate a drawing or stand-by if the member failed to comply with the letter of intent. Moreover, the member is aware that it may need the fund's help again in the future. The member is equally aware, however, that these sanctions are never—well, hardly ever—invoked, at least in their most drastic form. Nevertheless, through this mechanism the IMF exerts substantial influence over the economic policies of drawing members relating to balance of payments adjustment. Indeed, the extent of the fund's powers is a frequent source of bitter complaint in the Third World, where policies adopted at the fund's insistence have sometimes contributed to political upheaval or the overthrow of governments.

Procedures for exchange rate surveillance draw heavily on this earlier experience. They date from the late 1970s, after the collapse of the par value system originally adopted at Bretton Woods, when the Fund Agreement was amended to give members a free choice of exchange arrangements. The obligations in the amended agreement with respect to exchange practices are expressed in the most general terms. Members agree "to collaborate with the fund and other members to assure orderly exchange arrangements and to promote a stable systems of exchange rates." The only concrete prohibition is against "manipulation" of exchange rates.

The agreement provides that "the fund shall . . . oversee the compliance of each member with its obligations [as set forth above]" and to that end "shall exercise firm surveillance over the exchange rate policies of its members. . . ." Under this broad mandate, executive directors' decisions have identified specific suspect exchange rate practices and have established an elaborate surveillance procedure.

The fund conducts routine "consultations" with each member about once every eighteen months and special consultations on the initiative of the managing director when there is trouble. A team of staff economists prepares a study raising both factual and policy questions. The team then visits the country concerned for an intensive review of its findings with the responsible officials, sometimes consulting private industrial and financial groups as well. Thereafter, the fund staff revises the study and transmits it with recommendations to the executive directors, who discuss the study at a regular meeting. The director representing the concerned member makes the opening presentation. At the end, the managing director's summary of the discussion is adopted as the conclusions of the directors. Although couched in diplomatic terms, these conclusions often include pointed suggestions for changes in the member's exchange rate and related economic policies. As in the human rights case, the surveillance activities of the fund plug into a far-flung network of public and private financial institutions.

According to Professor Andreas Lowenfeld of New York University Law School, this surveillance process "seems to have been successful in keeping the system together and making it difficult for a state openly to defy the rules. . . ." He interposes the reservation that the executive directors may not be as effective in constraining "a major state." However, in contrast to human rights enforcement, IMF surveillance procedures are confidential. Given the sensitivity of financial markets, publicity might be counterproductive. An environmental organization would surely exploit the glare of publicity to achieve results. Its decisions, resonating against the sounding board of sophisticated and well-organized political constituencies, might well have impact even in the largest states.

Surveillance of state performance against targets established by treaty or accepted by the member is becoming a more familiar feature of international regulation. It is now a regular element in GATT dispute resolution. The ILO follows a similar procedure when its review of a country report reveals a failure of the member to comply with treaty standards. In negotiation with the offending state, it defines specific targets and policies designed to correct the deficiency.

Although as noted, this technique exerts strong pressure for compliance, it is premised on the notion that noncompliance is not necessarily, perhaps not even usually, the result of deliberate defiance of the legal standard. Major policy changes affecting politically entrenched important countervailing interests are difficult to achieve, especially in democratic countries. The surveillance process, by keeping the issues high on the government's agenda and focusing on concrete and realizable targets to which in most cases the member has agreed, can help to offset this resistance.

Negotiation and Conciliation. The only method for settling disputes that arise under bilateral arms control agreements between the United States and the Soviet Union is bilateral negotiation. The 1972 ABM Treaty formalized this process by establishing the SCC composed of representatives of the two countries "to consider questions concerning compliance with the obligations assumed and related situations that may be considered ambiguous."

Over the past two decades, the SCC has considered a number of difficult compliance issues. The mixed results reflect the problems of dispute settlement in the national security area. In the 1970s, when detente was in the air, a number of complaints were successfully resolved, and the Nixon, Ford, and Carter administrations all expressed satisfaction with the operation of the commission. The Reagan administration in its first six years criticized the commission as "an Orwellian memory hole into which our concerns were swept." The differences in response reflect the highly charged nature of efforts at dispute settlement in the sensitive national security area.

Through all the high politics, the SCC has continued to work systematically at the compliance issues on its agenda and has settled a good many of them. Much of the discussion and analysis that led ultimately to the Soviet acknowledgment that the Krasnoyarsk radar was a treaty violation took place in the SCC. All subsequent arms control agreements establish similar forums for dispute settlement.

Like a global environmental treaty, the GATT is a multiparty agreement dealing with activities in which long-run benefits are in constant tension with insistent short-run domestic economic interests backed by powerful political constituencies. The method contemplated for settlement of disputes is negotiation between the parties concerned, and in the absence of a negotiated settlement, reference to the contracting parties (that is, all the parties to the agreement acting jointly) who "shall make appropriate recommendations to the . . . parties . . . or give a ruling on the matter, as appropriate." In serious cases, the contracting parties may authorize the aggrieved state to withdraw trade benefits from the offending state.

The contracting parties soon adopted the practice of referring controversies for investigation and recommendation to a panel of three or five experts, chosen by the director general, with the consent of the parties. Panel members are knowledgeable about international trade and the GATT. Usually they are members of the GATT secretariat or trade officials of states other than the disputant states. They serve in a personal capacity, and are not subject to governmental instruction.

The United States originally thought of GATT dispute settlement as essentially an adjudicative process for applying and enforcing GATT rules. As late as 1962, in the first major dispute between the United States and the new European Economic Community (EEC), the United States was represented by lawyers and filed a legal brief, which the GATT panel largely ignored. The EEC presented its case through economists and diplomats, and got the better of the settlement.

The adjudicative mode gave way, over the 1960s and 1970s, to an approach emphasizing conciliation by the panel in cases where negotiation between the parties failed to produce a settlement. The United States and free-trade partisans have complained that in contrast to adjudication, which they believe would result in strict enforcement of GATT norms, the move to conciliation has inevitably meant fuzzy compromises and erosion of the rules. The critics argue that the result is an overall decline of free trade and the rise of protectionist sentiments among GATT members. They cite the reduced percentage of world trade conducted on a most-favored-nation basis, as mandated by Article I of the GATT.

Such criticism misconceives the nature of the agreement. The GATT does not enshrine a doctrinaire free-trade position. From the experience of the interwar period, the drafters learned not only the virtues of a liberal trading system, but also that domestic political leaders would not always be able to resist demands for protection from foreign competition. They learned too that unilateral trade restraints and retaliation could be disastrous. The agreement is itself a pragmatic compromise that expresses a general orientation and broad principles favoring continuing liberalization of international trade, but at the same time makes generous allowance for escape clauses and safety valves by which members can assuage political pressures from domestic producing interests. It insists on consultative procedures for invoking the exceptions.

A balance between these two conflicting tendencies was the essential requirement for the acceptance of the regime in the first place, and maintaining that balance, in a constantly shifting world economic and political context, is the essential requirement for the regime's survival. Former Deputy Secretary of State Kenneth Dam observes that with "the recognition by all contracting parties that legalism does not contribute to trade liberalization, the emphasis has shifted from the normal role of the GATT as third-party arbitrator to its informal role as catalyst for the resolution of disputes by the disputing parties themselves." "Compliance" is secured by a plastic process of interaction among the parties concerned in which the effort is to reestablish, in the microcontext of the particular dispute, the balance of advantage that brought the agreement into existence.

Of course, in the process of interpretation and application over forty years of tumultuous economic change, GATT norms and rules adapted and changed, as do all legal rules if they are to remain vital. Over those four decades, the overall volume of world trade has grown exponentially, with widespread, if unevenly distributed, benefits. It is doubtful that a more judicialized settlement approach, generating frequent formal interpretive opinions and precedents, would have provided the assurance of compliance needed to preserve the regime as a foundation for the expansion that has occurred.

The 1979 Draft Understanding Regarding Notification, Consultation, Dispute Settlement, and Surveillance essentially reaffirms the prior GATT procedures, despite a determined U.S. effort to tighten up the process. The exercise reflected a fair degree of satisfaction with the conciliation procedure as it has evolved. The understanding states explicitly that "the use of the dispute settlement procedures . . . should not be regarded as [a] contentious act."

Beyond the State System

In the traditional conception, international law operated between and among states. Obligations under it ran to states, and only a state had standing to challenge breach. If a state was party to an international agreement, it alone was responsible for ensuring that the requirements of the agreement were satisfied. In the case of a regulatory treaty, this meant that the state was obligated to enact measures on the domestic plane to ensure that individuals and entities subject to its jurisdiction conformed their behavior to the treaty requirements. If it failed to take such measures or if they proved ineffectual, only another state party to the treaty could complain.

That conception of international law has been rapidly eroding in two dimensions. In the first place, international organizations are fully recognized as subjects of international law. In the second, though more hesitantly, individuals and private entities are becoming the bearers of rights and to some extent obligations under the international legal system. Both developments have wide importance for the tasks of international environmental regulation.

Rights and Duties of
Private Persons and Entities

Even during the classical period of international law, in the United States at least, some treaty obligations gave rise directly to individual rights. Two centuries ago, for example, aliens were subject to widespread disabilities, including limitations on the right to hold or inherit land. If the United States made a treaty with a foreign state stipulating that the nationals of that state were entitled to inherit property, the alien could enforce the right to inherit in his/her own name in a U.S. court. The treaty, known in American parlance as "self-executing," in effect created individual rights and obligations. Other systems have similar concepts.

Today, international law recognizes a widening range of rights of individuals as against the state. Duties to aliens, once rationalized as derivative of the duty to the alien's home state, are now recognized as creating rights directly in the alien. Formerly, what a state did to its own citizens was its own business, a matter of domestic jurisdiction and not of international concern. It is now well accepted, notably in the field of international human rights, that states have obligations under international law to their own citizens, and that they can be called to account for violation of those obligations in both domestic and international forums.

If private parties can be the bearers of rights under international law, there is no longer any conceptual objection to the idea that it can also give rise to private obligations. Indeed, that was the point of the Nuremberg trials. Today, the notion of private obligation underlies the work on codes of conduct for multinational enterprises. Although these have not borne fruit in the shape of international agreements, many of the provisions worked out at the international level have been enacted in the investment laws of developing countries.

It would be possible to draft some kinds of environmental agreements establishing simple and well-defined prohibitions in such a way as to give rights of action to private citizens in national courts against a nonstate entity acting inconsistently with the agreement. An example would be a total ban on chlorofluorocarbon production if the intention to create such a remedy were clearly expressed. It is doubtful, however, that the international system is ready to employ this technique on any very large scale. For the present, the impact of international regulatory regimes on private action is likely to be mediated by national governments.

Nongovernmental Participation in Adjustment and Compliance Processes

The energy and intensity of the many nongovernmental groups and organizations in the environmental field is one of the heartening phenomena of recent years. A prime objective of international environmental lawmaking should be to empower and enfranchise these groups. As we have seen, individuals and human rights organizations are entitled to complain of human rights violations to UN human rights organs and to the European and Inter-American Commissions on Human Rights. In addition to formal participation in the proceedings, all these international institutions rely heavily on documentation developed and presented by nongovernmental groups.

In the ILO, national delegations have a tripartite form, consisting of representatives of the government, labor, and management. Labor and management representatives are free to take, and often do take, positions differing from those of their government representative. The same tripartite structure is repeated on the committees and subcommittees of the organization, including the compliance organs.

A further step would be to open national processes to the participation of outsiders. A path-breaking move of this kind is the Nordic Environmental Protection Convention, permitting each of the three Scandinavian countries to appear in the administrative or judicial processes of the others on matters dealing with the environment. Although justly celebrated, this agreement is not unprecedented. For example, interested foreign parties have long been entitled to appear and be heard in their own right in proceedings before the U.S. International Trade Commission on antidumping and countervailing duties, escape clause actions, and the like.

In these cases, identifiable outside parties—the neighboring state or the exporter of the goods in question—are likely to be directly and uniquely affected by the domestic action. It seems natural to permit such interests to be heard. When the consequences are more generalized—as with activities affecting climate or the atmosphere—it is harder to identify in principle those who should be permitted to represent the external interests.

This "standing" problem could readily be addressed by international agreement designating entities authorized to appear in relevant administrative and perhaps judicial proceedings in states that are parties to the treaty. If, for example, a framework convention on global climate change creates an ongoing climate organization, as seems likely, that institution could be authorized to appear in domestic proceedings in member states to represent the interests embodied in the convention. Another possibility, not mutually exclusive, would be for the treaty to authorize the organization to maintain a roster of qualified nongovernmental organizations that would have standing in domestic proceedings in member states. The same result could be reached unilaterally by any state willing to do so without benefit of an international agreement.

International Organizations

The international organization, not its member states, is the primary guardian and enforcer on the international plane of the regulatory norms expressed in the treaty that creates it. As shown above, international organizations are capable of acting and of creating rights and obligations within the scope of their charter authority. The adjustment and compliance processes discussed in this chapter are characteristically institutional processes, with the states that make up the organization playing a major, but by no means the exclusive, operational role. The director and staff have a range of powers and possibilities for initiative that decisively affects institutional outcomes.

The major existing international regulatory organizations are the product of a remarkable burst of institutional innovation in the aftermath of World War II. The World Bank and the IMF were created at Bretton Woods. The companion International Trade Organization never came to full fruition, but the GATT is a fragment of it. Functional organizations—the

ITU, ICAO, the Food and Agriculture Organization (FAO), the World Health Organization (WHO), the World Meteorological Organization (WMO), and a host of others—were refurbished or newly created. Perhaps, as is often said, this architectural effort was overly ambitious. There is much complaint about the rampant bureaucracies that it spawned. But these organizations are still in being, performing an increasing array of essential tasks for the international community.

The world appears to be on the verge of a major period of international lawmaking in the environmental field. To be effective, this effort must be accompanied by a new and equally imaginative burst of institutional creation. That does not necessarily mean the establishment of a single comprehensive super-organization to manage the problems of the global environment. On the contrary, as in the postwar period, different tasks can be assigned to different organizations. A certain amount of overlap and departure from elegant hierarchical order can be tolerated and may indeed be an asset.

To date, however, the proponents of international cooperation for the protection of the environment have shown an impoverished institutional imagination. International environmental norms, however sound in substance, will not be made effective without international organizations to maintain the regime that is established, adapting it to the exigencies of rapid change and giving assurance of compliance adequate to induce continued commitment.

10

The Implications
for U.S. Policy

JESSICA TUCHMAN MATHEWS

T he end of the cold war and the decline of the United
States relative to Japan and a coalescing Europe leave
the geopolitical landscape fundamentally altered. In all likelihood, international problem solving in the decades ahead will,
for the first time, be achieved through collective management,
not hegemony. It is to precisely this form of governance that
global environmental problems will yield—if sufficient vision
and political will can be mustered. The challenge is to initiate
change in human activities of a scale and rate comparable to
the change in global circumstances.

Two broad political strategies are possible. One might be
called the quantum leap approach. It emphasizes the immen-
sity of the problems, and the distance between present policies
and those that are needed. It urges vast, bold policy leaps,
attempting to make the very challenge of such an approach
into a political asset: a way to capture attention and to galva-
nize support for action. It calls for the expenditure of large
sums of money, especially in North-South transfers. Today,
proposals for a system of global environmental taxes would
fall into this category.

The other strategy might be called ambitious incremental-ism. It urges following the path of least resistance: eliminating policies that are both environmentally and economically coun-terproductive; taking steps that cost little or nothing or those that have immediate economic payoffs; aggressively exploiting existing technology; using well-tested policy instruments, and avoiding the highest political hurdles. It emphasizes the rela-tively modest steps needed to weave environmental concerns into the fabric of mainstream economic and foreign policy.

The first approach in effect makes the global environment the most important single issue on the international horizon, with concomitant shifts in spending. The latter concentrates on using present public and governmental concern to embed environmental values and goals in international policy, and focuses immediate action on initiatives with little or no cost.

A strong case can be made for the quantum leap strategy, given the risks that fall within the range of present uncertainty. However, the incremental approach is more likely to perma-nently change the policy context, so that when the next issue captures the center stage spotlight—as it inevitably will—envi-ronmental reform and sustainable policies will move steadily forward. Globally, public concern for the environment is very high and growing rapidly. But no matter how real the prob-lems, if concern and political attention do not produce solu-tions within, perhaps, a decade, fatigue and apathy will set in. The greatest risk lies in losing this opportunity in debate over quantum leap policies that elude consensus and do not leave permanent change in their wake.

The two approaches are not mutually exclusive, of course. Moreover, the distinction would disappear if international change continues at the pace of the past few years. In that case, what qualifies as a quantum leap today may seem little more than a sensible next step in a year or two. For now, however, ambitious incrementalism offers a crowded and challenging policy agenda. It recognizes the cash shortages many govern-ments face and puts the most difficult policy steps first into the domestic, rather than the international, domain. For the United States, this approach would begin with steps to put its

house in order, correcting egregious failures of both substance and process that damage its credibility and weaken its
capacity to exercise international leadership.

Three substantive policy changes are most important: correcting the present underpricing of gasoline; ending large
government subsidies for the cutting of U.S. forests; and reducing the federal budget deficit. The real price of gasoline in
the U.S. today is lower than it has been since 1918. The combined state and federal tax of twenty-five cents per gallon compares to a tax of double that amount in Canada and taxes of $1
to more than $2 per gallon in all of the other industrialized
market economies. The illusion that the real price of gasoline
is cheap chains the U.S. to a single ground transportation option—the single-passenger automobile—and blocks Detroit
from producing high-mileage automobiles like the 70–120
mpg four- and five-passenger prototypes being tested by
European and Japanese manufacturers in countries where gasoline taxes are high. Since transportation accounts for nearly
two-thirds of U.S. oil consumption, the underpricing of gasoline is also a major factor in the growing U.S. dependence on
imported oil (now close to 50 percent) and, therefore, in its
large trade deficit.

The U.S. is in no position to urge tropical countries to take
difficult steps to protect their forests while it subsidizes the
cutting of its own forests and the sale of publicly owned timber
at far below market prices, even in most of its few rainforests.
Through its effect on interest rates, the federal budget deficit
slows Third World debt repayment and raises the costs of new
borrowing, as well as weakening the domestic economy.

On the procedural side, steps should be taken to shift from a
diplomacy based on the primacy of bilateral relations to one
that emphasizes multilateral concerns; to restore respect for
international law; and to allow the U.S. to play a stronger role
in the UN and other multilateral institutions. Specifically, the
U.S. should as promptly as possible pay the $350 million
owing in past dues to the UN, and restore financial support for
the UN Fund for Population Activities. Appointments to UN
headquarters and specialized agencies, as well as to institu-

tions outside the UN system, should go to the most talented individuals available, making this the track to success in the foreign service. The State Department should be reorganized to give greater power and prestige to the multilateral and crosscutting bureaus and relatively less to the regional desks. Coveted policy appointments at State, Treasury, and the National Security Council should go to individuals experienced in multilateral diplomacy. The U.S. should demonstrate a greater commitment to be bound by negotiated agreements in which it participates, such as the Law of the Sea. And it should either refrain from armed excursions into other countries, such as those in Grenada and Panama, or avoid making a mockery of international law in justifying them.

Beyond these corrective steps, new initiatives are needed to bridge two traditional divisions in the policy cosmos: between foreign and domestic policy, and between "environmental" issues and everything else. National security in the coming decades will rest less heavily on military strength and, as this volume demonstrates, will include a growing environmental component. Security measured against the strength of an opponent will steadily give way to the measure of global security, defined principally by environmental threats and the conditions of economic interdependence. This shift calls for a strengthening of environmental expertise and influence at the Departments of State and Treasury, especially, and in the White House.

In the State Department, environmental concerns are represented at the assistant secretary level in the catchall Bureau of Oceans, Environment and Science (OES), an undersized, low-ranking bureau that, with only a few exceptions, has been a career cul de sac. The OES bureau needs to be upgraded, and the under secretaries' portfolios rearranged to give one of them a logical and direct responsibility for this increasingly important aspect of the department's business. At Treasury, environmental expertise, such as it is, is subsumed under the assistant secretary for international affairs. Yet the department's policies have a major impact on global environmental trends through U.S. influence at the World Bank, the International Monetary Fund (IMF), and the General Agreement on Tariffs and Trade (GATT).

The World Bank's ability to leverage other private and public funds, its influence on technology development and transfer, its powerful role in shaping development strategies, and its structural adjustment lending, all make it a key player in achieving environmentally sustainable development. Today the U.S. plays a passive and sometimes uninformed role in the World Bank's environmental decision making, too often urging that the bank avoid, rather than face, major policy choices. The IMF, through its influence on natural resource pricing; government subsidies; export, agricultural, and land tenure policies, also plays a vital role, though to date environmental concerns and expertise on its staff have been notably absent. Trade decisions made in the GATT have immense environmental impact. For all these institutions, the choice is not whether to get involved in environmental matters; they *are* involved, like it or not. The only choice is whether to recognize the extent of that involvement and acquire the necessary expertise to understand its environmental impact. For all these reasons, the Treasury Department needs a high-level, influential environmental policy position.

Presently, the executive branch lacks an effective mechanism for producing coherent policy on issues that are equally foreign and domestic. Integration of policy on the economy, environment, energy, drugs, and many other issues is accomplished, if at all, on an ad hoc basis, through short-lived White House offices, czarships, and special advisors, often bringing debilitating turf battles in their wake. Nor can the creation of ever more Cabinet Councils do the trick, for these are associations of equals. Proposals have been made that a new post, assistant to the president for international economic affairs, be created, comparable in rank to the assistant for national security. Down this road lies an ever-expanding White House, bulging with new assistants and their staffs. Moreover, the National Security Council's influence derives from history and from its origin in legislation and cannot be recreated by fiat or built up quickly.

The logical answer to the changing nature of national security and to the need to integrate foreign and domestic policies is to change the profile of qualifications for the assistant for national security affairs, and by extension, the background and responsibilities of his or her staff. Past appointments to this post have heavily emphasized U.S.-Soviet relations and military security. Five recent national security appointments have been career military officials. Future criteria could emphasize expertise on global issues, especially economics and environment. By the same token, nine of the thirteen presidential science advisors have been either nuclear physicists or engineers. Given the new threats to planetary security, future appointments should emphasize the natural and physical earth sciences—ecology, climatology, oceanography, and so on.

Even among the once wholly domestic issues, global trends demand new approaches. One of the most difficult of these lies in forging an integrated policy embracing clean air, energy, and transportation. Each is presently managed by a different department, under different laws, with its own library of regulations and army of lawyers. Yet they are, in reality, separate manifestations of the same activities. Energy use produces 80 percent of air pollution. Transportation accounts for more than two-thirds of oil use and 40 percent of acid rain–forming nitrogen oxides and ozone-forming organic compounds. President George Bush rightly decided that his environmental policy would be based on "pollution prevention," that is, on reducing pollution before it is produced, rather than after-the-fact regulation. Clearly, for the atmosphere, source reduction can *only* be achieved through energy policies. Ultimately, therefore, it will prove futile to try (as Congress and the executive branch are now doing) to fashion a national clean air policy without a national energy policy or an integrated transportation strategy. This accounts, in large part, for the endless legislative thrashing on the Clean Air Act, and the general sense that whatever the outcome, it will not produce the desired result. After more than a decade without one, the United States needs an explicit national energy policy that abandons long outdated assumptions and sets annual goals for decline in energy demand, priorities among fuel options with congruent research and development (R&D) spending, and realistic fuel pricing policies.

The most subtle process change that needs to be addressed is a reevaluation of the nature of American leadership in international affairs and, therefore, of U.S. priorities among global environmental issues. There are still calls from foreign policy experts for "America to hold firmly to the reins of global leadership. There is no substitute." Yet given economic realities, and weak U.S. energy productivity (the U.S. needs twice as much energy to produce a dollar of GNP as do the other advanced market economies—see Rathjens, Table 1), these calls sound like a wistful harkening to the past rather than a clear-eyed understanding of the present and likely future.

Nations other than the two cold war superpowers are already more adept and adapted to multilateral diplomacy. This is particularly true of Western Europe, now entering the longest period of uninterrupted peace in its history. It would be no surprise, in fact, if the 1990s turn out to be the European Decade, with the U.S. and the USSR turned inward, preoccupied with their domestic difficulties, Japan unready to offer political leadership, and Western Europe, especially after 1992, invigorated by its new-found political and economic strength, pioneering mechanisms for regional governance. These include solutions to regional environmental problems through Europe's new institutional machinery and leadership on the most difficult issue of all—global climate change. In these circumstances, demands that the U.S. must be in the policy forefront on every important issue seem both unrealistic and ill-advised.

On the other hand, America has in the past provided such strong leadership in areas such as population growth that it is hard to imagine much progress being made without at least its active participation. In many other areas, especially fossil fuel consumption as it relates to climate change, the U.S. is such a global presence that it has no choice but to play a leading role. The U.S. accounts for 23 percent of global carbon dioxide (CO_2) emissions from fossil fuel use: the other six of the G-7 nations together account for 18 percent.

The matter is even more complicated. During this decade of

transition to a still undefined future, there will be a substantial policy hangover: the widespread assumption based on long postwar experience that little can happen without U.S. leadership. We can expect to hear demands from abroad for U.S. leadership—especially from European governments—even while the same countries are themselves leading the way. A careful sorting out of priorities is therefore in order. On some issues it will be appropriate for the U.S. to pave the way, to provide an example, even perhaps a success story. In certain circumstances, as in the 1978 banning of chlorofluorocarbon (CFC) use in aerosols, unilateral action may prove beneficial. In others it may well impede an international response. The U.S. should choose those areas in which it will exercise strong leadership. At the same time it should do what it can to erase the expectation that international solutions in *every* arena depend on its leadership. It should expect and encourage others to take the lead in certain areas, but without reverting on those issues to either hostility or passivity. In short, in some cases the U.S. will have to relinquish stardom for the demanding and unfamiliar role of supporting player.

A still unanswered question is whether such a role will prove acceptable to the American public and politically feasible in practice. Historically, U.S. foreign policy has swung between the poles of isolationism and interventionism. Can a middle ground—what former Ambassador Richard Gardner calls practical internationalism—be a lasting alternative? Polling data suggest that there is a very high degree of public concern on the global environment and support for much tougher policies, including a larger role for the UN and other international agencies and greater American deference to international law. However, support for domestic policy changes stops short of new taxes, the most economically efficient response in many instances. Polls also suggest a dramatic shift in Americans' perception of threats to their national security and perhaps, therefore, in their willingness to spend public funds in these new areas. How long these views will persist, and whether they can be translated into support for a steady internationalism, remains to be seen.

A number of important substantive steps toward solving global problems should also be taken domestically. Foremost among them, U.S. policy on greenhouse warming should be based on the understanding that despite the many scientific uncertainties, the phenomenon itself is not a subject of controversy: what is important is the direction of change, not the details. The science will shift constantly over the coming years, but its central policy implication—that humankind will eventually have to stabilize greenhouse gas concentrations in the atmosphere—will almost certainly not. It is this core truth, not the newest piece in the scientific puzzle, that should guide policy.

Two considerations should shape U.S. policy. The dimensions of the planetary risks inherent in global warming demand an "insurance" policy. The uncertainties in both the science and the costs of slowing the change mean that a "no regrets" approach is called for, that is, steps we will not regret however the scientific questions are answered. Together they mean that action to reduce greenhouse gas emissions should begin now if policies can be identified that are low in cost or produce substantial non-greenhouse benefits.

The most obvious of these is a decision to eliminate CFC production and use no later than 2000. A much stronger and better funded multinational effort to slow tropical deforestation, to which the U.S. should contribute its fair share, also qualifies. Most important for the U.S. is a national energy policy based on a steady decline in energy intensity of at least 3 percent per year, approximately the rate of improvement that was achieved during the high oil price years 1973–86. This would double the efficiency of U.S. energy use in about twenty years. It is a substantial initial target, though even more may well be achievable.

In fact, comparisons of current energy use practices to best-available technologies suggest that the efficiency of the major energy-use sectors—transportation, utilities, and residential and commercial buildings—can be doubled with technologies that are currently available or now in development. There is no telling what might result from a concerted research and development effort that shifts priorities away from coal and nuclear power and toward energy efficiency, solar, hydrogen, and other advanced alternative energy technologies. The technological burst that followed the Montreal CFC treaty is a timely reminder that modern technology can reap bounteous harvests in previously unplowed fields.

Finally, the "insurance/no regret" policy should include active U.S. support for the creation of an international mechanism to coordinate global policy on climate change. A GATT-like approach, involving more or less continuous negotiation and adjustment, or an IMF model in which national goals are individually negotiated by a neutral staff empowered to make binding decisions, both look more promising at this juncture than the framework agreement followed by separately ratified protocols that is being discussed by governments.

Together with drastically improving its energy productivity, the U.S. should take steps to improve its overall environmental productivity, that is, to steadily reduce the use of natural resources and the consumption of environmental services (including those of air, land, and water for waste disposal) per unit of economic output. If appropriate economic incentives are adopted and an indicator of industrial environmental productivity can be developed, the private sector will most efficiently accomplish the required changes. The U.S. should also follow West Germany's example and revise its system of national income accounts to include consumption of environmental capital. Unilateral action of this kind by enough countries will accelerate revision of the official international methodology by the UN statistical office.

On the international scene, needed procedural and institutional initiatives are less clear. Many proposals have been made for new institutions, mergers, upgrades, and new responsibilities for existing institutions. All seem to entail at least as many negative consequences as positive ones. One clear exception is the need for additional financial resources for the United Nations Environment Programme (UNEP), whose $40 million budget is unquestionably inadequate to its responsibilities.

However, broad guidelines for procedural progress seem clear. Following a global analogy to federal-state relations in the U.S., problem solving at the global level should be reserved for those things that cannot be done locally or regionally. The global interest is not strongly represented among existing institutions, and global organizations will likely always be more cumbersome than smaller groupings. On both counts it makes good sense to do what can be done through regional and quasi-regional organizations such as the Organization for Economic Cooperation and Development (OECD) and the Economic Commission for Europe (ECE). Many of the regional groups are far too weak for effective action, but the stronger among them enjoy shared cultural values and comparable levels of economic development, which will smooth the way for agreements on policy. Dividing responsibility among the regions also allows responses to global issues to be tailored to regional differences. For example, the causes and appropriate responses to deforestation are quite different in Latin America and Southeast Asia. Moreover, the global trends significantly overlap important regional concerns on which these organizations are already taking action. The U.S. ought to work to strengthen Western Hemisphere institutions as well as the OECD and ECE, and support others such as the Amazon Pact, of which it is not a member.

A second guideline is that, wherever possible, institutional reform or innovation should make greater use of the private sector, including both the corporate community and nongovernmental organizations (NGOs). Partnerships with governments and multinational organizations in various types of public/private hybrids are especially promising. The U.S., with the strongest, best-funded, and most diverse NGO community in the world, has a special role to play in pioneering these new models. International organizations might, for example, usefully be able to adapt the principles of regulatory negotiation, in which nongovernmental constituencies are directly involved in developing regulations, to international decision making.

The greatest threat to international cooperation on the

global environment, one that already shows signs of provoking a debilitating North-South deadlock, is the question of who will pay for the necessary changes. Attention to possible new sources of funds in the developing countries could help provide a solution. This is not to suggest that additional money does not also need to flow from the industrialized countries. But it would be a fatal mistake to base ambitious global plans on the promise of large North-South transfers that are not in the offing. The result would be something like the sad outcome of the recent Plan of Action for Africa, when, despite a genuine crisis and the development of an excellent international strategy, nothing happened because no additional money was forthcoming from the developed countries.

A more successful approach will pair commitments of additional funds from the North with steps to redirect substantial funds in the South. Three large sources of money are potentially available: capital flight, debt payments, and military spending. Capital flight, by its nature, is extremely difficult to pin down. Estimates range from $10–$50 billion annually. Third World debt payments are about $125 billion each year, and military spending is just under $150 billion annually, having grown twice as fast as global military expenditures for the past thirty years. In each case, releasing some of these funds for more productive uses will require cooperative North-South action. Reforms of tax policy and banking regulations in the North will help squeeze capital flight. On debt, forgiveness for the poorest countries and greatly expanded use of debt swaps, together with a more aggressive pursuit of debt reduction negotiations and involvement of commercial banks by the U.S. and other lenders, are badly needed.

Military spending offers a largely ignored opportunity to redirect the most rapidly growing use of public funds in many developing countries. The dynamics of the arms trade also makes this an opportune moment to take action. Arms exports by developing countries are already growing rapidly, making these new suppliers increasingly interested in expanding this new source of export earnings. As arms control agreements and defense budget cuts in the North cut deeply into weapons manufacturers' incomes, these producers will also turn more aggressively to Third World markets. Arms purchases are known to reflect the intensity of sellers' efforts, so that if action is not taken soon to slow the trade, weapons spending in the Third World might well rise substantially. Despite the growth in Third World exports, about three-quarters of all arms exports to developing countries are supplied by five industrialized countries (USSR, U.S., France, United Kingdom, West Germany). Therefore, an international initiative to slow military spending will require North-South negotiations organized on a regional basis to reflect the differences in the levels and sophistication of armaments in different parts of the world. Some of the foundation for such an effort was laid in the U.S.-Soviet Conventional Arms Transfer Talks (CATT) in the late 1970s.

It remains to be seen whether reduced defense spending in the USSR and the NATO countries will produce a peace dividend that can be diverted to environmental or any other needs. But the end of the cold war should mean a useful peace dividend in the intelligence sector through the adaptation of existing satellites for other needs and through the redirection of funds for spy satellites to desperately needed global scientific studies and monitoring of environmental trends. If studies show that U.S. space intelligence assets can be used in this fashion, the U.S. could also approach the Soviet Union and the other space powers to explore a pooling of these resources in the interests of long-term common security.

The gravity of human impact on the earth also suggests the need to reappraise the nation's space program. Scientific exploration of space remains a valid national priority, but hugely expensive manned projects ultimately aimed at colonizing other planets seem badly out of place so long as the longer-term livability of our own planet remains in such jeopardy. Funds from those projects would be better spent on the global security goals outlined in this volume.

The shrinking Soviet military threat offers one other important opportunity to redirect money and scientific and technological know-how toward solving the long-term environmental dilemma. Worldwide, one-quarter of all R&D funds are devoted to military uses. In the U.S. the figure is much higher: in fiscal 1990, two-thirds of publicly supported R&D was allocated to military purposes. The U.S. should shift some of that money to a significant new research and development initiative: a long-term commitment to sophisticated, high-technology research in the civilian sector. The goal would be the development of new materials, processes, and technologies in energy, agriculture, communications, transportation, materials science, and manufacturing that will allow continued economic growth with greatly diminished environmental stress. Research would be directed both at fundamental advances in basic science and at the applied research and engineering necessary to reverse the United States' now chronic inability to turn its scientific strength into commercial products. The Defense Department's Advanced Research Projects Administration (DARPA) provides a highly successful model on which this new agency could be based.

The economic benefits of such an investment ought to be sufficient justification for it. But since Americans are so distrustful of federal economic investments, its environmental motivation may provide the only convincing public argument. Harvard economist Robert Reich points out that for the past forty-five years, Americans have had to clothe major public investments in the spurious guise of military security in order to command political support, calling the highway system the "National Defense Highway Act" and the post-Sputnik push in education the "National Defense Education Act." Without the cold war to justify such investments, Reich believes, the U.S. will be unable to act in its own economic interest. Global environmental security could provide a compelling rationale, blending real security fears with the positive motivation of a far more attractive future. Japan's first response to global climate change has been to launch exactly such an effort, the Institute of Industrial Technology for the Global Environment, due to start operations in 1992.

Taken together, these steps would have an enormous impact on the global environment. Individually, many are easy, some cost nothing, and some will return a sizable economic benefit. Others, like a gasoline tax and reducing the federal deficit, are politically very difficult, yet command broad bipartisan support. Most would require a degree of political commitment to the environment and a readiness to exercise leadership that has been absent from the White House for the past decade.

Ambitious as it is, this agenda does not come close to including everything that needs to be done, especially through international agreement. But the actions it proposes are largely or entirely within the power of the U.S. to adopt on its own, and as such constitute a realistic goal for U.S. policy. If carried out, this program would change the way we think about, and act to protect, national security, the U.S. role in the international community, and the way we measure economic success and, therefore, deploy economic resources. The results, in short, should be anything but incremental.

Final Report of the
Seventy-Seventh American
Assembly

At the close of their discussions, the participants in the Seventy-seventh American Assembly, on *Preserving the Global Environment: The Challenge of Shared Leadership,* at Arden House, Harriman, New York, April 19–22, 1990, reviewed as a group the following statement. This statement represents general agreement; however, no one was asked to sign it. Furthermore, it should be understood that not everyone agreed with all of it.

Three indivisibly linked global environmental trends together constitute an increasingly grave challenge to the habitability of the earth. They are human population growth; tropical deforestation and the rapid loss of biological diversity; and global atmospheric change, including stratospheric ozone loss and greenhouse warming. These trends threaten nations' economic potential, therefore their internal political security, their citizens' health (because of increased ultraviolet radiation), and, in the case of global warming, possibly their very existence. No more basic threat to national security exists. Thus, together with economic interdependence, global environmental threats are shifting traditional national security concerns to a focus on collective global security.

The 1990s offer a historic opportunity for action that must not be allowed to slip. Not only do the global environmental trends pose an urgent threat to the planet's long-term future, but the waning of the cold war also lifts a heavy psychological and economic burden from both governments and individuals, freeing human, physical, and financial resources to meet the new challenge.

There is evidence that developing countries are ready to become partners in this global endeavor. However, their willingness to act will depend on help from the industrialized countries to alleviate the poverty that is a major aggravating cause of population growth and environmental degradation. It will also depend on the industrialized countries' demonstrated commitment to reduce their heavy per capita consumption of natural resources and ecological services. The industrialized countries, in short, must prove through concrete action that they take environmental issues seriously. The other side of the equation that determines environmental stress, which must be addressed, is population growth: 95 percent of which will otherwise occur in the developing countries.

The global response must therefore be launched as a mutual commitment by all countries. The certainty that all nations will share a common destiny demands that they work together as partners.

The global environmental challenge is fundamentally different from previous international concerns. Unlike the effort to avoid nuclear war that dominated international relations for the past forty-five years, success or failure will not hinge on the actions of governments alone. It will rest equally on the beliefs and actions of billions of individuals, and on the roles played by national and multinational business. The importance of individual behavioral change and the major new roles to be played by these non-governmental actors demand profound change in the institutions and mechanisms of international cooperation.

Population Growth

The degradation of the global environment is integrally linked to human population growth. More than 90 million people are added each year—more than ever before. On its present trajectory, the world's population could nearly triple its current size, reaching 14 billion before stabilizing. With a heroic effort, it could level off at around 9 billion. However, today's unmet need for family planning is huge: only 30 percent of reproductive age people in the developing world outside of China currently have access to contraception. Women's full and equal participation in society at all levels must be rapidly addressed.

Policy makers must recognize that actions taken during the critical decade of the 1990s will largely determine whether human population will double or triple before stabilizing. Nigeria, for example, could grow from about 30 million in 1950 to around 300 million in 2020—a tenfold increase in one lifespan. In the absence of rapid progress in family planning, future governments may be tempted to restrict human freedom in order to deal with unmanageable population increases.

The pressure of population on the environment is bound up with poverty: in the Sahel as well as other areas threatened by famine and environmental deterioration, poor people have no other option but to consume all available local resources. Sustaining the environment thus requires a balance between wise environmental management, active efforts to slow population growth, and equitable economic development.

In many developing countries, population pressures on the land threaten national security as people migrate in search of sustenance, aggravating territorial disputes and often creating violent conflict.

While population pressures affect the planet as a whole, they must be individually addressed by each nation and its citizens. Countries must make their own assessments about population levels and growth, ordering their development priorities and incentives accordingly. Industrialized nations can offer much needed technical support and experience in family planning to help developing nations and individual couples achieve their goals.

Despite its complexities, the problem clearly calls for several policy initiatives aimed at:

• Universal access to family planning by the end of the decade—this will require a global expenditure rising to reach $10 billion a year by the year 2000.

• Giving priority to investment in education for women and in bringing women into full economic and political participation.

• Greatly increased research to provide a wide array of safer, cheaper, and easier birth control technologies.

• Stepped up mass communication aimed at increasing support for family planning.

Since 1981, the United States has retreated from the strong leadership role on world population it exercised in the two previous decades. The ideological debate has destroyed a bipartisan consensus that laid the groundwork for crucial international cooperation. Money for research has fallen sharply, and the global family planning effort has been gravely weakened. Positive U.S. leadership needs to be reestablished, through the restoration of U.S. support for the major international population and family planning organizations and annual population assistance budgets more commensurate with global requirements. Ultimately, no administration can be regarded as serious about the environment unless it is serious about global population growth.

Tropical Deforestation and Loss of Biodiversity

Tropical deforestation and the loss of a diverse set of species rob the earth of its biological richness, which undermines long-range ecological security and global economic potential. Nearly 20 million hectares of tropical forests are lost every year. Conservative estimates put the extinction rate at one hundred species per day: a rate unmatched since the disappearance of the dinosaurs. Escalating human populations, deforestation, disruptions of watersheds, soil loss, and land degradation are all linked in a vicious cycle that perpetuates and deepens poverty, and often creates ecological refugees.

Because deforestation and the loss of biodiversity result first from mismanagement at the local level, effective interventions must also occur at this level, building upon local norms, traditions, and cultures that will promote sustainable management. Recent efforts to restore common property management by indigenous peoples in the Amazon basin of Colombia and Ecuador are notable initiatives. This approach respects the rights of indigenous populations and the wisdom of their institutions, and is likely to be low in cost.

At the national level, effective management will require a commitment to conservation, land use planning, secure property rights, and sustainable agroforestry, so that forests provide a continued flow of goods and services with minimal ecological disruption. Timber harvesting must reflect long-term scarcity values, consistent with full environmental and social cost accounting. Tropical forests are often sacrificed for a fraction of their real value by nations in search of quick sources of foreign exchange. While "debt-for-nature" swaps by the private sector are helpful and should be expanded, they are unlikely to be sufficient *either* to save forest ecosystems *or* to relieve debt loads. However, the opportunity exists to include government debt in this process and to complement the international debt strategy by linking reduction in public sector debt to policy reforms with environmental benefits.

What policy goals and means are appropriate locally, nationally, and internationally?

- While respecting local and community property rights that promote ecologically sound management, national governments can help most by eliminating distorted economic incentives that encourage mismanagement, such as the granting of property titles in return for forest clearing, and below-cost timber sales. International institutions should encourage such reforms that, at the same time, relieve the pressure on remaining tropical forests and help bring about their sustainable exploitation.
- Forest conservation is not enough; it must be accompanied

by aggressive, ecologically sensitive reforestation and land rehabilitation, especially on arid lands and where fuelwood demands are high.

• These measures will be costly. Current international funding levels (such as called for in the Tropical Forest Action Plan) should be increased tenfold from about $1 billion to $10 billion. The additional funds will only achieve their goals if accompanied by increased training and broad nongovernmental participation in the planning process.

• An international Strategy and Convention on Biodiversity would provide a means to actively engage many institutions, and to formulate a global action plan for identifying and funding critical needs in ecological "hot spots." The Strategy and Convention should be readied for the 1992 Conference on Environment and Development.

• The World Bank in its lending policies should be sensitive to encouraging land use and forest practices that are consistent with environmental sustainability.

Atmosphere and Energy

Human activities are substantially changing the chemical composition of the atmosphere in a way that threatens the health, security, and survival of people and other species, and increases the likelihood of international tensions. Depletion of the ozone layer and global warming are two salient examples, but other unforeseen effects cannot be ruled out.

Ozone

The depletion of the ozone layer by chlorofluorocarbons (CFCs) allows increased ultraviolet B radiation from the sun to enter the earth's atmosphere, threatening human health and the productivity of the biosphere.

The 1987 international agreement to limit production and use of CFCs in the Montreal Protocol to the Vienna Convention was a landmark achievement and a promising precedent for international agreements on other global environmental issues. However, the protocol itself is an unfinished story. Full participation by the less developed countries has not yet been achieved, issues of acceptable alternatives and technology transfer remain unresolved, and the treaty itself must be revised to require complete elimination of CFC production and use by industrialized countries no later than 2000. How these issues are resolved will have important implications for addressing climate change and other global ecological problems.

The Greenhouse Effect

There is a scientific consensus that rising concentrations of greenhouse gases will cause global climatic change. Atmospheric levels of carbon dioxide have increased 25 percent since the beginning of the industrial era. Most of the CO_2 emissions derive from energy use. About 90 percent of the world's current energy use is met by the burning of carbon-based fuels. Tropical deforestation is also a major source of carbon dioxide. Other greenhouse gases, methane, nitrous oxides, and CFCs, are collectively as important as carbon dioxide in their greenhouse effect and are increasing more rapidly.

Therefore, the earth is set to experience substantial climate change of unknown scale and rapidity. The consequences are likely to include sea level rise, greater frequency of extreme weather events, disruption of ecosystems, and potentially vast impacts on the global economy. The processes of climate change are irreversible, and major additional releases could be triggered from the biosphere by global warming in an uncontrollable self-reinforcing process (e.g., methane release from unfrozen Arctic tundra).

"Insurance" actions to reduce CO_2 emissions and those of other greenhouse gases are therefore needed, starting now. The associated risks are much less than those of not acting and in some cases require no net increase in cost.

Past and present contributions to greenhouse gases come largely from the industrialized countries. However, the less developed countries already contribute significantly through deforestation, and their share will increase sharply with development and expansion of fossil fuel use, especially coal.

The international community should work quickly toward a multilateral framework ultimately involving national targets for reducing emissions of carbon dioxide and the other greenhouse gases. There is no need for the industrialized countries to await universal agreements. They should act now: individually and/or in concert. Indeed, some in Western Europe have already begun.

Initial steps involve the deployment of a range of policy instruments to achieve energy conservation and efficiency, demand-side management, and changes in the fuel mix. A considerable expansion of support for research and development into alternative energy sources is urgently required. There may be a future for nuclear energy if credible assurances can be provided with respect to safety, waste disposal, nuclear proliferation, and comparative costs.

This American Assembly strongly endorses the global target now under study by the Intergovernmental Panel on Climate Change (IPCC) of a 20 percent reduction in CO_2 emissions by 2005 as a minimum goal.

Goals and Means of International Cooperation

Global environmental damage threatens the physical as well as economic security of individuals and nations without exception, giving new reality to traditional concepts of collective security. Environmental threats are also likely to create new sources of conflict. The risks of collective insecurity call for an unprecedented strategy of international cooperation.

The health of the global environment is the product of behavior by billions of individuals. National governments must increasingly take into account the views of their citizens as they design policies to confront environmental concerns, and can increasingly rely on the influence and impact of changes in individual behavior. Coalitions of non-governmental actors can be a powerful force in hammering out bargains, hardening scientific consensus, and developing legal concepts and new institutional frameworks. Governments and international institutions can then set widely applicable norms and standards.

In this new international context, institutions and mechanisms are becoming more fluid: the complex and swiftly evolving environmental dilemmas demand it. Thus we need to seek global consensus in the United Nations as work proceeds in many other arenas to reach more limited agreements. These include unilateral action by individual governments, small groups of nations bargaining on discrete issues, an active role by companies and non-governmental organizations (NGOs), regional arrangements, and hybrid public-private partnerships (such as the collaboration between pharmaceutical companies and the World Health Organization on new birth control measures—a pattern that should be copied for ecological restoration). Actions and decisions should always be taken at a level as close as possible to the people affected by them.

Within the UN system, the United Nations Environment Programme (UNEP) has demonstrated its capacity to serve as innovator, monitor, and catalyst—notably in the Mediterranean cleanup and the 1987 ozone treaty. UNEP should be strengthened and much more dependably funded to continue this important role.

Among key priorities for international action are the following:

Establishing Norms and Setting Goals

The first task of the international community as a whole is to develop a broad consensus on norms of global survival, and to establish specific environmental goals—for example, boundary conditions on pollution of the atmospheric commons, targets for the protection of biodiversity, and population policy goals—toward which public and private efforts should be directed.

Meeting the Costs

Industrial countries must make major investments to improve their own performance. Developing countries must, in their own interest, increasingly incorporate sound environmental practices as part of their own development programs. Resolving the debt overhang is crucial. But industrial countries will also need to make a special effort to expand flows to developing countries if needed investments in global environmental priorities—slowing population growth, protecting the ozone layer, limiting greenhouse gas emissions, preserving biodiversity, and many other non-global environmental needs—are to occur. Because of resource scarcities, developing countries are otherwise unlikely to act.

The UNEP, United Nations Development Program (UNDP), and the World Bank have proposed a $1 billion, three-year pilot facility for this purpose; it deserves strong support. Much larger resource flows will be needed in the future. As a source of such funds, serious consideration should be given to establishing an international fee (for example, on carbon use) because conventional sources of finance are simply not adequate to, or appropriate for, the task of reducing global environmental risks.

Policy Reforms

While additional financing is required, many other measures can make a major impact. International agreement is needed to introduce into national accounting methods the full costs incurred in depletion of natural resources and use of the global commons; this could serve as a valuable guide to all nations' decision makers to use scarce resources well. International trade is a major source of revenues for development; the current Uruguay Round of the General Agreement on Tariffs & Trade (GATT) negotiations should be used to strengthen environmental considerations in trade policy. All international financial and planning institutions should take account of how policy recommendations affect environmental policy.

Technical Assistance and Research

All countries need additional environmental expertise and research. An International Global Environmental Service Corps should be established to provide technical help and build local environmental capacity.

Expanding the Role of the Private Sector

Government and international organizations have special responsibilities, but the private sector may have the most impact. Where central planners and government bureaucracies have tried to replace free markets, neither economic development nor environmental protection has been well served.

The private sector should be spurred to anticipate—and benefit from—the changing structure of regulation and market demand by developing environmentally superior technologies. Governments need to encourage such environmental entrepreneurship through the use of taxes, subsidies, and other signals, including codes of conduct. An international structure of targets and standards is needed to support this approach.

Within the private sector, an enormous number of citizen organizations now play an important part in establishing priorities. In all the actions we propose, active and early participation by representative groups at the local, national, and international level should be encouraged.

The 1992 U.N. Conference on Environment and Development

None of these environmental challenges can be met without a new era of heightened cooperation between the industrial and developing countries. This will come in many shapes and forms, using *ad hoc* coalitions of governments, active participation of NGOs and the private sector, and other new arrangements designed to meet varying needs.

The 1992 conference provides a unique opportunity to build on these initiatives to advance international action on the points noted here—in short, to achieve a global compact for environmental protection and economic progress. The conference should affirm that slowing population growth is an integral part of meeting the environment and development challenge. It should agree on how the additional resource needs of the decade should be met. It should establish a new official methodology for calculating national income accounts. And it should complete legal agreements on conventions already under negotiation—for protection of the atmosphere, and biological diversity.

A Challenge to the United States

As the world's largest economic power and consumer of environmental resources, the United States must play a key leadership role both by example and through international participation. This calls for strong action at every level from private households to the White House. Change is difficult and not cost free. It will take commitment and courage. But the long-term benefits will be worth every penny.

Essential to this drive is the development of a national environmental strategy, through the joint efforts of government, private industry, NGOs, and individual leaders. It should be aimed at global goals that include:

- A halt to the buildup of greenhouse gases;
- A lower per capita environmental cost of industrial and agricultural practices and consumption patterns, particularly in the United States and other wealthy nations;
- Slowing and then reversing deforestation;
- A drastic reduction in the rate of human-caused species extinction; and,
- Stabilization of world population before it doubles again.

To develop and carry out such a strategy will require integration of policies and more effective coordination of agencies within the U.S. government, and a major review should be launched to determine the needed changes. Equally important, the strategy can benefit from close cooperation between private industry and environmental experts to identify, develop, and adopt environmentally superior technologies.

With its preeminent scientific research capacity, the United States is in a position materially to aid development, improve the environment, and increase the planet's carrying capacity. Government research and development funding should be shifted from a preoccupation with defense to greater concern for the environment, to increase knowledge of natural phenomena and trends, to expand our understanding of the human dimensions of global change, and to develop more benign technologies, particularly in energy, manufacturing, and agriculture. Incentives for private environmentally related research and development should also be considered.

In addition to lending strong support to the multilateral initiatives identified above, U.S. action is needed in the following areas:

Adopt New Policies on Global Warming and Energy

Despite considerable uncertainties, enough is known about the risks of global warming and climate change to justify an immediate U.S. policy response. Without waiting for international consensus or treaties, the United States should take actions to reduce substantially its emissions of carbon dioxide, CFCs, and other greenhouse gases. The United States should promote a global phase-out of CFC production by 2000. U.S. energy strategy should emphasize reducing fossil fuel use through aggressive energy efficiency improvements, especially in transportation and in the production and use of electricity, backed by greater efforts to introduce renewable energy sources. Research on nuclear energy should be pursued to determine whether designs can be developed that might resolve safety and proliferation concerns and restore public and investor confidence.

In addition to performance standards and other regulatory approaches, economic incentives are essential to achieving energy efficiency. Most important is a large, phased-in increase in the federal tax on gasoline and the adoption of a carbon dioxide emissions fee applicable to users of fossil fuels. To avoid competitive imbalances, other industrial nations should be urged to adopt similar policies.

Strengthen Cooperation with the Developing Countries and Eastern Europe

Recognizing that meeting many of today's environmental challenges will require major actions by the developing countries, the United States should launch new programs and strengthen existing ones that can encourage and support these undertakings. Operating in concert with international partners whenever appropriate, these programs should: 1) provide strong financial and other support for universal access to family planning and contraceptive services, accompanied by efforts to improve the status of women and their employment opportunities; 2) launch major new financing initiatives aimed at facilitating developing country participation in international negotiations, and at meeting the large need for investments in sustainable forest management, biodiversity protection, watershed rehabilitation, fuelwood production, and techniques adapted to the needs of small-scale farmers; 3) facilitate the transfer of needed technology, expertise, and information in energy, environment, and population; 4) assist the developing countries with training and capacity building both in government and in NGOs; and 5) redeploy a substantial fraction of military and security-related assistance to help developing and East European countries to alleviate their environmental problems. Two important objectives of these efforts should be to make improved technologies available to developing countries at affordable costs, and relatedly, to assist in finding environmentally acceptable ways of meeting their energy needs.

Recent political changes in Eastern Europe afford an immediate opportunity to reduce environmental stress of local and global importance. Resolving the region's severe environmental problems requires collaboration and assistance from the United States, including the private sector. Such collaboration is a commercial opportunity, and should be one of the more economically efficient ways of reducing environmental degradation. It is vital, however, that the needed transfer of technology and funds from the West should not be made at the expense of resource flows to the developing countries.

Revise Agricultural and Forestry Policies

The United States, through negotiations abroad as well as unilateral actions at home, should phase out agricultural subsidies that encourage overproduction, excessive use of chemical fertilizers and pesticides, and mismanagement of water resources. Eliminating overproduction and adopting full cost pricing will open U.S. and other markets to developing country producers who enjoy a natural comparative advantage, thus aiding their economic development and intervening in the poverty-population-environment degradation cycle. Similarly, U.S. national forestry policies should be amended to eliminate the federal subsidization of timber sales at below market prices, and jointly with Canada, to conserve the last remnants of old growth temperate rainforests.

A Final Word

On this Earth Day 1990, we call attention to the need for immediate international action to reverse trends that threaten the integrity of the global environment. These trends endanger all nations and require collective action and cooperation among all nations in the common interest. Our message is one of urgency. Accountable and courageous leadership in all sectors will be needed to mobilize the necessary effort. If the world community fails to act forcefully in the current decade, the earth's ability to sustain life is at risk.

Preserving the Global Environment:
the Challenge of Shared Leadership
April 19–22, 1990
Arden House, Columbia University

TIMOTHY ATKESON
Assistant Administrator
Office of
    International Activities
United States Environmental
    Protection Agency
Washington, DC

JAMES D. ATWATER
Professor
Editorial Department
School of Journalism
University of
    Missouri-Columbia
Columbia, Missouri

†† NICOLE BALL
Director of Analysis
The National Security
    Archive
Washington, DC

ANTHONY C. BEILENSON
Congressman from California
U.S. House of
    Representatives
Washington, DC

RICHARD E. BENEDICK
Senior Fellow
The Conservation
    Foundation/World
    Wildlife Fund
Washington, DC

†† LINCOLN P. BLOOMFIELD
Department of Political
    Science
Massachusetts Institute of
    Technology
Cambridge, Massachusetts

ZBIGNIEW BOCHNIARZ
Senior Fellow
Hubert H. Humphrey
    Institute of Public Affairs
University of Minnesota
Minneapolis, Minnesota

SEYOM BROWN
Chair & Professor of Politics
Department of Politics
Brandeis University
Waltham, Massachusetts

GERARDO BUDOWSKI
Director of Natural
    Resources
University for Peace
San Jose, COSTA RICA

* IAN BURTON
Director
The International Federation
    of Institutes for Advanced
    Study (IFIAS)
Toronto, Ontario, CANADA

SHARON L. CAMP
Vice President
Population Crisis Committee
Washington, DC

ROBERT G. GILPIN, JR.
Eisenhower Professor of
   International Affairs
Woodrow Wilson School of
   Public & International
   Affairs and Department of
   Politics
Princeton University
Princeton, New Jersey

PETER H. GLEICK
Director, Global
   Environment Program
Pacific Institute for Studies in
   Development,
   Environment, & Security
Berkeley, California

U.V. HENDERSON, JR.
General Manager
Environment & Product
   Safety Department
Texaco, Inc.
Beacon, New York

PERDITA HUSTON
Senior Advisor to
   International Planned
   Parenthood Federation
Regent's College
London, UNITED
   KINGDOM

PAUL IBEKA
Development Economist
Anambra-IMO River Basin
   Development
   Authority
Owerri, NIGERIA

†† ANDRZEJ KASSENBERG
Institute of Geography and
   Spatial Economy
Polish Academy of Sciences
Warsaw, POLAND

HISAKAZU KATO
Director
Office of Policy Planning &
   Research
Environment Agency
Government of Japan
Tokyo, JAPAN

NATHAN KEYFITZ
Leader, Population Program
International Institute for
   Applied Systems Analysis
   (IIASA)
Laxenburg, AUSTRIA

* T.N. KHOSHOO
Distinguished Scientist
   (CSIR)
Tata Energy Research
   Institute
New Delhi, INDIA

JANUSZ KINDLER
Professor
Institute of Environmental
   Engineering
Warsaw University of
   Technology
Warsaw, POLAND

†† MICHAEL KLARE
Director & Associate
   Professor
Five College Program in
   Peace & World Security
   Studies
Hampshire College
Amherst, Massachusetts

SEEISO D. LIPHUKO
Deputy Permanent Secretary
Ministry of Local
  Government & Lands
Gaborone, BOTSWANA

ABRAHAM F.
  LOWENTHAL
Professor of International
  Relations
University of Southern
  California
Los Angeles, California

C. PAYNE LUCAS
Executive Director
Africare
Washington, DC

THOMAS F. MALONE
Scholar in Residence
St. Joseph College
West Hartford, Connecticut

JOAN MARTIN-BROWN
Special Advisor to the
  Executive Director, &
  Chief,
  Washington Office
United Nations Environment
  Programme
Washington, DC

JESSICA TUCHMAN
  MATHEWS
Vice President
World Resources Institute
Washington, DC

DONALD F. MCHENRY
Georgetown University
Washington, DC

BERNARD MCKINNON
CAP Director
United Auto Workers
Farmington, Connecticut

ROBERT MCNAMARA
Former President of The
  World Bank
Washington, DC

DANA MEAD
Executive Vice President
International Paper Company
Purchase, New York

JAMES W. MORLEY
Professor of Government
East Asian Institute
Columbia University
New York, New York

MARTHA T. MUSE
Chairman & President
The Tinker Foundation, Inc.
New York, New York

YVETTE M. NEWBOLD
Company Secretary
Hanson PLC
London, UNITED
  KINGDOM

MATTHEW NIMETZ
Partner
Paul, Weiss, Rifkind,
  Wharton & Garrison
New York, New York

ROBERT PAARLBERG
Associate Professor
Wellesley College
Wellesley, Massachusetts

†† ROBERT H. PRY
Director
International Institute for
Applied Systems Analysis
(IIASA)
Laxenburg, AUSTRIA

KEVIN F.F. QUIGLEY
Program Director for Public
Policy
The Pew Charitable Trusts
Philadelphia, Pennsylvania

KILAPARTI
RAMAKRISHNA
Senior Associate
International Environmental
Law
The Woods Hole Research
Center
Woods Hole, Massachusetts

GEORGE W. RATHJENS
Center for International
Studies
Massachusetts Institute of
Technology
Cambridge, Massachusetts

WALTER V. REID
Associate, Program in Forests
& Biodiversity
World Resources Institute
Washington, DC

ALDEMARO ROMERO
Executive Director
BIOMA
Caracas, VENEZUELA

ANNIE BONNIN
RONCEREL
Coordinator
Climate Network-Europe
Louvain-La-Neuve,
BELGIUM

** CARLISLE FORD RUNGE
Associate Professor &
Director,
Center for International
Food & Agricultural Policy
University of Minnesota
St. Paul, Minnesota

JOSE SARUKHAN
Rector
Universidad Nacional
Autonoma de Mexico
(UNAM)
Mexico City, MEXICO

JOHN C. SAWHILL
President &
Chief Executive Officer
The Nature Conservancy
Washington, DC

YURI N. SAYAMOV
First Deputy Chairman
Committee of Soviet
Scientists for Global
Security
Moscow, USSR

†† JAROMIR SEDLAK
Krupp Senior Associate
Institute for East-West
Security Studies
New York, NY

ALEXANDER SHAKOW
Director
Strategic Planning
 & Review Department
The World Bank
Washington, DC

LEONARD SILK
Economics Columnist
The New York Times
New York, New York

BRUCE SMART
Former Chairman & Chief
 Executive Officer of
 Continental Group
Former Under Secretary of
 Commerce for
 International Trade
Upperville, Virginia

JAMES GUSTAVE SPETH
President
World Resources Institute
Washington, DC

† MAURICE F. STRONG
Secretary General, 1992 U.N.
 Conference on
 Environment
 & Development
Geneva, SWITZERLAND

†† KOSTA TSIPIS
Director
Program in Science &
 Technology for
 International Security
Massachusetts Institute of
 Technology
Cambridge, Massachusetts

MARTIN VON
 HILDEBRAND
Head of Indigenous Affairs
Office of the President
Bogota, COLOMBIA

EDITH BROWN WEISS
Professor of Law
Georgetown University
 School of Law
Washington, DC

CASEY E. WESTELL, JR.
Consultant
(Formerly Director,
 Industrial Ecology)
Tenneco Inc.
Houston, Texas

** JENNIFER SEYMOUR
 WHITAKER
Director
Committees on Foreign
 Relations
Council on Foreign Relations
New York, New York

JOHN WILLIAMSON
Senior Fellow
Institute for International
 Economics
Washington, DC

GEORGE M. WOODWELL
Director
The Woods Hole Research
 Center
Woods Hole, Massachusetts

TAIZO YAKUSHIJI
Professor of Political Science
Saitama University
Urawa City, Saitama, JAPAN

ORAN R. YOUNG
Director
The Institute of Arctic
  Studies
Dartmouth College
Hanover, New Hampshire

CHARLES ZIEGLER
Senior Vice President,
  External Affairs
Ciba-Geigy
Ardsley, New York

KARL ZIEGLER
Financial Consultant to the
  World Wide Fund for
  Nature and
  Friends of the Earth
Former Executive Director of
  Bankers Trust
  International
London, UNITED
  KINGDOM

** Rapporteur
† Delivered formal address
  †† Panel Member
*Discussion Leader

Index